LIVING A
FULFILLED LIFE

SELF-EXPLORATION AND PERSONAL GROWTH WITH POSITIVE PSYCHOTHERAPY AFTER PROF. DR. NOSSRAT PESESCHKIAN

Including
an in-depth understanding of the psyche,
evolutionary human and individual development,
happiness, and flourishing.
With mindfulness, meditation practices,
and communication skills.

DR. RICHARD-CHRISTIAN WERRINGLOER

PAPERBACK: ISBN 978-3-910225-13-8

EBOOK: ISBN 978-3-910225-14-5

Book Design by HMDpublishing

Published by WAPP Press

World Association for Positive and Transcultural Psychotherapy

Luisenstrasse 28, 65185 Wiesbaden, Germany

www.positum.org

DEDICATION

I am delighted to dedicate this book to my parents, Margarete and Jürgen. They were models who gave me the love and the fundamental life experiences necessary to write it.

I would also like to thank my siblings, Gunver and Stephan, for our shared childhood and youth, when we all learned love and tolerance and had loads of fun.

I furthermore am pleased to dedicate this book to my loving wife, Libertad Ordóñez, and her caring parents, Blanca Cecilia and Henry Ordóñez. They welcomed me with love and inspired me with conversations on philosophy, spirituality, and history.

I would also like to mention Erika and Ernst Zölß, who have always been like second parents to me.

My warmest gratitude is due to Professor Dr. Nossrat Peseschkian, Manije Peseschkian, Dr. Nawid Peseschkian, and Dr. Hamid Peseschkian for all they have taught me and for treating me like a family member for many years, which made their collaboration on this book all the more joyful and inspirational.

As my personal spiritual and developmental guide, John Okoro has been of the greatest and dearest value to me.

I am indebted to Elena Bellavia because, through her fortuitous circumstances, Professor Nossrat Peseschkian found his way into my life.

I am very indebted to my dear friend Peg Marrin and her family for a lifetime of friendship and the wonderful and drawn-out work she has done revising and correcting my book with me.

I also want to thank Carmen Kauffmann for her years of friendship and continuous exchange of coaching, philosophical and spiritual knowledge, and experience.

"If you only do what you know how to do, you will always stay the same."
- Nossrat Peseschkian

CONTENTS

FOREWORD

The right book at the right time!

Sometimes a book comes into your life at just the right moment. There's something in it that speaks to your specific place in space and time. In a time of collective and individual crises, the question how to live a happy and fulfilled life has become an existential question. Living a fulfilled life is a goal that resonates with all of us, regardless of our backgrounds, ages, or aspirations. We all strive to find meaning, purpose, and joy in our lives, and yet the path to fulfillment is not always clear or easy to navigate.

When Positive Psychotherapy was developed by Nossrat Peseschkian, he applied the Positive to mental health at a time when the term positive implied some strange feelings. Since the development of Positive Psychotherapy in 1977 and Positive Psychosomatics in 1991, the Positive has led to the development of Positive Psychology (1998) and Positive Psychiatry (2012). Today Positive Psychotherapy is being applied in many different settings in more than 45 countries worldwide.

Richard Werringloer, one of the students of Nossrat Peseschkian, is presenting in this book not only the application of Positive Psychotherapy and its techniques in daily life but based on the author's rich experience, he offers a thoughtful and practical guide to living a fulfilled life. Drawing on his own experiences and insights as well as the wisdom of philosophers, psychologists, and spiritual leaders, the author provides a roadmap for readers to cultivate inner peace, deepen their relationships, pursue their passions, and find fulfillment in their work and personal life. But this is not an ordinary self-help book—it is based on an integrative humanistic-psychodynamic psychotherapeutic approach and rooted in medical knowledge.

The author's approach is both inspiring and accessible, making this book a valuable resource for anyone seeking to live a more fulfilling life. Whether you are just starting out on your journey or have been searching for meaning and purpose for years, the insights and guidance offered in these pages will help you create a life that is rich in meaning, purpose, and joy.

I am confident that this book will become a treasured companion for anyone seeking to live a fulfilled life. And that is both the beauty and tragedy of the right book for the right time. It can save you and transport you—but there can be no going back again.

Wiesbaden (Germany), March 2023

Hamid Peseschkian, M.D., D.M., D.M.Sc., I.D.F.A.P.A.

German Board-certified psychiatrist, neurologist and psychotherapist

International Distinguished Fellow, American Psychiatric Association

Managing and Academic Director, Wiesbaden Academy of Psychotherapy

Medical Director, Wiesbaden Psychotherapy Center

INTRODUCTION

The art of self-realization: Flourishing as the expression of success in life by developing and manifesting our personal talents and desires

"If you want something you've never had, you have to do something you've never done."
- Thomas Jefferson

My name is Dr. Richard Werringloer. I am a medical doctor, naturopath, and positive psychotherapist, and I treat my patients' physical and emotional pain with a holistic psychosomatic approach. I use osteopathy and acupressure to relax muscle and fascia tension and unblock vertebrae, and Positive Psychotherapy to help my patients overcome their mental obstacles and find balance in their lives again. I aim to enable each individual to live their life freely and fully and progress toward their life's objectives. As an international trainer for Positive Psychotherapy, I am happy to spread the knowledge Nossrat Peseschkian has bestowed on me, and I give training in many places worldwide.

This book has grown from twenty-five years of medical and psychotherapeutic studies and therapy. It consists of the core knowledge I have acquired, and I believe this knowledge has been helpful for understanding and helping myself and my clients. In the process of writing the book, I have become clearer about the wonderful nature of the human being and what we humans are capable of. The book is directed to all who are interested in discovering themselves and undertaking the permanent voyage of self-development. Whatever situation we may be in now, if we want to tread the path of self-exploration and development or if we simply want to live a happier, healthier, more meaningful and fulfilled life, this book can help us reflect on who we are, our current situation, how we can search for new ways to thrive and flourish. It is further directed to all my colleagues who are curious about life and want to share further knowledge and growth techniques.

Through the book, I also pay tribute to my teacher, Nossrat Peseschkian, who not only helped me professionally but also aided me in overcoming my personal difficulties and realizing my vocation in life.

This book is based on Professor Dr. Peseschkians Positive Psychotherapy (PPT). It gives a meta-theory and a structure for understanding ourselves and is the basis of the self-help we can receive through it. At the same time, it goes beyond PPT in theory and practice, encompassing many other therapeutic schools and my own discoveries that seamlessly fit in with Dr. Peseschkian's teachings, thereby making a more profound understanding of PPT and ourselves possible. The book is my very personal interpretation and elaboration of PPT, which isn't necessarily that of all the World Association of Positive Psychotherapy members. I intend it to help us understand ourselves more profoundly and to flourish as human beings and as a world community.

What is Positive Psychotherapy (PPT)?

"There is nothing more powerful than an idea whose time has come."
- Victor Hugo

Rather than begin with a definition, I would like to start with a story by Mowlana that my mentor Nossrat Peseschkian often relayed.

"The Sightseers and the Elephant"

A long time ago, a sultan received an elephant as a gift from a ruler of another kingdom. It was so big and magnificent that he wanted to show off the honor bestowed upon him by the other sultan. Since he was a very playful guy, he thought he would exhibit it by night in a big palace room with the curtains closed so nobody could see what it was. He then invited some people to the darkened room to try and guess what the present was. One touched the enormous legs and exclaimed, "What great new pillars; it must be a new palace room!" Another stretched out on the back, saying, "What a wonderful new lounger for the hot summer days." Another one added, touching the ears, "Wow, some big fans to go with it!" Then another man got the trunk in his hands and exclaimed, "No, this is a big hose for watering the garden." But then, when touching one of the enormous tusks, one person started wailing, "No, no, he is going to go to war! He got a huge saber for fighting!" Luckily at that moment, the sun came up and slowly lit up the room through the cracks between the curtains. Now everyone could see that the sultan had received a majestic elephant.

– Retold after Nossrat Peseschkian (Oriental Stories, p. 82)

What can this story tell us? There are usually as many opinions as there are observers of an object. One explanation is that each guesser had limited knowledge; in the shadows, each speculation was based on a single aspect of the whole. With the sun's illumination, all could see the whole, and they came to the same conclusion. Metaphorically, we can extrapolate from this tale that we must open our eyes to life so we can find out more about it. We often come to the wrong conclusions when we limit ourselves to our own narrow perspective of observation and interpretation. Especially in difficult situations, our focus tends to narrow the problem, and we lose track of possible resources. Positive Psychotherapy allows us to see the world in the sunlight and open our eyes to its beauty and depth. It is about getting to know ourselves and the world to an ever greater extent.

Happiness, self-realization, and world peace lie at the heart of Nossrat Peseschkian's Positive Psychotherapy (PPT), which is taught and practiced around the world. As a pedagogical and therapeutic method, it proceeds from the bottom up, from the individual to the family to the community, the city, and then the country, and extends to all humanity. This is not a revolution or dogma imposed from the top down but a natural learning process, beginning with the personal growth of the individual and expanding outward with unity in diversity to all the inhabitants of our world.

This book, *Living a Fulfilled Life,* is about letting go of our fears and learning to love ourselves and the world more completely while developing all our potentials, healing our wounds, and integrating our shadow-self. It is also about revealing our hidden talents and treasures, called our golden shadows. The methods described in these pages are meant to help us go beyond our fears to reach our life objectives, unite our search for a sense in life with our desire to find it, and pursue the goal of creating ourselves anew, creating a fuller, more integral and beautiful personality every day. We have been bestowed with so much potential waiting to be brought into the light for the glory of Nature/God/the Universe. Let's allow the Universe ("One Song") to sing through us.

I studied Positive Psychotherapy beginning in 2000 in Wiesbaden, Germany, for more than four years with Nossrat as my teacher and mentor. In his classes, he used to ask us students: "What would you prefer sharing, an apple or an idea?" If we share an apple, we can all have a taste of it. But the bigger the group, the less we get. On the other hand, if we share an idea, we can all have an entire idea, and if it's a good one, all humankind can benefit from it. So, let's share the idea of personal growth in harmony with life using the tenets of Positive Psychotherapy as a methodology. **Personal growth** means we get what we really want, and we get on course for life. Adopting this methodology means we must try something new. In Nossrat's words: "If you want something you've never had, you have to do something you've never done before." So, let's get off our couch, out of our comfort zone. Let's make the difference between wanting and deciding to change our lives and fill ourselves with enthusiasm and energy, just like a kid heading outdoors to play with his friends. The world needs warmhearted, wise, and empowered people who use and express their individual creativity to manifest the beauty of their inspirations and desires and help others use their personal resources so we can all make a difference. We want to grow in the sense of "unity in diversity," mutually helping one another, so the entire world can radiate joyously in its art of self-expression, simultaneously fulfilling us with love.

"A vegetable soup doesn't result from individual vegetables but from the composition of all the individual vegetables. If one vegetable claims that the flavor is due to its particular taste, then this isn't true."
- Nossrat Peseschkian

In Positive Psychotherapy (PPT), we begin personal change by re-perceiving our world. When we come as a client with regret, hate, and sadness for the past and fear of the future, we must learn how to see the world differently. From the onset, the empathic presence of the psychotherapist, counselor, or coach who attends to us will give us hope for a better future. This effect will be stronger the more certainty the therapist can exude by drawing on his own experience of personal growth and that of other clients through the method. He can help us become aware of, appreciate, and be proud of all we have previously achieved in our life. The psychotherapist helps us recognize the beauty and creativity we have already expressed as children and adults. More importantly, a skilled counselor helps us recognize our dormant potentials and possibilities, which can motivate us even more when they are awakened and brought to life. Guided by a counselor, we can learn to become open to the present moment and filled with life energy. Embracing the present gives us the energy to redevelop and bring balance to our lives as we examine difficult or even collapsed areas. We can learn to resolve problems by addressing the inadequate personal concepts and ideas we have about our future and the negative stories and wounds that drag us down from the past. Working with PPT helps us take away the dark shades that cover life in the present so we can come to find thankfulness, forgiveness, and happiness for the past and go on into a hopeful future. "A sorrow we share is already half cured" refers to the healing power of empathy. "It is never too late to have a beautiful past and bright future." We can learn to solve our present problems, and in overcoming our personal difficulties, our past will shine in the light as a gift that brought us growth and allowed us to mature into the marvelous person we have always been. "It is never too early to experience the beauty of what is" shows us that by opening our eyes, we can experience, relish, and appreciate that which lies before us, all the possibilities we hadn't even seen in our anger and despair. We learn how mindfulness and gratitude change the perspective we have of our life.

Changing our thinking is an incremental but uplifting and eventually selfless process. Through time we begin to see ourselves as beautiful incarnations.

We are the flowers of life blooming for ourselves and others, rising above ourselves from moment to moment, growing day by day in our capacities of love, comprehension, and creativity.

Plato considered "the good, the true, and the beautiful" to be celestial essences or ideals on which virtuous human actions are based. These three qualities have for millennia served as benchmarks or guideposts to help people find meaning and make sense of their life. Our heart, head, and abdomen represent these three ideals anatomically. Extending the metaphor, we shall use our warm-heartedness, intelligence, and intuitive creativity to benefit humankind. Learning to see ourselves and others in light of these qualities is at the heart of PPT.

What are the centerpieces of PPT's therapeutic approaches?

PPT is a meta-theory and a psychotherapeutic method at the same time. This humanistic method seeks to help us recognize our conflicts and inner wounds and let us heal them from our core to alleviate our symptoms. It is conflict-centered and resource-oriented, focused on helping us develop concrete strategies for overcoming problems, coping, and thriving in life. Among the various tools of PPT, we find the **four dimensions of life** for bringing our life to bloom, **primary and secondary capabilities** for entering into contact with others and shaping the relationship for the benefit of all and for becoming healthy, happy, and successful. We also have the **Differentiation Analytical Inventory (DAI)** and **Wiesbadener Inventory for Positive Psychotherapy and Family Therapy (WIPPF)** for analyzing these capabilities and using the discoveries we make for our further personal development.

The **five steps of conflict resolution** serve as a key to solving disputes within ourselves and with others and for growing toward new goals in life with our partners. PPT shows us a path to growing a positive attitude for approaching ourselves, others, and of course, clients, empathically and with open understanding. PPT also consists of using Middle Eastern and international stories for education, coaching, and therapy. These act as a mirror for us to recognize ourselves as a model for changes in behavior and a mediator in difficult situations. Stories also serve as deposits, since they usually stay in our memory much longer than a piece of simple advice. They convey traditional values as intercultural mediators, serving as aids for regression, contrasting concepts, and changes of perspectives. We also use **transcultural mediation**, using contrasting examples from diverse cultures to open new perspectives for partners in conflict. An example of two culturally different approaches to a health issue is the difference in treating a sick person in the Middle East and in many countries of the western world. In Germany, we say a sick person should rest and stay alone so he can recuperate. Visits are often seen as social control. In the Middle East, on the other hand, it is customary to put the sick person's bed in the middle of the living room so they can receive attention and healing company. Both approaches can be helpful; in excess, both can also be harmful. We can find a middle way that suits us by reflecting on both customs.

Positive interpretation is a centerpiece in PPT's way of seeing the world, since there is always more to a situation than we perceive now. For example, a "lazy" guy just hanging around, a "good-for-nothing" type can also be seen as someone who can say no to other peoples' expectations and can go his way and take care of his personal needs. Within the PPT method, we have behavioral change strategies such as **situation control,** with which we can analyze a behavior and the feelings, needs, and reactions behind it. We can conceptualize and then practice new strategies to create healthier reactions and habits. We also have a method for analyzing the situational interaction of partners and bringing more connectedness into their dialogues—**phases of conversation,** which we can call a sort of "pacing."

I have woven into this book knowledge and lessons that I've gained from other fields, from other friends such as Marshal Rosenberg, Michael Bohne, and Jon Kabat Zinn. I have added all this knowledge with the sense of *positum*—the whole, the real—so we can gain an even wider perspective of the human being, of coaching, and of therapeutic possibilities.

What are PPT's objectives?

The overall objective of PPT is to liberate our full potential and to use it to achieve our common goals of growth, happiness, and flourishing with humankind and in the world. We strive to learn to use our gifts to participate in the "world symphony orchestra," creating a "musical piece" played by humanity and the universe in its full diversity. When we all work together in a collaborative team, we represent enormous potential for knowledge, love, and creativity.

We come from a variety of cultural backgrounds, and each of us is unique. We want to be individuals. Each of us wants to be respected, understood, and seen reciprocally with his own particularities for his contribution to our venture. Yet we can fly together under one single flag, that of humanity, while at the same time keeping our personal identity and using all our talents and potential together. We fly together and elevate one another by cultivating opportunities for transcultural dialogue. This, of course, must be learned and practiced.

At the International Association of Positive Psychotherapy, our primary goals are to help the individual develop and thrive within the world community and go from pedagogy to coaching, counseling, and psychotherapy all the way to transcultural conflicts. Positive Psychotherapy is a humanistic, transcultural, and psychodynamic psychotherapeutic method.

Research and recognition: A study published in 1999 in the *European Journal of Psychiatry* showed a highly significant improvement in the symptoms between pre- and post-measurement of PPT patients as assessed through the Global Severity Index. In comparison, no significant differences could be found for the control group. The basic principles of PPT have been proven to be true and the interventions demonstrated to be effective by basic research. Martin Seligman, pioneer in Positive Psychology and Cognitive Behavioral Therapy and various other psychotherapeutic institutions, has done further affirming studies, for which the community of PPT therapists is grateful. Nossrat Peseschkian has received various merits throughout his life, including the 1997 Richard Mertens Prize for his computer program, Computing Quality Assurance in Positive Psychotherapy, a tool that evaluates the results of a psychotherapist's work with a client. Dr. Peseschkian also received the prestigious Order of Merit, the distinguished service Cross of the Federal Republic of Germany (the Bundesverdienstkreuz).

Our personal path to life fulfillment through PPT

"You are what your deepest desire is. As is your desire, so is your intention. As is your intention, so is your will. As is your will, so is your deed. As is your deed, so is your destiny."
- Upanishads

"The Miracle of the Ruby"

In a country so far away that not even the delicious smell of its famous oriental spices and herbs could travel, there lived a sultan who ruled his people through the excellent advice of his knowledgeable vizier. The sultan was pleased with his advisor's work since his people worshipped him for his wise rule. But as the years passed, he became increasingly unnerved by the high-pitched voice with which his vizier sang. The advisor followed him wherever he went, singing throughout the workday and in the morning and in the evening when he was in the baths. From the baths, the vizier's annoying voice echoed throughout the whole palace. Soon the sultan got so fed up with the awful sound that he forbade the vizier to sing even a single note. So, in his grief, the vizier stopped eating and got thinner and thinner until he died. The sultan was surprised and struck to the heart. He couldn't believe what had happened, so he had his medical doctors perform an autopsy to find out the reason for the vizier's death. When they examined the dead man's heart, they found a big red ruby hidden there. When they showed it to the sultan, the sultan wanted to touch it on the spot and to have it since he was a curious and greedy chap at the same time. The moment he touched it, his hands and then his arms and then all his body turned red, and he began singing.

– Retold after Nossrat Peseschkian (Oriental Stories, p. 63)

What can this story tell us? What does it mean to us and our personal lives? Let's think about it for a moment before reading on.

One of the meanings—as there are innumerable interpretations depending on the reader and interpreter—is that we must live our personal essence, our deepest desires, and express them throughout our lives. If we don't, as the vizier couldn't after being prohibited from singing, we begin to somatize or manifest our psychological problems in our bodies. We become sick and bring mayhem to our health just as the health of the vizier began to wither and fade away. Maybe the sultan's intuitive understanding of this led him to start singing in the end. But there can be many more interpretations of the story. Let's keep looking for hidden messages that resonate with our personal essence and issues. They may be important and meaningful to us.

The basic principles of Positive Psychotherapy:

- **Principle of hope**

- **Principle of balance**

- **Principle of conflict resolution**

As the story has shown, knowing what we really want, becoming conscious of our purpose in life, and expressing ourselves resiliently are important keys to becoming happy and flourishing. The **three basic principles of PPT** give us a firm basis for expressing these and living an intense and fulfilled life. As we will see in detail, the **principle of hope** gives us roots in a healthy, positive perception of ourselves and our life in the form of vision, motivation, and purpose. The **principle of balance** brings us into resilient harmony with ourselves and our environment. And the **principle of conflict resolution/consultation** gives us the tools to face and solve conflicts and problems we encounter on our individual life paths. We can express this with a short metaphor in the following way: *When we set sails on the seven seas of life, we want to lift the anchors of the uniquely crafted sailboat we call our individuality and set sail towards the unknown, the destinations of our lives, knowing we have the best sails for catching the wind, the best skills for riding it, and the best hull for weathering any storm that confronts us.*

Next, knowing what we are looking for in life and expressing our personal gifts in balance with life is important. This way, we can be in flow with existence, experiencing and actively expressing who we are. At the core of all our ambitions, aspirations, and striving lies our innermost desire to be happy. Happiness is our indicator or our barometer for perceiving how far we can live in accordance with our inner values and needs, and where we are on our path to life fulfillment. It indicates to what extent we are in balance with ourselves and life.

Where are we on this path to happiness and fulfillment?

Let's ask ourselves:

1. Why are we reading this book?
2. Are we living a fulfilled life, or are we frustrated? How does our frustration reflect how we are feeling physically, emotionally, and mentally?
3. What are we especially happy about, and what are our main pre-occupations?
4. Is there anything we want to change?

Happiness is finding inner peace through harmony within ourselves on a path towards our higher goals while taking joy in life.

Living a fulfilled and happy life is like the art of surfing; when a surfer rides the waves, despite the biggest difficulties and excitement all around, he finds his center and gets into balance with everything. Ivan Kirilov, PPT trainer, calls this stress-surfing. We can also call it life-surfing.

The morning pages

To activate our innate ability to understand ourselves and to begin listening to our intuition and inspiration, we might try to write morning pages, as Julia Cameron suggested in her book *The Artist's Way*. After getting up in the morning, we take a small book and start intuitively writing down all the thoughts that come to our minds for five to fifteen minutes. We just let our words and inspirations flow, and the pen writes on its own. Sometimes the results will be truly inspiring; other times, we will wonder why we are sitting there. Eventually, this practice opens our minds to more inspiration and consciousness about ourselves. Our inspiration opens us up to creativity and shows us where we want to make changes in our life. Creativity enables us to get out of our routine mode of living, which is often nothing more than repetitive sets of habits, until we can become true artisans of the life we were meant to live.

In the second step, after a few months, we go back and read our morning pages. Now we ask ourselves, what do we notice about them? What can we learn? About what and whom have we complained repeatedly? What have we postponed repeatedly? What did we change? We take two colored pens. With one, we mark our successes, and with the other, we mark what we want to change in our life. Once we have marked everything, we congratulate ourselves for the good things and plan the changes. We pick a day and hour for beginning and finishing.

"If you want something you never had, you have to do something you've never done before."
- Thomas Jefferson

CHAPTER 1

THE THREE PRINCIPLES OF LIFE AS KEYS TO MASTERING AND FLOURISHING CREATIVELY IN LIFE

A surfer needs to be addicted to the beauty of the waves, have a keen sense of balance, and have a deep intuitive knowledge of how to ride the surf.

The principle of hope: The art of being our own visionary and creator of our life-script

When *we unite the skills and experiences we have acquired in the past and marry them with our passion and calling for the future, our present will be a fest of creativity.*

The art of being our own visionary is based on Nossrat Peseschkian's first principle, the **principle of hope**. It is based on a positive concept of life and of ourselves. It is nothing more and nothing less than our ability to come to believe in ourselves and life by opening our eyes and recognizing who we really are while we discover the world as it is. Explained in the simplest of ways, it means that we are an intrinsic part of the world and, therefore, the creative force of life itself in its continuous evolution with infinite possibilities. The universe and we ourselves are a living, vibrating organism that originates from intelligence and energy. We are personified knowledge and love with the capability of letting life live and create through ourselves. An essential prerequisite for living a flourishing life, though, is that we always stay connected to ourselves and life itself.

The descriptive word "positive" in this therapeutic approach comes from the Latin word "positum," which emphasizes the given, the real. Positive Psychotherapy is not about avoidance or seeing the world through rose-colored glasses; it focuses on seeing ourselves and life holistically, with all the beauty, difficulties, and possibilities within us that life has to offer us every day. There is always much more beauty and opportunity around than we tend to believe and see, especially when we are enmeshed in a period of crisis and despair. In PPT, humans are seen as intrinsically good, and conflicts are described as a source of and catalyst to our personal growth. A so-called "conflictive personality" is based on a personality structure with a core self that is inaccessible to its holder and, therefore, incapable of expressing itself and its beauty completely. The causes are rooted in emotional wounds, imbalance, and immaturity, which lead to conflict within the personality as well as a distorted perception of its true self. But our personality in its entirety consists not only of the difficulties and wounds we have suffered but also of all our capabilities and gifts, including the personality and talents we have already developed and manifested but never consciously recognized, observed, or respected. Our personality also entails our inherent ability to heal, get into balance with ourselves and life, find happiness, and keep evolving and growing beyond ourselves. Often healing is simpler than we believe.

"Regard man as a mine rich in gems of inestimable value. Education can, alone, cause it to reveal its treasures, and enable mankind to benefit there from."
- Bahá'u'lláh

It is in our hands to discover and develop our potential and help our children discover and develop theirs. During their childhood, we can help them cultivate their innate gifts so they can develop them throughout their lives.

"A teacher's work is like that of a gardener who takes care of various plants. One plant loves the sunshine, the other the cool shade; one loves the shore of the stream, the other

the barren mountain peak. One thrives on sandy soils, the other on rich loam. Each requires the care best suited for it; otherwise, the result is unsatisfactory."
- Abdu'l-Bahá

As disciples of PPT, we begin with ourselves, of course. For the following exercise, we might want to set aside a day or at least an afternoon for tranquil reflection. In any case, take as much time as possible because it can be life-altering to reflect on our past and present and what we want to realize in the future. I remember how my own experience helped me reevaluate myself and create stronger self-esteem by discovering all the personal growth I had gone through as a child, youth, and adult and all the strengths I have developed through the challenges I have encountered. I reflected on my transcultural experiences living in different countries. From my perspective today, I view these experiences in a positive light. I know that having the chance to live in different worlds meant that I learned to express myself in different languages and to connect with diverse cultures. PPT has also helped me find hidden strengths, such as my ability to connect with an audience and to be an effective teacher. Before I met Nossrat Peseschkian, I was an extremely timid person, unable to express myself in public. Dr. Peseschkian enabled me to liberate myself of my inhibitions, let me become who I have come to be, and gave me the chance to become an international PPT trainer. I want to continue sharing this liberating experience with my friends and audiences, helping them find and liberate themselves.

Manifesting ourselves through our calling in life

A basic question in life: Who are we, where do we come from, and where are we going? When we find the answers to these questions, we find our core motivations in life, and we become able to manifest ourselves through our endowed gifts. At the same time, we exude the energy and enthusiasm fueled by these unique desires and goals. We then express ourselves naturally and with integrity, living from our core self. Our core motivations give us the energy to set out toward new horizons, develop the skills to become who we want to be, and display the will to persevere through challenges when our objectives seem difficult to achieve. The more experience we have, the more challenges we have mastered, and the more our inner resources grow. When we have mastered our challenges, we find fulfillment in looking at our past. So, a key to our happiness is discovering what we really desire and acquiring the inner resources, the capabilities, and the will to achieve it.

Discovering our resources and capabilities

If we want to look positively at our past, we must view our life with integrity: our difficulties, accomplishments, resources, and future potential. By answering the following questions, we dig deeply into our lives:

1. Who are we? We write down our personal and professional biography.

2. What are the five most important experiences in our lives that forged us and our values? What are the character strengths we manifested through these situations and life periods?

3. What were the most difficult situations we have mastered in life that can give us strength and show us that we will always find a way when facing challenges? What were the qualities we manifested that let us master these situations?

4. What we love and want is often what we know how to do. What have we realized? Where did we really excel and experience our greatest professional or private success, and which made us the proudest? What special capabilities did we use, and can we grow the capabilities we have mastered into excellence?

5. What is our sense of life? What gives our life meaning, makes us feel like we belong to something bigger than ourselves, and even gives us the sensation of inevitability?

6. Which qualities do we admire most in a human being?

7. Who are the five most important people in our past and present who have been our models and can give us strength in times of hardship?

8. Which people really inspire us, and can we learn from them? What makes them attractive to us? What character strengths do we find in them?

9. If we imagine an alien coming to take possession of our body, which qualities and joys would he put into action?

10. Which three doors have closed on us and taught us that adverse events are only temporary, changeable, and local? What new doors opened?

11. Where do we really feel at home? What place gives us the most security?

When looking back at our answers, what makes us special and powerful? And where can the qualities, strengths, and capabilities that we identified lead us to more happiness, pleasure, and fulfillment in the future?

Resource meditation

After we have thoroughly pondered our answers, we sit down with our backs straight and inhale and exhale a couple of times in full awareness and with focused attention. We recapitulate and synthesize what we have gone through, remembering visually what we see as our meaning in life and all the greatness we have achieved. We remember the people who sustained us throughout our strife, and we see all the ones whose company we want. We envision the place we love the most and acknowledge our greatest potential. We create a beautiful place in our imagination where we, as individuals with our talents and powers, are surrounded by the people we adore and an environment where we feel at home. We imagine this powerful inner haven vivaciously in all its details and aspects, including its intense smells and sounds. We choose a color to frame this experience and then make a motion of our hand to create an anchor. We repeat this visualization at least three times in the following days so it becomes imprinted in our imagination.

"If you want to get what you really want, you have to open your gate to phantasy."
- Nossrat Peseschkian

Creating a vision for our life

When we share our unique gifts, we have a purpose in life. Everything we think now, everything we thought in the past, and everything we will think in the future charts the destiny of our lives. If we want to be the artisans of our life and not just leave everything up to chance, it is fundamental that we become conscious so we can purposefully direct the creative process and craft our own future. Learning how to visualize purposefully will help us on our way.

Creating a better future is an intentional and serious pursuit. We should be reminded that "when we sow potatoes, we get potatoes, and when we sow tomatoes, we get tomatoes." Just as we don't expect to harvest tomatoes when we sow potatoes, we must be attentive to the seeds we plant. We are all a unique expression of the universe; let's express ourselves and, at the same time, be careful about what we desire because we may get it.

Finding our purpose in life is part of becoming mature. It can take us a while, and we may live through a whole spectrum of different vocations as we pass through different life periods with different motivations. The moment we find our true vocation and create our personal objectives, our motivational energy is set free, and we begin our voyage toward our personal destination. The problems that get in our way and seem to thwart us usually solve themselves on the way. When we stay open-minded, forward-looking, and trusting, the solutions to all our challenges will come to us in given time. New opportunities will arise, and our problems will fall along the wayside. Since things always turn out differently than expected, there is no use in planning every detail meticulously beforehand.

Usually, our fears never come true. When we think back on the fears we suffered—the exams we might fail, the devastating opinions others might have of us, what people might be gossiping about, financial problems that might ruin us, fears of not living up to our parents' expectations, and so forth—we find that most never came true or simply had no impact on our life. When we look back on our lives, we see that imagined catastrophes caused many moments of fear or even panic. Although things go differently than we expect, and we fight against their outcomes, they typically turn out well, often even better than we think. We usually appreciate the results in the end. So why are we so fearful?

When we meet our challenges with a good attitude and open mind, and we give our best, we will always find a way through. Challenges force us to grow and achieve new capabilities. When we look back, we are grateful for them and happy with what we have accomplished. We can learn to meet the inevitable new challenges in our life by appreciating the obstacles and difficulties we have already encountered.

If we learn to live in appreciation of the wonders and beauty that unfold before us, we will be fulfilled. Suppose we live in the expectation that new horizons with ever-new destinations will be revealed. In that case, we will always be able to grasp a renewed, wider, more adventurous vision of our future. As we travel, we grow and become stronger and more mature. Fulfillment makes us radiate happiness and project a strong personality. The more we live in sync with life and its natural flow, the more open we will be to seeing new opportunities.

"You don't paddle against the current, you paddle with it. And when you get good at it, you throw away the oars."
- Kris Kristofferson

In the following part, we will go through a three-step process. First, we will discover our desires, vocations, and personal destination in life with *meditation* and *inquiry*. Second, we will take an inspirational trip, elaborating on our desires, vocations, and personal destinations on a *vision board*. Third, we will create a *visualization*, an inner picture that we can always have at hand to remind us of our goals and give us the motivation to strive for them.

1. **Finding our desires, vocations, and destination with a meditative trip to our dreams**

We sit upright and comfortably, leave our eyes open, focus softly a few feet in front of us, take a few deep breaths, and imagine: What did we dream of as a kid, as a teenager, and young adult? What have we already accomplished, and what do we love doing? And what dreams are still unfulfilled? What is it we want to have achieved at the end of our lives, and how do we want our family and friends to remember us when we depart from this world?

After this thoughtful reverie, we want to inquire even deeper into this magical space of our personality. We investigate and focus on our personal desires, vocations, talents, and resources with the following questions:

1. When have we felt really happy and full of enthusiasm?

2. What do we love doing and do on a regular basis? What have we loved doing but haven't done in ages? What gets us into a flow for hours and days and feels so rewarding that we finish our activity energized instead of exhausted?

3. What were our childhood, teenage, young adult, and adult desires? Which ones have we fulfilled? What dreams are we still waiting to take on? Which are still relevant to us looking from where we are today?

4. What are we after in life? What is our innermost desire, our passion, and what makes us feel realized, happy, and most alive?

5. What do we desire for our personal and professional life?

6. Imagine that within twenty years, we will be honored on a podium, and someone will give a speech about us. What would we like him to say?

7. What resources do we have to help us realize our dreams? What kind of friendships, connections, and other resources and opportunities do we have and enjoy?

8. Let us look back at the questions and summarize the essential messages we have discovered about ourselves through this personal inquiry process.

Letting our dreams give us inspiration for our future

We keep quiet again for a couple of moments, close our eyes, and after three deep breaths, dare to dream of where we will be in five years. How will our personal and professional life be? What values will be important to us? What important change do we believe we'll have made?

"Nothing would have been created if someone had not thought it up before."
- Reinhold Messner

2. Creating a vision board

We now create a vision board to visualize our future perspective and imbed it deeply into our imagination. We take magazines that we like and find interesting, a big piece of cardboard, scissors, and glue. Then we cut out the images that correspond to the vision we have created of our future. We take an hour for the exercise and play meditative music to help with our creativity. We allow twenty minutes to look for and cut out the pictures and slogans that correspond to our dreams in life. Then we make our personal collage. We address as many of our goals as possible in terms of our health, profession, and social life, as well as our spiritual and cultural goals. We envision how we want our life to look in the future. We make our life an inspirational adventure and can add powerful affirmations connected to our goal onto our map. We also put a picture of ourselves in this collage. Once we have finished, we put it where we will see it every day (on the refrigerator, for example). Our map will remind us of our goals and provide a source of inspiration on our path to achieving them. In the beginning, the world we have created will seem a bit surreal, but with time, as we get closer to it, we will experience its reality.

3. Creative visualization

To strengthen the inner image of the goals and dreams we have created on our vision board, we can use creative visualization. Every day, millions of images of the future and the past rush through our minds. They influence our feelings, our perception of life, and how we act and react. With creative visualization, we take this usually unconscious process and make it a conscious tool for shaping our future. This way, we become the ones who decide what will influence us. We decide on a voluntary positive input instead of a random one and, thereby, on the direction we want to go.

Creative visualization is part of purposefully taking the wheel and taking command of our life, choosing between constructive and destructive future perspectives, empowering or disabling ones, and making them part of the internal image we have of ourselves and the life we want to live. Creative visualization helps us in all aspects of life—attaining our professional and private goals, improving self-esteem, and bolstering our resilience, as well as preparing for high-performance and sports events. We can choose to make our life our conscious creative work of self-expression or to let it go adrift. We can become the artisans of our health, vitality, relationships, profession, and spirituality when we connect to our inner essence and let our passions radiate through us. We take the opportunities that life offers us along the way, keeping our eyes open for synchronicity—the appearance of the right chance at the right time—and turn them into our synchro-destiny. After defining our objectives as a first step and creating a vision board as a second, we now do creative visualization.

Creative visualization meditation

We sit up straight and take a few deep breaths, observing our breath for a couple of minutes until we are relaxed. Then we start visualizing our future life in the way we have already created it. We are specific and bring all the details on our vision board into our imagination. We let it come to life in the present, with all its details, including colors, smells, sounds, and feelings as if it were already true. By doing so, we root our future into our deepest selves and strengthen our resolve and motivation to get there. We start living our tomorrow today. We visualize as long as possible. At the same time, we try not to get fixated on the result. We just create it in our minds and then let it go. Once we have experienced our future deeply, we can dive into it each morning and each night right before falling asleep.

"Beauty lies within every beginning."
- Hermann Hesse

Although we have clearly visualized our goals and resolutely keep to them, we also keep our eyes open for other opportunities and chances life has to offer us.

As time passes and we grow older and change, our perspectives also change, and we may want to go through this process of self-exploration again. We can always use these techniques for other objectives on other occasions and with whatever goals we have in mind. The vision board and the creative visualization techniques help to keep us evolving as our perspectives and desires change.

To fill ourselves with more energy and to stay enthusiastic in situations when we are in competition with others and our desires collide with theirs, it can help to wish for them to become happy with something wonderful but different from what we are striving for—and do so from the depth of our heart.

We must always remember that we have to create and manifest our goals and dreams through practice, action, and hard work. Getting there isn't just about dreaming and visualizing them.

"Commitment is what transforms a promise into reality."
- Abraham Lincoln

The principle of balance: The art of creating resilience through interior and life balance

"Standing on One Leg"

In the splendid gardens of a city, a man was once standing on one leg, crying, and complaining because of the pain he felt in his overburdened, cramped-up leg. A person passing by felt pity and wanted to help him, so he stopped and massaged his leg. The man standing on one leg immediately felt relief and thanked him. But as time passed, his pains returned, and his neck and back started hurting from standing stiffly for such a long time too. Another passerby saw him, felt compassion, stopped, and said, "Hey, let me help you!" and started massaging his neck and back. Of course, the man felt better and was grateful for the help. But again, as time passed, the pain returned. Then a person observing the two giving the one-legged stander relief thought he had an even better solution. He told them, "Wait a second, I know what can help him. He needs someone to lean on. That will relieve his pain for sure." So, the observer stood next to the one-legged stander and allowed him to lean against him. And, of course, it was helpful until the guy giving support had to run errands. Soon the one-legged stander's pain returned. Then another well-meaning person stopped and told him that the pain would be easier to endure if he meditated on a feather. So, he meditated on a feather, and sure enough, at least temporarily, the pain subsided but only to return even stronger as his muscles ached even more. Finally, sometime later, a person who had come to the gardens to seek peace was so upset by all the wailing and screeching of the man standing on one leg that he asked, "Why are you such a wimp? You have a leg to stand on!" Now, apart from having physical pain, the man standing on one leg also felt guilty and began to sulk. Luckily a perceptive and forthright young woman saw him in his awful state and inquired, "Why are you bending your other leg and not using it? Let me help you extend it and help you walk again." So, before the man standing on one leg could respond, the young woman helped him straighten his leg. She put his other foot on the ground, massaged the intensely cramped muscles, and showed him some exercises. Relief spread across the man's face; joy filled him as he shifted his weight from leg to leg and started jumping and dancing around in gratefulness, as he had not imagined doing for years.

– Retold after Nossrat Peseschkian (Oriental Stories, p. 12)

Among other things, this story tells us is that we must get to the root of our problems and not just cure the symptoms, and to bring *balance* into our life, we must use the resources we have been given. We must learn to let people help us, but we must help ourselves by using our resources intelligently.

The principle of balance is about being an equilibrated individual and living a balanced life. Creating and cultivating this balance within ourselves and in our lives creates resilience for flourishing in life. Looking at it from this perspective, we can differentiate between inner and outer resilience. When we look at resilience as a wheel, our inner resilience—existing within ourselves as our core values, personal capabilities, and positive inner representations—represents its axle. Our four dimensions of life—health, work, social life, and spirituality, and how we have chosen to live them (creating strong health, a meaningful and empowering professional life, fun and sustaining social relationships, and motivating and inspiring spiritual and creative life)—are the spokes and outer part of the wheel. When the axle is weak, the wheel risks breaking, and if the spokes are out of balance, the wheel will wobble. Our lives are fragile when inner and outer resilience are weak and out of balance. They then need to be strengthened and brought back into balance. Taking care of our four life dimensions is taking care of ourselves and results in happiness, life fulfillment, and a strengthening of our inner resilience.

Our balance within: Our inner resilience

According to Martin Seligman, the founder of Positive Psychology, the following aspects of resilience are important for living a fulfilled life: We need a **spiritual core** that consists of our most central values and beliefs. The truths we have recognized and acquired in life nurture us and guide our inner potential. A second aspect is **self-awareness**, which is our capacity for introspection and reflection. Self-awareness helps us gain insights into our personal identity and the meaning, purpose, and truths about our interior life. It lets us grow to fulfill our potential, be authentic, and create a life worth living. A third aspect is a **sense of agency**, which means that we feel responsible for our continuous quest to develop ourselves and put our insights into action for a higher purpose. With a sense of agency, we can express our potential as well as accept our shortcomings and imperfections. Through this aspect of resilience, we realize that we are the primary authors of our lives. A fourth aspect is **self-regulation**, which is necessary for controlling our emotions, thoughts, and behavior so we can act in our own interest and the interest of all in a socially acceptable way. A fifth aspect is **self-motivation**, which is the ability to perceive that our personal path will lead to the realization of our deepest aspirations and inspires us to move towards it. A sixth aspect is **social awareness**, which reminds us that relationships play a vital role in our development and that we need to be able to understand others and communicate with them. Additional aspects of resilience are tolerance and acceptance. These qualities are especially important in dealing with others. We recognize that other people have the right to hold different values, beliefs, and customs and that we must be considerate and open to alternative viewpoints without giving up our own beliefs. We do so just as we expect others to do with us. All these internal capabilities add up to our ability to resiliently live our own lives and head towards our personal destinations. We shall foster them!

"The Merchant and the Parrot"

A merchant once had a parrot he loved very much. He spoiled him every day with sugar he had stored in a big linen sack that stood in the corner of his store. Since he was anxious that his store would be robbed, he slept in a little bed in the office of his store. One evening, when he was unusually weary and tired of sleeping on the hard mattress of the office as well, he decided to make an exception and sleep in the big comfortable bed he had for himself and for his wife in the apartment upstairs. But before going to bed, he told his parrot to screech and call him if a burglar took anything of value. During the night, a burglar entered, put a lot of the merchandise from the shelves and floor into big bags, which he then hauled away. However, the burglar didn't touch the sugar standing in the store's corner. The parrot observed everything with his keen eyes but didn't screech. When the merchant woke and came downstairs in the morning, he couldn't believe his eyes. No more jewels, no more carpets, no more spices. All that remained of his valuable merchandise was the sugar sack in the corner. He froze on the spot and exclaimed in an exasperated voice, "How can it be, dear parrot, that I spoil you every day, and you aren't even able to warn me of a burglar?!" The parrot replied, "But you told me to take care that nothing of value was stolen."

- Retold after Nossrat Peseschkian (Oriental Stories, p. V)

Finding the core values of our spiritual core

What is more important, ethics or values? What we care about or value is the most important. A mother doesn't rescue her child because she learned ethics in school but because she loves and values her child. So, it is important to foster what we value. Values resonate with us on a far more basic level than ethics. Values are profound convictions that cover our most essential needs at the core of our personality and provide a foundation for our life. We all develop values and value-sets differently. They influence us in every moment of our lives, in every choice and decision we make. To become conscious of how essential values are to our lives and become aware of the deepest roots of our motivation, we can do the following exercise.

Core value exercise

We find a quiet place, sit down comfortably, inhale and exhale a few times, and reflect on the following value table. Which twenty of these 110 values are the most important ones for us? Let's take fifteen intuitive minutes, no more!

Sharing, education, self-realization, gratitude, friendship, obedience, sexuality, patience, happiness, effectiveness, contact, punctuality, beauty, efficacy, doubt, curiosity, thrift, wisdom, discovering, passion, time, courage, nobility, optimism, pride, rationality, courtesy, humility, culture, honesty, knowledge, independence, diversion, speed, relaxation, faithfulness, harmony, faith, balance, flexibility, charity, wealth, perfection, unity, leadership, loyalty, realism, spirituality, self-control, intimacy, influence, earning, orderliness, reputation, family, innovation, respect, benevolence, empathy, marriage, integrity, humor, compassion, responsibility, well-being, change, power, justice, sacrifice, conscientiousness, excellence, coherence, love, science, satisfaction, comfort, knowledge, maturity, security, simpleness, self-esteem, commitment, confidence, tranquility, creativity, generosity, originality, tolerance, truthfulness, cleanliness, perseverance, justice, achievement, reliability, freedom, precision, role-modeling, elegance, trust, health, team, confidence, work, resilience, certitude, sustenance, fame, skill, equality, strength

So now, which are our twenty most important values?

To reduce the number of values even further, we can imagine we are traveling to a remote island. Each of us can take only ten values along on the plane, and we must leave the rest behind. As we arrive at the airport before our departure, we are told that we will need to hike for two days to get to the little port from which we will make the final leg of the trip to the island. Therefore, we must get rid of another five values. As we walk, our backpacks get heavier with every step, and we decide to get rid of two more. But as we trudge along, these two still seem too heavy, so we discard another value; now we are left only with two. As we finally get to the boat, we discover it is nothing more than a tiny canoe, and we once again must choose which of the last two values we will keep. We ask ourselves, which one doesn't make sense without the other one? One of the two will still be valuable without the other. This one is the most valuable for us right now. Let's hold our chosen value quietly in our minds for a couple of moments.

Returning to the exercise above, we consider our three most important values. We do an honest assessment by asking: Are we living according to them? If not, what changes do we have to make to bring ourselves into harmony with them? Let's start with small steps that will pave the way to living our lives according to what is important to us today.

Our values and value system change as we ourselves change, grow, mature, and become more ourselves throughout life. We can check our values every year to see if they have changed and determine if we are in line with our new values. People have different values and different value systems. They aren't necessarily better or worse than ours but simply different, and they belong to their personal stage of development. We can try to discover and understand the values of the people we especially like and those who are closest to us. By doing this, we get to know and respect our fellow human beings better, understand the basis of our differences and conflicts, find ways to evade and solve quarrels, and love them more.

Discovering more factors of our inner resilience:

- *Self-awareness:* Have we gone on a trip of self-discovery, and do we know ourselves?
- *Sense of agency:* To what degree have we taken responsibility for and command of our lives?
- *Self-regulation:* How much control do we have over ourselves, and do we get what we set out to get?
- *Self-motivation*: How motivated are we to really fight for what we desire in life?
- *Social awareness:* How aware are we of our social surroundings, and how well do we manage within them?

As we work our way through this book and live with intensity, we will slowly acquire the skills and strengths necessary for healthy resilience.

Our balance in life: Our outer resilience

Next to the balance within our individual self, we must take care of the balance in our external life, within our four dimensions of life: Body/health, professional life/achievement, social life, and spirituality/vision.

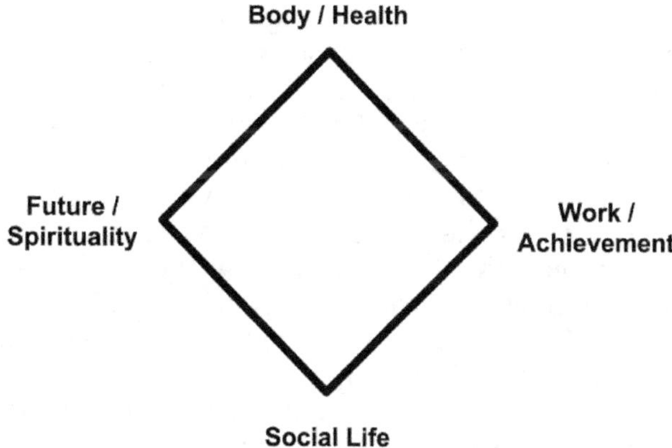

Nossrat Peseschkian describes them in the following way: "The four dimensions are like an equestrian who is motivated for performance (professional life/achievement) and rides towards a goal (spirituality and creative life). He needs a healthy and well-attended horse (body/health), and in case he falls, he needs assistants to help him back into the saddle (social life)."

These four areas are our four dimensions of flourishing, thriving, blossoming, and becoming who we really are. When we live our four dimensions of life intensely, they are never-ending sources of happiness, self-esteem, and sustenance. If we nurture all four dimensions, they will be our source of strength and resilience, four pillars on which we can truly rely. Any one of these pillars offers us refuge when times get tough: We take refuge with our friends and talk about our problems, take refuge in our spiritual life, and use our creative ideas and plans to find a solution to the problems when we have difficulties in our professional life. And if we have strong health on which we can rely, we will leave a bad situation with a headache but nothing more. Relying on any one of the pillars to escape our problems will not work. Hiding from life by gossiping with one's friends, burying one's head in religious fantasies, or using one's health problems—caused by somatizing—can be excuses for not solving one's problems. We must solve our problems where they originate. We must solve a health issue by caring about our health, a problem at work by talking with our boss, a social problem by resolving a dispute, and so forth.

If we consider the cycle of life from inception to adulthood, we see the wonders of nature unfolding before our eyes—the miracle of a microcosmos growing into a macrocosmos through the marvelous process of differentiation, from an egg and a sperm all the way to an adult person. When born, a child isn't simply a blank piece of paper or a tabula rasa, as once thought, but more like a sponge with enormous capabilities of assimilating, apprehending, growing, and shapeshifting at an amazing pace. When we observe children, we see how incredibly in motion they are. They physically, emotionally, and mentally discover the world around them, learn about everything they encounter, and then become creative. New challenges for learning new capabilities for our children arise in our ever-changing world. In our modern world, televisions, computers, and cell phones give new types of stimuli and offer new dimensions for discovery that didn't exist before. These new media should be used wisely and in moderation, together with all the other areas of learning and discovery that existed before.

Understanding the giant leaps of child development is mind-boggling. Beginning with its physical differentiation from its surroundings, a baby, in moving its hands and observing them, with time experiencing its whole body, becomes aware that it is the one causing the movement and discovers it belongs to itself. Then, as development continues through childhood, she slowly begins to experience and recognize herself as an *I*. Later on, conscious of her individual emotions and thoughts as her own, she understands that others don't experience them since they are individuals separate from herself. The child develops and differentiates in all four dimensions of life, step by step, according to the laws of nature and what developmental stimuli it receives. In the physical domain, it starts bringing everything to its mouth to determine its qualities and begins to learn how to roll over on its stomach, crawl, stand up, walk, run, and then even hop on one leg. Cognitively, it begins with syllables, then says *mama* and *papa*, to formulate two-to-three-word sentences and later to communicate complex abstract contents, to read, write, think logically, use phantasy, and become creative. In the emotional domain, it learns to become interested in others, connect with them, be affectionate, and finally, even share. The spiritual domain unfolds later with thoughts of one's individual existence, mankind's origins, and the existence of God. Awareness and gratitude for the miracles of nature and human growth help us remain open to life's wonders.

> *"The real voyage of discovery consists not in seeing new sights, but in looking with new eyes."*
> *- Marcel Proust.*

We receive health from our parents, nature, and God so we can flourish as individuals. We must take care of our health responsibly to live up to our possibilities. This encompasses getting the nutrition we need from food, the sleep and relaxation necessary for recuperating from mental and physical stress, the strength, energy, and stamina through sports, as well as finding physical pleasure through our body with sexuality and esthetics.

We can develop competencies from our talents to have a meaningful and empowering professional life. We can either find a profession with meaning or give the profession we have meaning. We can contribute to creating a professional team that works flexibly together, in which everyone can give their best. We also want to receive appropriate remuneration to provide material security for our family and allow us to realize ourselves and our dreams in our free time.

Rewarding and sustaining family ties and friendships are important for a fulfilled life too. We must learn to develop emotional stability so we can maintain social ties and get what we want from our relationships instead of exploding in anger or falling into despair at the slightest irritation. We also need counselors and role models to help us in moments of crisis. Furthermore, we need the ability to make and maintain contacts through socializing and communication skills so we can have family and friends with whom we can laugh or cry. Nossrat Peseschkian advised cultivating our sense of humor since "humor is the salt of life, and if you are salted well, you'll stay fresh longer." It is scientifically proven that happiness and laughter are more contagious than loneliness and depression, so let's go for it. If someone new moves into the neighborhood and radiates happiness and friendship, their pleasant emotions will spread to and beyond their next-door neighbors. But at the same time, we should remember that a few sad and angry apples can spoil the morale of the entire group. So let's project joy.

An inspiring and motivating spiritual and creative life, with a solid faith as a foundation and interesting hobbies for inspiration, gives us energy and motivation to meet our objectives. They are profound roots for happiness and flourishing: We nourish these roots by cultivating our life philosophy and connecting to nature, life, the universe, the all, God—whatever we want to call it—through meditation, mindfulness, and prayer. These practices help us base our lives on our spiritual values and give us a healthy mental foundation. When we create our vision for a wider and brighter future by developing our desires, values, and capabilities into motivating future perspectives, we give our life a personal taste, fragrance, and color that is unique to ourselves and lets us ride with optimism and high energy towards our goals. A motivating spiritual life keeps us solution-oriented and our eyes and mind open to new horizons.

Our four dimensions: *body/health, professional life/achievement, social life,* and *spirituality/vision,* are not primarily inborn. They are, for the most part, grown, so we must exercise them regularly and attend to each daily. We will find life fulfillment by keeping them strong and in balance, solving their conflicts, and enjoying the resources they have to offer us mindfully and with appreciation. By cultivating our four dimensions, we cultivate our source of sustenance, happiness, and self-esteem; we become resilient and prosperous and will always have safe havens to fall back on when we are in difficulties.

Balance in our personal four dimensions of life

Now let's look at our personal four dimensions. How much energy are we putting into each one, and how much satisfaction are we getting out of them? How well are we doing in each of them? How balanced are we in our four dimensions? How do we feel about them, and what do we want to change? Look at the three diagrams below and systematically answer the following questions.

The Four Dimensions Questionnaire

The body dimension:

1. How do we feel in our bodies? How do we see our own body? What is our attitude towards it?

2. Do we suffer any health problems? If so, what type?

3. What are our eating habits?

4. What type of sports and physical fitness do we do?

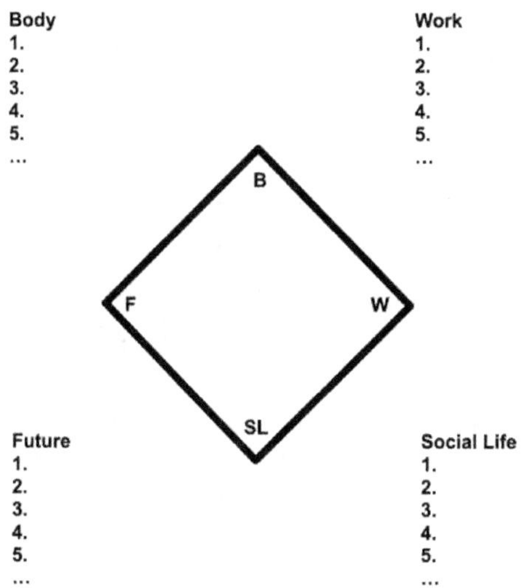

5. Do we sleep well? How many hours (7-8)?

6. Do we take time to rest during the day?

7. What do we do for our physical well-being?

8. Do we smoke, drink, or take any drugs?

9. What is our attitude towards sex? Do we enjoy it?

10. How would we like to change our health and physical well-being in the future?

The achievement dimension:

1. Do we like going to work?

2. Are we happy with our work? Does it bring us fulfillment? Can we call it a profession?

3. Can we excel and develop ourselves at our workplace?

4. Does our profession give us enough income and security?

5. How many hours a day do we work?

6. Are we insufficiently tasked or overly challenged? Are we bored or scared of failing?

7. Do we have a good team and boss; how are our relationships at work?

8. How do we react when our performance is questioned?

9. How do we feel when we don't have anything to do?

10. What would we change to become happier and more content at work? What could we contribute to change our working atmosphere?

The social contact dimension:

1. How happy are we with our partners, family, and friends? How do we see our relationships?

2. Who are the five people closest to us? What do they bring to our life? What are they helping us with?

3. Are there people with whom we can talk about everything? Is there someone we can call in the middle of the night if we are in difficulty?

4. Are we happy with our partner? Do we help each other and have compassion for one another? Why or why not?

5. Do we and our partner like socializing? Do we have hobbies together?

6. Do we spend time with our partner, our family, with friends? What do we like doing together?

7. How is our relationship with our parents? And with our grandparents?

8. Do we feel in balance with our family and social contacts?

9. Do we receive social/emotional warmth? Do we give emotional warmth?

10. How would we like to change our social life in the future?

The future/spirituality dimension:

1. What usually goes on in our mind? What do we think about? (About our body, work, social life, past, and future?)

2. What are our hobbies and cultural activities? How happy are we with them?

3. What is our life philosophy, meaning of life, spiritual or philosophical background, and anchor in life? Do we belong to a faith?

4. How do we live our personal philosophy and our spiritual life? Do we spend time practicing our spirituality or thinking about life and spiritual concepts?

5. What do we value in life? What do we like living and being healthy for?

6. Do we take time to plan our future?

7. What would we like to do and change in the coming five years?

8. What needs to change most urgently?

9. What would we do if we had no more fears or worries?

10. What is our greatest wish?

11. How would we like to change our spiritual life in the future?

The balance model as four dimensions

Now we go back and reevaluate all our questions about the four dimensions. Then we utilize the **balance models**:

1. *Energy-distribution/contentment* (diagrams below): We diagram how much energy we expend in each of the four dimensions (total 100%). Contentment: We evaluate how much satisfaction we get out of each of the four dimensions. (The outer rings equate to high contentment, inner rings to lower contentment.) We evaluate and compare our estimation of how much energy we invest in each, how much satisfaction we get from them, and what we would like to change.

2. *Strengths and difficulties*: We look through our answers for our strengths or what we feel especially good about, as well as our difficulties and what we would like to change.

3. *Specific contentment* (diagram below): We make a list of the twelve critical areas of our lives according to the four dimensions of life: For example: Work, health, family, friends, money, sport... We assign a score of 1-10 on every one of them according to our satisfaction. (See the arrows; outwards high satisfaction, inwards low satisfaction).

4. We imagine four of our best friends delivering a eulogy for us after our death on our ninetieth birthday. What would we like them to say?

5. What advice would we give ourselves for achieving these merits and goals if we had the chance to meet ourselves at the age of ninety, reflecting on our life? How would our best friends advise us to achieve the goals we have set for ourselves?

"New ideas bring new change."
- Nossrat Peseschkian

Four dimensions energy and contentment and specific contentment, blank diagrams:

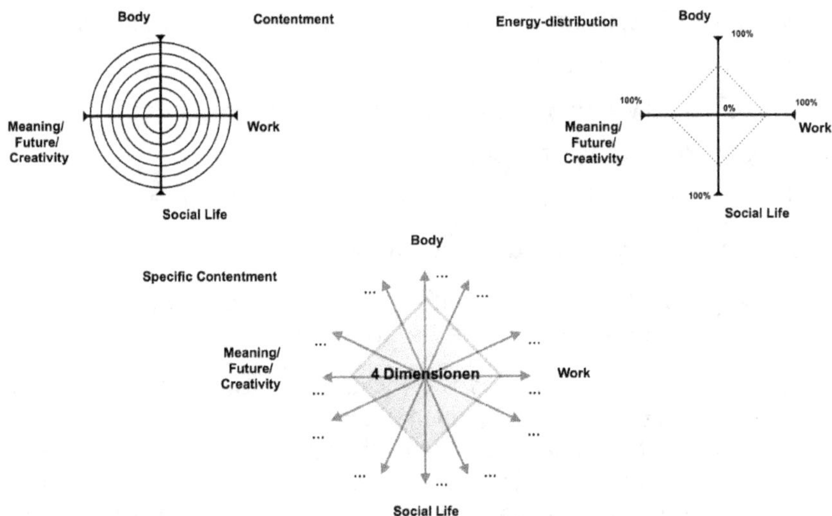

Four dimensions energy, contentment, and specific contentment diagrams, filled in:

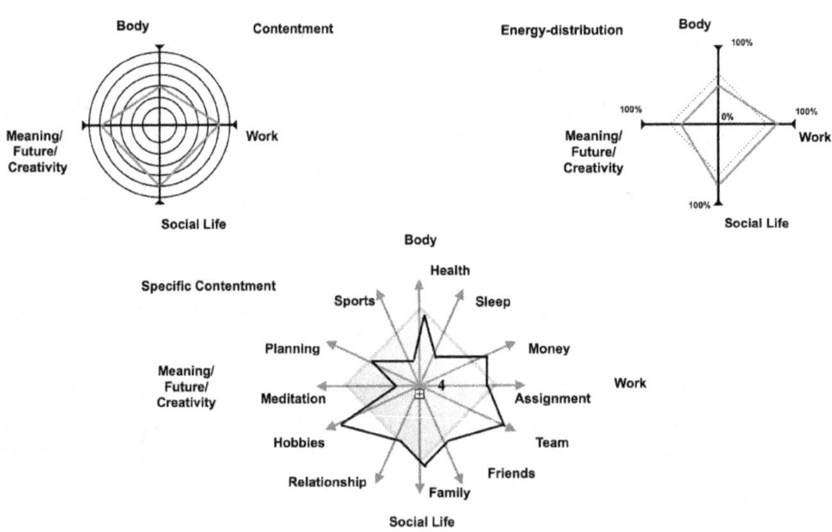

The four dimensions planner

1. Now we review what we have worked through in our previous exercises, including the vision board and the creative visualization. We evaluate and envision all of what we want to have reached and lived up to by the end of our life and classify these goals according to the four dimensions. We fill these ideas into the spaces— In my Lifetime Body, Work, Social Life, Future—at the end of the four dimensions planner.

What do I want:	In the next 90 days	In the next year	In the next 5 years	In the next 10 years	In the next 30 years	In my Lifetime

2. Using the four dimensions planner, we make a concrete plan about which steps we must take to reach our goals. How exactly do we want to get there starting today and beginning over the next few weeks? It is important to plan meticulously. The more precisely we plan, the easier and quicker it will be to realize change.

3. What must we do today so we can achieve our plans?

Balance in psychodynamics

The principle of balance, as described earlier, addresses our individual inner and outer life balance, yet this principle encompasses much more. It also encompasses our personal vulnerabilities and how we deal with conflict—how we are in balance with ourselves and the world. When an external situation, **actual conflict,** provokes a crisis, that situation ignites a conflictual part of our personality structure with its vulnerable concepts. We call these vulnerable concepts our **basic conflict**. We learned these vulnerable concepts in the past, and while they once protected us, they are no longer adequate if they become conflictive. They could also be emotionally laden through micro or macro trauma, such as a big loss or continuous admonishment by parents. The conflict resulting from the collision of the actual and the basic conflict sparks a whole chain of reactions within the individual. This we call the **interior conflict**—with all the emotions, indecisiveness, being torn in different directions, hurt feelings, sadness, frustration, fear, and anger that come with it. If the conflict is solved immediately, the symptoms subside. But suppose the conflict persists, and no inner or outer solution is found. In that case, the person who is dis-eased (not at ease) develops chronic problems, starts somatizing, and changes his life habits, takes to conflict compensation reactions such as drinking alcohol, developing risky behaviors, working harder or less, venting his anger on his family, and so forth.

Therefore, restoring balance to the personality structure is important to healing the wounds and finding fresh solutions to the basic conflict. Consider this example: Two young boys are ridiculed by their teacher. Both boys grow up with the same injustice, but one rebels against his parents. The other never learns to stand up for his rights. They react in diametrically opposite ways to the same situation. One curses and screams at the teacher and runs out of the room; the other cowers with guilt and shame and blames himself for not standing up for himself. So, the **basic conflict** or personality structure would be that when faced with injustice, one boy explodes and uses his mode of honesty to direct the conflict outwardly with aggressiveness, and the other, with his mode of courtesy, remains silent and blames himself. The **actual conflict** would be the situation with the teacher; **the inner conflict** the inner turmoil caused by the actual conflict meeting the **basic conflict** and resulting in the external reaction. We can say that a situation has awakened a "sleeping dog," which is the slumbering basic conflict. Carl Gustav Jung called it the shadow self.

Actual capacities

According to Aristotelian wisdom, it is necessary to live one's virtues to become happy. Dr. Peseschkian expanded on that wisdom by saying, "One has to fulfill one's actual capacities if one wants to live a happy and fulfilled life."

PPT asserts that all people are endowed from birth with two sets of actual capacities: the **primary capacity to love** and the **secondary**

capacity to comprehend or acquire knowledge. These capacities are not absolute values and are expressed distinctly in different cultures. These two **basic capacities** are basic human needs from which the **primary** and **secondary capacities** differentiate and transcend. They are like two seeds from which two trees with their trunks and then their branches grow, the trunk being the *basic capacities* from which the *actual capacities* in the form of *primary* and *secondary capacities* grow as branches. The *primary capacities* such as love, modeling, patience, and time enable us to enter into and maintain contact with other people. The *secondary capacities* such as punctuality, cleanliness, orderliness, and obedience shape our mode of contact to become an effective member of society. They are both learned, developed, and individually expressed through experience with our parents and social contacts in our formative years, and they continue to evolve throughout our life. Children learn the capacity to love and trust when their parents spend time with them, exhibiting patience and unconditional love. The importance of this capacity cannot be underestimated. Primary relationships provide the capability to enter into a relationship with and be at peace with oneself, to feel and develop a consciousness of oneself and the world, to find interest in the outside world, to play, discover, learn, and finally, to react adequately to conflicts.

Basic and Actual Capacities	
Primary Capacities	**Secondary Capacities**
Love	Punctuality
Modeling	Cleanliness
Patience	Orderliness
Time	Obedience
Contact	Courtesy
Sexuality	Honesty
Trust	Faithfulness
Confidence	Justice
Hope	Diligence
Faith	Thrift
Doubt	Reliability
Certitude	Precision
Unity	Conscientiousness

So, just as we all go through a differentiation process within the four dimensions during our childhood, we also differentiate in our capabilities for interacting with the world and people. Differentiation is a process we all experience in all areas of life. To explain the differentiation process in more detail, let's look at the following example of learning to discern between round things. There are round things one can play with and round ones one can eat. Among the edible ones are those you must wash before eating, like apples and pears, and those you should peel, like oranges. Among round things are also those that are recreational, like soccer balls and marbles. The process of learning through differentiation generally goes through various stages. We first instinctively distinguish between pleasure and pain, then learn to differentiate between dangerous and safe. Later, we learn what is acceptable and unacceptable and what is good and bad, which is then often reinforced by punishment and reward.

As there are differences between cultures, there are differences between human beings. These differences are simultaneously strengths and causes for conflict. Since the way we learn our values has passed from our conscious to our pre-conscious and is stored in our subconscious, the causes of our conflicts are usually not directly accessible to us. Nossrat Peseschkian developed specific tests, such as the Differentiation Analytic Inventory and the Wiesbadener Inventory for PPT, to reveal these conflicts systematically, making them accessible to our consciousness. Once we are aware of the causes of our conflicts, we can address them and develop strategies to resolve them.

As with our four dimensions, we must bring balance to our system of primary and secondary capacities so we can live in harmony with ourselves and express ourselves effectively to the outside world and work harmoniously with others. As we've seen in the example of the two young adults insulted by their teacher, the combination of courtesy and honesty are especially important here. These two secondary capacities combine to create the key conflict, directing the conflict energy outwards or inwards. *Honesty* is the capacity, or we can also say the capability, of openly expressing one's needs and conflict energy to the outside world, and *courtesy* is the ability to be polite, keeping one's needs to oneself and confining the conflict energy within oneself. We need both, and a person with an integrated personality uses them in balance as strengths. If we are overly courteous, we have many internal conflicts and rarely get what we want. If we are overly honest, we create external conflicts, getting what we want in the short term but losing in more conflicts in the long run. Therefore, it is important to bring honesty and courtesy into balance, having equal respect for ourselves and for others, and in doing so, creating connections and building a working team. As Dr. Peseschkian often said, if you work alone you add; if you work together you multiply.

Science has shown that the capability of being openly aggressive (Latin *aggredior*, "to approach") and selfish is of great importance to the expression of the human being. (*The Selfish Gene* by Richard Dawkins discusses this at length). At the same time, we humans also need the social capabilities of bonding and being able to work together (as noted by evolutionary biologist David Sloan Wilson). Being social is a successful form of higher adaptation through compassion, love, kindness, teamwork, and self-sacrifice, collectively known as the hive emotions. Mirror neurons that reflect other minds enable social groups to cooperate, hunt in groups, and create agriculture together. It has been shown that if you use only single best egg-laying hens for breeding, the descendants will fight each other to death within a few generations. On the other hand, if you allow the whole flocks of best egg-laying chickens to breed, the descendants will continue producing more and bigger eggs. This way, the group genes that include the greater hive emotions are cultivated and produce better egg-laying broods.

"Shadows on the Sundial"

A king once had a sundial installed in the marketplace of his city. He had bought it on one of his trips and thought it would be an amusing gift for his people. The people, in fact, were very curious about the sundial and soon used it exclusively to tell time. As the years passed, the country became prosperous and flourished. Everyone venerated the king, the benefactor of the sundial. But one day, he died unexpectedly, and his subjects mourned. Since he had been such a popular king, they decided to build a mausoleum. And what better place than the marketplace, where his memorable gift had been installed? So they erected his magnificent sepulchre on the ground near the sundial. However, the high walls of the new edifice blocked out the sun. In the beginning, the subjects were unaware of the damage they had done; they were still pleased with the honor they had bestowed on their departed king. However, as months progressed without the reliable sundial, the people became less punctual. With the loss of punctuality, many of the other accompanying virtues faded, and with it, the country's wealth.

*– Retold after Nossrat Peseschkian (*Oriental Stories*, p. 53)*

"Intelligence without love is cold, love without intelligence is naive, intelligence with love is wisdom."
- Nossrat Peseschkian

Primary and secondary capabilities are based on our basic capacities to love and comprehend

"With a childhood of love one can household for half a lifetime of coldness in the world."
- Nossrat Peseschkian

Here is a description of the primary and secondary capabilities Dr. Peseschkian gave us:

Primary capabilities based on the basic capacity to love:

- *Love*: The capacity of a positive emotional relationship that can be directed to many objects in different degrees
- *Modeling*: The ability to imitate others or to provide a model for others to imitate
- *Patience*: The ability to accept oneself, another person, or a situation the way they are
- *Time*: The ability to shape the course of time and to establish a relationship with the past, the present, and the future
- *Contact*: The ability to establish and cultivate social relationships
- *Sexuality*: The ability to establish with oneself or with a partner a sexual or sexually motivated relationship
- *Trust*: The ability to place oneself in the hands of another and to feel secure
- *Confidence*: The ability to depend on certain accomplishments and qualities and to expect them
- *Hope*: The ability to develop positive attitudes toward one's own capacities and those of one's partner and group, which go beyond the present moment
- *Faith*: The ability to establish a relationship with the unknown and unknowable and to approach it step by step until a part of this unknown becomes known

- *Doubt*: The ability to call a belief into question, to make distinctions, and to weigh matters against one another
- *Certitude*: The ability, after an attack of doubt, to make decisions that no longer provoke any guilty feelings
- *Unity*: The ability to integrate the configurations of the actual capacities, the basic capacities, the value system, and the experiences.

> *"Zeal without knowledge is a runaway horse."*
> *- English proverb*

Secondary capabilities based on the basic capacity to know/comprehend:

- *Punctuality*: The ability to hold an expected or agreed-upon distribution of time
- *Cleanliness*: The ability to maintain purity related to the body, clothing, objects of daily use, premises, and the environment and, in an analogous sense, to character
- *Orderliness*: The ability to organize and arrange one's perceptions and environment
- *Obedience*: The ability to accede to requests and follow orders and commands from an external authority
- *Courtesy*: The ability to shape interpersonal relationships. Its manifestation is manners, in which social rules are recognized.
- *Honesty/candor*: The ability to express one's opinion openly, to share one's needs or interests, and to give information
- *Faithfulness*: The ability to enter a stable relationship and to maintain it for a long time; to behave in a trustworthy manner
- *Justice*: The ability to balance one's self-interest against the interests of others
- *Diligence/achievement*: The ability and readiness to maintain a mostly exertive and fatiguing type of behavior over a prolonged period, to reach a certain goal
- *Thrift*: The ability to practice economy with money, valuables, capabilities, and energies
- *Reliability*: The ability to carry out a task even in the absence of supervision

- *Precision*: The ability to accomplish a task in the assigned way
- *Conscientiousness*: The ability to work according to one's own inner standard that is compatible with the conscience.

For all primary and secondary capacities, there are two opposite extremes. For example, in cleanliness, there is rigid orderliness on one side and messiness at the other extreme. Finding the balance between the extremes and living our capabilities without fear is important. If strong fear is driving cleanliness, it becomes compulsive; likewise, thrift becomes greed, love becomes jealousy, and time becomes stress. Therefore, we are reminded that every value has its counter value, and we are best situated somewhere in the middle between the extremes. We can always learn from our opposite. They are often shadow elements when at their extremes, and we react to them with overly strong emotions.

The four dimensions of role-modeling

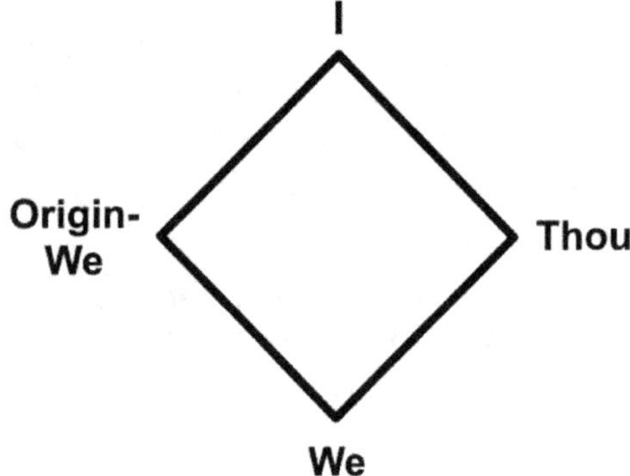

"Children who aren't loved become adults that can't love."
- Pearl Buck

Looking at human development, we can differentiate four dimensions of role-modeling for the capacity of love.

- **"I"**: How I experience myself, my self-perception, and the relationship "I" have with myself depends strongly on how I experienced myself through my parents. Did they love me, neglect me, or beat me? How did they exhibit their love, their happiness, or their anger toward me? How did they punish me? Did they use loving words, look at me lovingly, touch me tenderly, give me loving kisses and caresses, or did they neglect me or even verbally and physically hurt me?

- **"You":** The way we experience partnership, the "you" relationship, depends on how we experienced our parents' partnership. How did they live it? Were they in love, did they treat each other respectfully, did they have a marriage of convenience? Was one of them dependent on the other? Did they relate to one another through verbal and physical violence? How did they express their love, live their conflicts, and what was their relationship to sexuality?

- **"We":** What was the social life of my parents like? Were they sociable? Did they meet with many friends, invite friends over, did they participate in any clubs? What was the relationship with the extended family?

- **"Origin-We":** How did my family live spiritually? Did they live it with me? Did they pray, read holy scriptures, or go to the temple, church, or mosque with me? What general worldview and picture of God did they have? Was it a benevolent or a violent and punishing godhead?

The four dimensions of comprehension

We also differentiate four dimensions of comprehension through which we apprehend our world and learn to understand it. One, we use our senses (**means of the senses**) to gather information about our surroundings. Second, we then elaborate on the information we gather using our intellect (**means of understanding**). Third, we refine that information through education with knowledge that is passed on from generation to generation (**means of tradition**). Fourth, our inspiration combines with the information we have gathered and refined to create new ideas (**means of intuition**).

By differentiating our four dimensions of comprehension and the experiences we make through them, we develop the following capabilities:

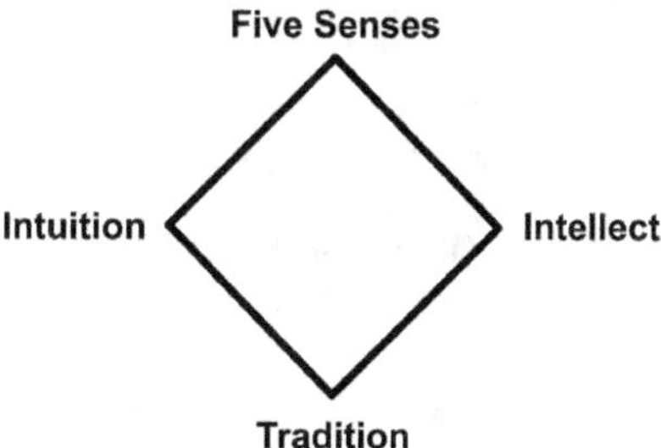

- **Means of the senses**: The structural capability to experience the body and our feelings.

- **Means of understanding**: Our capability to check reality and control activity.

- **Means of tradition**: The capability to enter relationships and maintain them, as well as our emotional communication with ourselves, the capacity for empathy, and the capability to anticipate the thinking and behavior of others.

- **Means of intuition**: The way we live meaningfully and intuitively, the ability to project into the future, and the capacity for fantasy or imagination. Intuition reaches beyond our immediate reality. It can include all that is meaningful, desirable, or utopian. It also includes the capability of bonding to ideals, people, and objects.

In addition to the four dimensions of comprehension, we also gain experience through our social connections in all our roles as grandparents, friends, teachers, coaches, and so forth. All social connections help form our capabilities and the picture we have of them and ourselves.

"Justice without love sees only performance and only compares. Love without justice loses control over reality. Learn to balance justice and love."
- Nossrat Peseschkian

The WIPPF Test

The Wiesbadener Inventory for Positive Psychotherapy and Family Therapy (WIPPF) is a wonderful tool for discovering the characteristic expression of our primary and secondary capabilities, conflict reactions, model dimensions, and social behavior. (A copy of the WIPPF is in the Appendix.) We can evaluate ourselves individually or in comparison to another person since the table gives us the space to fill in our own results on one side and those of a partner on the other. When we fill in the tables and mark the scales using a different color for each survey participant, we can immediately see where differences and potential conflict areas exist within a relationship.

- The **primary and secondary capabilities** indicate where we land on each scale of the actual capacities between the possible extremes of expression. Whenever expectations are not met on any one scale, we have the potential for conflict with ourselves or others. On whatever scale of the actual capacities, we find ourselves at an extreme; conflict potential with others or with ourselves exists whenever expectations are not met.

- Our **conflict reactions** show us in which of our four dimensions we usually react when we enter conflict and how we do so. We may react to conflict by developing psychosomatic symptoms or becoming alexithymic, unable **to identify and express or describe our feelings** (*body/health*). We may begin working harder or the opposite, abstaining from work (*work/achievement*). We might seek social support (*social life*) or try to make it on our own. Or we may seek a haven in spirituality and fantasy or remain purely materialistic (*spirituality/fantasy*).

- The **model dimensions** show us where we come from and the form of connectedness we have learned from our close ones. This section of the WIPPF reveals whether we feel distant or attached to our mother, father, or other people we grew up with (*I-dimension*). It addresses whether we experienced our parents' relationship as symbiotic or in opposition (*you-dimension*). It also reveals if our parents lived a life open for contact with others or closed within their relationship (*we-dimension*). And last, it reveals if our parents expressed strong ideals fervently or if they were insecure about them (*primary-we-dimension*).

- The **social behavior** with the secondary capabilities has a number of scales. The *active scale* shows us how passive-adaptive or overly self-controlled we are. The *reactive scale* shows how tolerant or rigid or controlling we are. The *concept scale* reveals how free of or fixed to concepts we are in general. It also shows us our emotional reactions, how intensely we react emotionally to transgressions of our values towards ourselves (*ego*), others (*we/you*), or more general concepts (*ideals*).

Working through the WIPPF and finding balance in life

We complete the entire WIPPF in one sitting. This assessment can be evaluated intuitively, and the results provide ample material for self-reflection. We can investigate our lives to find out where our strengths, difficulties, and conflicts with ourselves and others lie. Once we know ourselves better, we can enter a therapeutic process to heal using the five steps of therapy described further on in this book to find a greater balance in our lives.

Working on our primary and secondary capabilities and finding our balance in them

After reflecting on the results of the whole WIPPF, let's focus on the primary and secondary values next. We see our areas of strength and equilibrium and others where we might have room for improvement or mitigation. Then we choose the ones we can benefit from changing and take a six-week challenge to improve them. We make a checklist of these capacities and vow every morning to change them and then evaluate how we have done at the end of the day. If, in the evening, we notice that we didn't reach our targets, we start the six weeks over again. That way, we exercise our capabilities and make them a habit. We can improve our capabilities one by one, in pairs or groups, until we achieve our goals. If we want to address more capabilities at a time, we should allow more time for change.

Differentiation Analytic Inventory (DAI)

A valuable test for analyzing conflicts within a couple or two people in conflict is the DAI (Differentiation Analytic Inventory). It can be found in the appendix. It accesses our intuitive knowledge about the strengths and weaknesses of our actual capabilities in terms of our conflicts and conflict potential with our partner or others we compare ourselves to. It uses our intuitive estimation of the expression of our actual capacities and those of our counterparts using not a questionnaire but simple scales. It also asks about typical conflict situations. The DAI can be used as an abridged version of the WIPPF, giving a quick and valuable overview of conflictive topics between a couple or when there isn't time for a more in-depth investigation.

Further information can be found in the books of Nossrat Peseschkian and other PPT literature.

"There is nothing better in the world other than learning. When you stop learning, you sit down in a chair and it's over."
- Monserrat Caballé

The power of habits

Learning every day and putting your learnings into action is a prerequisite to thriving. We should always remember that knowing something without acting accordingly is as good as not knowing it. Theory remains nothing if we don't take charge and make the change. Let's make the commitment to having a pleasant life journey by being in charge of the four areas of life—body, work, social life, and future/spirituality. We demonstrate our care in these four areas when we take responsibility for the four pillars of our individuality—body, mind, emotions, and self.

We are all well versed on what it means to care for our bodies and the importance of lifelong learning, but we are not as conscious of what it means to care for our emotions. We can learn how to take charge of our thoughts by becoming aware of our emotions. Connecting to ourselves and paying attention to our emotions makes us aware of what is beneficial and toxic. We can regularly bring novelty for more happiness and well-being to our lives by creating new healthy habits in the physical, mental, and emotional dimensions. We change for the better when new habits replace the less healthy ones.

Although it may seem counterintuitive, being lazy is a great quality. By always trying to find a shortcut, our brain saves energy and simplifies its action so it will use less effort. Our repetitive, conscious daily acts are registered and gradually converted into automatic action. Repetition creates new pathways among the neurons in our brains, so the actions become easy and automatic, which is the essence of a habit. Our mind doesn't distinguish between good and bad habits, but it has the tendency to repeat them in similar situations so we can save energy. This pattern has always been essential to the development of humankind, beginning with primitive man. The more we do in automatic mode, the more energy we have for free decision. Habits are learned and then become unconscious.

A **habit** is created when we have a repeated trigger that is regularly followed by an action, which in time turns into a routine and stimulates a reward/compensation expected in the end.

One might say, for example, "When I got home tired and stressed (trigger), I used to sit down in front of the TV and watch the news followed by a movie. I ate Twix or ice cream (routine) and relaxed (compensation). Following that routine, I ended up feeling demotivated, weak, and lethargic afterward. This also led to a sense of guilt for abusing my body, so I consciously changed this routine by going for a walk after work. That way, I had time to relieve my stress before I cooked a delicious meal. With this new habit, I can feel the reward of true relaxation and well-being in my body."

Changing our habits is difficult in the beginning since habits are deeply engrained, but as we continue, our new habits also become routine and effortless. So, we create a new routine by first becoming conscious about which harmful habit we want to replace with a physically, emotionally, or mentally better one. The following step is to plan what we want to do differently, how, precisely, we will do it, and who or what can help us with the change.

There are some habits that can bring multiple benefits to our lives. Wholesome eating makes a significant contribution to our health. Quitting smoking ends a damaging habit. Therefore, we can call them powerful habits. Some of the most powerful and beneficial ones are sports, meditation, reading, and socializing. They bring immense physical, emotional, and psychological benefits within a noticeably brief time, enrich our lives, and are known to contribute to happiness and well-being.

Our motivation to discard bad habits can be seen in the light of an analogy. Consider the matches as our motivation and the wax of a candle as our willpower. Would we prefer having five matches or a strong candle? Our motivation gives us the initiative to create a new habit that must be practiced with willpower to become self-sustaining and to require minimal energy on our part.

"If you want to learn a language, don't get yourself a course-book about the language but a girlfriend from the country whose language you want to learn."
- Gerald Hüther

Changing our habits

We write down five habits that come to mind spontaneously because they get on our nerves the most. We want to change these habits by first looking at the benefits of changing them. We then go back to evaluating our primary and secondary capabilities as well as our four dimensions, and we systematically see where a change of a habit or two could bring essential benefit to our lives.

- What would we really like to change? What would we like to change it to?

- What would life be like after this change?

- How would we feel because of this change?

We will notice that small but essential changes can bring substantial changes to our level of happiness and state of well-being. We may notice that we want to change many of the habits we have acquired during our life, but we don't have to change them all at the same time. Changing selected ones will bring major changes. Just imagine changing or creating just one habit every month; that would add up to twelve beneficial new habits in a year.

The real magic begins when we get into action and stop thinking about change but really bring it about. There is nothing more important and effective than getting started. So, let's get moving! Not doing anything is also doing something. It is the conscious action of doing nothing. It is different from unconscious inaction because we are paralyzed.

Enthusiasm (from the Greek *enthousiasmos*, meaning "inspired or possessed by God") combined with commitment and discipline is the best way to change our habits. We might call this combination grit. When energetic motivation is paired with relentless commitment, we approach our habits with determination.

Thirty-day challenge

We begin with the first habit we want to introduce, the one we want to exchange it for, and a specific day to begin the thirty-day challenge. We may choose exercising every day, eating whole foods regularly, drinking enough water before and between meals, dancing a bit every day, smiling at our coworkers, giving a gift every day, or any other practice we deem as beneficial to our well-being. An important fixed rule is that if we miss a single day, we must begin again. When we get to day twenty, we count backward: ten, nine, eight... When doubts arise, we detach from them and say yes to our challenge.

If we want to change more than one habit at a time, keeping a list of them nearby to read and reread during the day is helpful. This way, we don't forget them in the turmoil of our everyday life. We read the list in the morning when we wake up and read it again in the evening before going to sleep. We check them off one by one when we have reached thirty days and feel we have integrated them into our regular life. The more habits we try to integrate simultaneously, the longer it will take to bring them into automatic mode—if we are working with four to six changes at the same time, we must count on forty to forty-five days for integration.

Situation – concept – counter-concept for changing ourselves

We all have reactions that make us uncomfortable, but we know that they are typical and characteristic for us, even if we don't like them and would like to change them. They reoccur frequently, but nothing ever changes because we keep ignoring them. For changing such a behavior, PPT offers the following strategy. We keep a diary of these situations and see where and when they occur and immediately write them down when they happen. We can also use our WIPPF and DAI to search the actual capacities where we tend to any extreme and reflect on daily situations where we got unnerved. We then analyze the following:

- **Situation:** With whom did I get angry? In what situation?
- **Concept:** How did I react?
- **Counter-concept:** How could I have reacted?

Example:

- *Situation*: Little John didn't want to do his homework today when he came from school.

- *Concept*: His father says angrily, "If you don't do your homework now, you'll not be watching TV tonight!"

- *Counter-concept*: His father could say: "I understand that it is difficult for you to do all the homework right after school. You surely feel tired and need to clear your mind first. You will want to take a break first and go outside and play for half an hour. Then you can come in to complete your schoolwork. When you don't do your homework, I worry about your future. You know that your education is particularly important for you to be able to choose what you want to do one day."

We can show our consideration by trying to understand how the other person feels. We then also express what we feel and need and why we need it. We try to find a common solution. We must search for a new solution if this doesn't work out.

Another example:

- *Situation*: When Henriette gets home, she sees Andrew has already cooked dinner for her. But she also noticed he used the salad they had just bought and not the vegetables that had been in the fridge for a week.

- *Concept*: She says in an angry voice: "I've told you so many times to use the food that is going to expire first and not just cook what you like! You obviously don't care for our environment!"

- *Counter-concept*: She focuses on his effort first and says: "Thanks, Andrew, for cooking for me! I really appreciate that. It smells wonderful. We shouldn't forget to use the vegetables tomorrow, though. Otherwise, they will lose their flavor, and we might even have to throw them out."

As in this example, it is always helpful to express one's appreciation. This helps us create a stronger relationship with our counterparts. A strong, healthy relationship is always important for fulfilling both sides' needs. Putting ourselves in other peoples' shoes and trying to understand why they do something helps us connect. In addition, it helps us mitigate our extreme expectations, see the other side in a positive way, and grow personally. Every side has its positive perspective. If we look with new eyes, we will find it.

When we have found a solution to the behavior we want to change, we go over it repeatedly and practice it aloud until it becomes our first nature. We'll not be perfect the first time we need our new strategy again, but we surely will learn with further practice.

The influence of our shadow on our balance

We can call the limiting beliefs about ourselves and the world our **shadow self**. It is a part of our subconscious self that is based on fear and is anger-laden. It undermines our happiness and pulls us down. Our equilibrated, well-functioning self-parts, on the other hand, are empowering. They give us validation, openness, and the ability to connect and love, and they enable us to be creative and live up to our individual potential. A fearful and tormented childhood with neglect or a punishing education can cause us to un-love ourselves, limit and inhibit our self-expression, and keep us from expressing ourselves with joy and warmheartedness. We are born with a full set of capabilities and talents ready to develop and manifest in life. Before birth, they lay dormant in seed form within us, yet they are prepared to sprout and grow the moment we are born. They grow and differentiate quickly during childhood and adolescence, manifesting into a great fruit tree with many branches. However, negative experiences and education with punishment and reward force us to develop certain capabilities and personal traits while we neglect or even repress others completely. Example: Education is like pruning and taking care of a tree. If pruned and well cared for, it will bear excellent fruit. If pruned insufficiently and left in infertile soil, it will grow without any cultivation, not bearing fruit. If pruned excessively and treated badly, it won't grow straight and strong but will remain awkward and twisted. In the act of repressing our capabilities, we lose our awareness of them and deny their existence within ourselves, but at the same time, we see them in more dangerous forms in others. When capabilities have been laden with fear and anger in childhood through negative experiences as well as punishment and reward, every contact with situations or people that represent these will trigger negative emotions. Like a sleeping dog that growls menacingly when woken, we are expressing our shadow-self. The more we reject and repress certain capabilities in ourselves, the more we see them in others and our environment. Complete repression leads us to see everyone but ourselves as threatening.

When we haven't learned to express a certain positive capability—because of lack of opportunity or perhaps a repressive or over-protected childhood that resulted in shyness—its potential will lay dormant within us and may express itself in our admiration of it in other people. We call this our **golden shadow**. It is a trait we would instinctively love to express but still haven't developed. For example, consider our inborn ability to feel and express anger. Although it is a strong capability for getting what we want when expressed in a healthy, mature way, the more we have learned to despise and repress it in ourselves, the more we experience it in others, start to hate it, and subconsciously become envious of others who express it strongly. If we admire a jovial, expressive, and strong person, we probably haven't discovered these aspects in ourselves yet. We admire them in others without being conscious that we, too, may have these inborn capacities and could develop them ourselves.

Many things about people and our surroundings attract or infuriate us. The things about which we feel most negatively or positively are deeply connected to our interior selves and are, in fact, projections of ourselves. We know that when other people really get on our nerves, or we see something extraordinarily beautiful in them, their personalities resonate with us. They are activating something deeply related to us; the person who triggers us is acting as a mirror of internal motivation. When we become aware that this is happening, we can open ourselves to the unique opportunity to understand and recognize ourselves in greater depth. Once we are conscious of the reflexive reactions our shadow provokes, we can stop reacting to them. Instead, we can ask ourselves why we react and what we can do differently. We begin a process of discovering our shadow, becoming aware of the situations in which we react defensively or aggressively when we are angry and become condescending. With this self-knowledge, we are free to forgo the drama and scenes we once acted out. Becoming aware of our shadow and learning to find its positive sides and hidden treasures, we gradually integrate our repressed parts into a healthier form of personality and benefit from it for the sake of our own development. This means we mature into a more integral and creative grownup. To reintegrate our golden shadow, we open ourselves up to fulfilling the desires lying behind our exuberant admiration of the capabilities we see in others.

Some people do things that go against our personal beliefs, but we ignore these actions because they don't have anything to do with us. But other situations enrage us or kindle our admiration. In these instances, it is worthwhile to take a closer look at what shadow is lying behind our reaction and to see where we can heal and benefit from integrating its positive aspects. Perhaps the specific attribute is a part of ourselves that we strongly reject and repress and get angry about when we see it expressed by others; deep down inside, we are simultaneously envious of these individuals' capability of expressing it. Or we feel insecurity and anxiety about it because we haven't developed it well, and we would like to be able to live and express it. We can repress different aspects of ourselves, our drives, feelings, and capabilities. But they are all important for us to function integrally as human beings, and it is necessary to reintegrate them and have them functioning well. At the same time, we don't have to learn to love everything in life because this, too, would be an imbalance, a one-sidedness.

"The direction of your focus is the direction your life will move. Let yourself move toward what is good, valuable, strong, and true."
- Ralph Marston

Whatever we focus on, we create and attract more of in our lives. So, if we constantly focus on the things we don't like or hate, we will find more of them appearing in our lives. This negativity colors our view of the world. How often have we seen people and only seen part of them, not even recognizing that they wear glasses or the color eyes they have because we don't see with our eyes; we see with our brains. There is an experiment in which observers are asked to watch a group of people bounce a basketball among each other, and they are supposed to count the times the players pass the ball. The observers are so intent on their task that few notice a person crossing the court in a bizarre gorilla costume. The same thing happens with a movie showing bees in a beehive. If we were told to concentrate on a certain bee and afterward were asked to say which of the other bees were in focus, we wouldn't have noticed that the one we were watching was the only one in focus and not blurry. Here is another interesting study about our observational capabilities: In this experiment, a random person passes by on the street and someone asks for directions. Suddenly two workers carrying a large object pass between the two, and the person asking for directions is replaced by another person. The subject focused on giving directions doesn't even notice the exchange.

You can conduct your own experiment to demonstrate the degree of focus in humans. Look around your room for all the green objects. Then afterward, ask yourself how many yellow objects there are. It is likely that you will not know. We come to understand that by focusing on one specific aspect, others fade from our perception.

If we have only a hammer, we see everything as a nail. If we are a hairdresser, we see that everyone needs a haircut. Our intentions, convictions, and habits create our focus and provide the filters through which we see the world, just as a camera can create clear or fuzzy pictures of the same subject. If we believe that Volkswagen and Toyota build inferior cars, our personal experience will be reinforced by every Volkswagen and Toyota stalled on the roadside. This filter system works autonomically and is called **confirmation bias**. Our difficulties are less about what we don't know and more about what we know with certainty. These beliefs taint our view of life and affect our self-motivation. Typically, these beliefs aren't altered by scientific statistics. Normally, we see what we believe, and even statistics can't convince us of the contrary.

> *"Energy flows where attention goes."*
> *- Huna Principle*

- Create a goal for changing our focus: If we have mindless work, we make it our goal to try to fulfill it in a way so that we learn something new or we can relax during work time.

- Change our own filters: We note situations in which others changed our filter either consciously or unconsciously. (For example, we changed our opinion during a conversation.) We note a situation in which we have changed our filter consciously or unconsciously. (Think of a person or situation of which you have changed your opinion.)

This practice shows us how our attention works and gives us insight into how we see only what we are expecting and are easily fooled. In some circumstances, we act as if we were a bird caught in a room. We continuously fly against a window, seeing what we want beyond it but without being able to get to it. We bang our heads against the window without recognizing an open door next to it. Our false beliefs become the lifeboats we cling to, but they can't help us anymore since they were created for different life situations. We are always seeing life through the glasses created by our life stories, repeating our patterns of behavior yet blind to the great sea of possibilities in front of us. We are extremely set in our focus and ways. What we focus on becomes our reality, limiting our personal universe. If we don't open our eyes widely, we only scratch the surface of reality.

"If the doors of perception were cleansed, everything would appear to man as it is, Infinite. For man has closed himself up till he sees all things through narrow chinks of his cavern."
- William Blake

We determine our future by deciding what we want to see. We can change this attitude by consciously opening ourselves to the whole spectrum of reality and learning to accept and love our shadow.

"One needs much more strength to accept the truth than to defend a mistake."
- G. C. Lichtenberg

How to work with our shadow and bring balance to our subconscious

We all have our human traits individually developed to different degrees. When they are stressed to the extreme and are emotionally laden, they become difficult. Whenever we get into a situation that evokes strong emotions, such as rage, or whenever we feel that someone is pressing all our emotional buttons, we can choose either to react and get defensive or aggressive or to become more aware of ourselves, our triggers, and the shadows hiding behind them.

"Your laziness really gets on my nerves!"

- *To what extent is this something about me?*

It always has something to do with me. A moviegoer may be bored, moved emotionally, or even enraged by a film. Personal reactions depend strongly on the character of the person sitting in the movie, his family, and his social background. Although to a degree, all humans have certain reactions in common, we own our personal past and individual personality, the keys to how we interpret and react to outer circumstances:

- *It is something I get furious about, but is it an intrinsic part of me that I might not want to admit having and that threatens me? Am I avoiding, repressing, or actively trying to do the opposite of something?*

We investigate by *turning it around* from *you* to *me* and looking for the *hidden truths* of our shadow and the *positive interpretation* of the situation that can eventually alleviate our pain and let us grow.

"Your laziness really gets on my nerves!"

- *Am I sometimes "lazy"?*

- *Am I an "overachiever" and rigid?*

- *What are the advantages of the other side, the positive sides of "being lazy—the capability to take more leisure and time?*

There is always a positive interpretation, the other side of the coin. But in the moment, we react with fear, shame, doubt, or hate. We rigidly cling to the one side that has always been our lifeboat, our way of surviving as a child, and we repress the other, more beneficial side. We stay blind to a healthier, more beneficial lifestyle even when our current one is unhealthy and does us damage. We must consciously open our eyes to how we can heal ourselves by experiencing the repressed side, changing our view on a subject, re-owning our shadow, and bringing ourselves back into balance with life. Both sides have positive aspects, and it is in our interest to build inner strength and health throughout the whole scale of notes within the music of our personality and to become more flexible and resilient in new situations.

- *Where can we loosen up that rigid part of us and strengthen our opposite sides?*

- *We may question our strategy of making too many appointments.*

We can dig further into the depth of ourselves by asking:

- *What other fear may be lying behind our tendency to overschedule?*

- *Is it that we need attention (love) through excessive activity and success, or is it a deep-seated fear of not surviving because our parents were penniless (security), or is it our frenetic work to become independent (autonomy)?*

- *What are we gaining from our behavior? What false benefits are we clinging to that we might not need anymore? What can we do about this situation so it will not bother us anymore?*

We can recall experiences from our past where overscheduling was important and come to understand how we learned that behavior. The behavior might have made sense at the time, to protect us from the rage and anger of our uncaring, achievement-oriented parents. In today's context, filling our calendar doesn't make sense anymore.

After this examination of our past, we can learn new healthier behaviors and new capabilities.

- *Who would I be without these reactions and emotions? Having let them go, how would my physical and emotional body feel?*

We can visualize and live in opposite perspectives and practice them. In any case, we can always decide to keep or change our behavior, but we have the important chance to challenge our habits and question them.

> *"Medicine has three components: The disease, the sick person, and the doctor. All treatment is in vain if the patient doesn't participate in the treatment his doctor administers."*
> *- Paracelsus*

Shadow work, step by step

1. First, we write a *daily report* about the situations that really unnerve us during the day.

2. We then get a clear look at the *contents* (example: Achievement-punctuality).

3. Then we *turn it around* and ask ourselves if we possess this quality, and if so, when we express it.

4. When we have become clear on that, we look at *the positive opposite* side of the quality concerned and what we would gain by letting go of our rigid interpretation. (To do this, we can let the other person explain his position in our imagination.)

5. We can ask what we are getting out of it by *looking for the fear* that may be lying behind it (not getting attention/love or loss of security or autonomy, for example). Are these fears true? Are we still getting something out of it, or are these beliefs false and out of date? Do we live in a different world now, and have we matured into adults?

6. As a last step, we examine who we would be without these reactions and emotions and *who we would be with our changed attitude*. We *personalize this new skin* and take the challenge to work on this new trait we want to develop. We imagine it in the morning and at night before going to bed and take score of the changes and note the brilliantly jazzier tune we begin to play.

We can systematically go through the causes of stress our shadow weighs upon us by analyzing our relationships and ourselves by means of the DAI and the WIPPF. Here we can look for our neuralgic or painful points by searching for a combination of excessively high or low scores in an area that strikes a chord with us and expresses itself through rage in exemplary situations. These scores are clear indicators that we have an area that we can learn to re-own. Working on these reduces the amount of micro-trauma that adds up to rage, frustration, and depression with time. We can work the shadows we find here in the same way we work through the ones we notice spontaneously.

Further examples of shadow-forms according to Ken Wilber:

Symptom	Original shadow form
Resentment of outside pressure	<= Drive
Rejection ("nobody likes me")	<= Rejection ("I reject them")
Guilt ("You make me feel guilty")	<= Resentment (of other's demands)
Anxiety	<= Excitement
Self-consciousness	<= Outward focus (on others)
Sexual dysfunction	<= "I wouldn't give him/her satisfaction"
Fear ("They want to hurt me")	<= Hostility ("I'm angry and attacking without knowing it")
Sad	<= Mad
Withdrawn	<= Rejecting
I can't	<= "I won't, dammit!"
Obligation ("I have to")	<= Desire ("I want to")
Hatred	<= Self-hatred
Envy ("You're so great")	<= I'm better than I realize (A golden shadow form)

Working with our golden shadow

We can find our golden shadow by looking through our daily report and seeing where we admire someone excessively. We then ask ourselves if that person has traits or capabilities that we would like to develop in ourselves or if we already possess them and only need to express them more. We can then visualize ourselves in the future, manifesting these traits daily.

"It is not sufficient to only know, you should make use of your knowledge. It is not sufficient to only wish, you should make your wishes turn into reality."
- Goethe

When it isn't about us

If it isn't about us being the compulsive troublemaker, maybe it's about us not standing up for ourselves? If we find that it isn't about us and our personal shadow but that the other person is the one who is continuously hurting us, then it may be time to separate. We have to ask ourselves if our continuous efforts are lifting them up to their potential or if they are abusing us only for their own misguided, maybe self-destructive objectives. If they are continuously dragging us down and our efforts are merely helping them sustain their bad behavior. If, instead of being helpers and encouraging them to go forward in life, we have only become their enablers, permitting them again and again to continue their misguided vices. If, over time, they have perpetually expected more and more from us, draining our energy. We begin to see that all our failed attempts to help them have only led us into a downward spiral of resentment and depression. Once we realize this, it is time to say goodbye. It may be difficult to let go, especially if they are close friends. But we must get out of the trap of not wanting to hurt their feelings, always looking for their better sides, and the fear of leaving them to their own peril. If the relationship has become tiresome and toxic, the sooner we say goodbye, the better.

When we conclude that we must sever the friendship and go our separate ways, everyone will benefit. We will find more people with whom we will enjoy sharing a mutually beneficial friendship. We can attract and surround ourselves with people who inspire and motivate us instead of pulling us down. So let's stop letting others use us. When we stand up for ourselves, we can look into the mirror with pride instead of misguided compassion. Others will also start to admire us, since people admire strong, independent personalities. Declaring boundaries in a one-way friendship enables us to face our issues and stand up for ourselves. We don't want others to pull us down to their level so they can stand higher; we want to stand tall at our own inestimable height. We want to emanate worthiness and respect; we can't do that when we let others drag us down with their insecurity. We don't have to feel guilty, because we aren't being mean to others by being in balance with ourselves and reality. We give others a helping hand when we don't allow them to indulge in self-pity or when we stop enabling their maladaptive and self-destructive behaviors. It is "tough love but true love." It is the only way some people learn. We tell them what we genuinely believe, or if that openness is not possible, we just disappear out of their lives. If they object, we stick to our position and don't give way, don't let them open the door again with their arguments, accusations, and whining. It's over; we're not going back into that unproductive loop. Once we have decided to respect our own needs, we realize it's not about them anymore, and the relationship is not good for us, so we let go.

"Starting a war is like cutting through a knot instead of untying it."
- Nossrat Peseschkian

The principle of consultation: The art of resolving conflicts through communication and diplomacy

"The Prophet and the Long Spoons"

Mohammad once asked the prophet Elias the difference between heaven and hell. Elias told him, "Come along with me, and I will show you." He took him down into the depths of a big palace, where they entered a pleasant room well-lit by torches. The air smelled of a wonderful soup. In marked contrast to the pleasant room and wonderful aroma, there were sounds of people wailing. Those gathered around a huge soup pot had overly long spoons. As they tried to eat, they spilled the boiling soup on one another. Unable to nourish themselves, they became angry and resorted to hitting one another with the spoons. Elias said, "This is hell." Then they went on to another room that was just as pleasant, well-lit, and aromatic as the first, but this room was filled with laughter and happy chatter. Mohammad saw how the people in this room helped each other eat, feeding one another with the overly long spoons. Each one was happy to help the other. Now Mohammad said, "I understand. This, now, is heaven."

- Retold after Nossrat Peseschkian (*Oriental Stories*, p. 26)

While conflicts are inevitable, they can be a source of growth. Everything is changing and developing; nothing is perfect and finished. So, we must adapt and solve conflicts constantly and not deny their existence.

Being diplomatic and using empathic communication in conflicts is indicative of a respectful attitude. These skills emanate from a genuine belief in everyone's worth. What's more, we can openly express this belief by being able to say, "You are important to me" and "I respect you" to others. It is an expression of the knowledge that the secret of successful people is durable relationships, and it signals our will to respect and integrate all participants' desires, wishes, and intentions. Secondly, it consists of all the techniques of an empathic dialogue: Trying to be fair and friendly to the other and not to offend them. Always looking for sustainable win-win solutions for all conflict participants, not just grasping for one's own quick success. Acting in a way for as long as necessary and with the necessary means to cultivate a positive relationship with another person.

When going into a relationship, it is worthwhile to look at its quality and the dialogue existing between ourselves and our partner. Attitude and speech influence the outcome of our interactions with one another and make the difference between dialogue and one-sided discussion. Our affairs will benefit if we grow a strong connection with our work partners. Since a true capability for dialogue isn't inherited but developed, we can all learn it. People with a strong capability of politeness have an advantage in diplomacy: They think first, then they talk. People with strong honesty have the tendency to speak, then think, then speak again, hurting or making others defensive, often having to make up for the damage they have done. The core competence of diplomacy is becoming conscious of the conversation contents and the process during our discussion. We must be able to recognize conflict situations beforehand and analyze and manage them as objectively and diplomatically as possible. A helicopter perspective gives us the distance from the conflict we need, emotionally as well as contextually. With that distance, we can become less enmeshed and view it more objectively. We further need to be able to perceive our own feelings, needs, and thoughts as well as those of others and the state of our interpersonal relationship through sensitivity, good mentalizing, and empathic capabilities. We must simultaneously manifest good self-control and communicative capabilities for formulating our speech politely, smoothly, and appreciatively, and do this with high regard for our counterpart and good self-guidance/control—the fine line between openness and self-control. Straightforward appreciation of our counterpart is indispensable since any incongruence will be noticed quickly and will sow distrust.

"One thing is for sure: Rude people feel powerless in their own lives; they are terrified of not being in control. But that's not you, I'm sure!"
- Anonymous

Five steps toward dialogue and conflict resolution

To solve conflicts efficiently and compassionately with solution orientation, there are five steps of conflict resolution, according to Nossrat Peseschkian.

1. When in conflict, we first use **observation and distancing**. This means we take a step back, empathically listening to ourselves and our counterparts with all our faculties. We try to capture the whole picture of the situation, just as someone flying over in a helicopter would see the whole forest instead of each individual tree. Our openness and empathy create a connection with the person with whom we have a conflict. We can strengthen this process by paraphrasing and reflecting back feelings or needs wholeheartedly.

2. When we have heard the other person out, hear a sigh, or notice a change in their word flow, we **make an inventory**: We dig even deeper into the issue by asking specific questions about the distinct aspects of the conflict and explore its details profoundly. This inventory helps us gain an even deeper understanding of the conflict territory and the opportunities to map out its difficulties, beauty, and potential solutions.

3. The third step is called **situational encouragement**: We bring appreciation to the person we are against, appreciate his propositions and efforts to look for an optimal solution, as well as the positive sides of our problem and the situation we are in. Thereby, we create a durable connection with our counterpart and show him respect while we convey our own self-esteem.

4. In **verbalization,** we address the issues and problems honestly and courteously and assert the desires and objectives important

to us while still maintaining a durable connection. The stronger the connection we create in the first steps, the easier this will be.

5. **Broadening of goals**, the last step, involves creating new motivating goals and thereby directing our energy towards the future. This step is important because much of the energy that was consumed by and connected to the issues is now without direction and dispersed afterward. If no new goals are established, we will soon feel empty, void of meaning, without direction, or bored. Boredom can be just as unhealthy and unpleasant as the overload we feel in the conflict. New goals can strengthen our new relationship and direct us into a future partnership.

These five steps help us open our neurotic narrowness of mind and are a firm basis for connection and communication in conflict situations as well as normal dialogue in our social and work partnerships. They can help our partners and us lead a happy, prosperous life.

In PPT, we use these five stages as an integral treatment strategy, a therapeutic strategy in which psychotherapy and self-help intertwine. We use the five steps as the basis of therapy itself, and at the same time, give it to our clients so they can use it for themselves for self-help. They can share the communication strategy with their closest ones to facilitate communication and strengthen healing processes. In coaching and therapy, as well as in our everyday life, we can do the same. Let's use it for our personal communication and, at the same time, pass it on to others so we all can come to a greater mutual understanding.

*"Pick a person up where he is and not
where one wants him to be."
- Nossrat Peseschkian*

Using the three stages of interaction to improve communication with others and ourselves

In PPT, we distinguish between three stages of interaction: **connection, differentiation,** and **detachment.** We go through these three stages in our life and in communication. As infants, we begin our life in intense connection with our parents. We then differentiate and develop from childhood to adolescence, so we become individuals. When we have finally matured enough, we acquire the ability to detach from the protective nest of our parents and lead our own lives.

Connection - Differentiation - Detachment

We experience a similar process in communication. We say hello and connect with our counterpart when we meet her. After creating a connection, we then go into differentiation and discuss our issues, and after concluding, we then detach with satisfaction.

There can be disturbances in these processes. While maturing or as an already mature person, we can still regress into dependency (a stage of connection). When we are in a severe conflict with ourselves or others, we may somatize or **manifest psychological distress through physical symptoms** as an expression of being completely overwhelmed and feeling helpless. This regression can also be seen as a deep cry for help, for "Mamma." At its extreme, this can even lead to wetting the bed at night—"the capability for crying downwards."

- When we notice that we are in this process of regression, we can question ourselves about its cause, trying to understand ourselves and our needs more deeply so we can take the necessary action.

In communication, we can meet at various stages of interaction. It could be that we come home from work exhausted and seeking quiet and rest while our partner, on the contrary, is waiting for us, expecting conversation and connection. When making a professional phone call, our colleague might go straight into differentiating about a subject while we are expecting a greeting or standard connection first. In a misguided effort to nurture closeness with her granddaughter, a grandmother may assign the girl a list of chores. But wishing instead to have friendly chats, her frustrated granddaughter refuses to see her anymore. If both knew that they were both seeking connection, they could easily resolve the dissatisfaction, but without mutual understanding, they continuously upset each other.

- So, if we know about these various stages of interaction, we look, see, and understand where our counterpart is. Once we understand what he is looking for, we can address him where he is and get our own needs satisfied too.

The three stages—connection, differentiation, and detachment—are also aligned with different organs of our body. Connection is represented by our heart; differentiation is attributed to our brain, and detachment (or autonomy) to our abdomen. In addition to being rational adults, we want to feel alive, have fun, and listen to our body and what it needs. Being a mature adult means having all of this. We want to wake up full of energy and creativity, go out and enjoy taking part in life, assume responsibility, and live our dreams with our fully conscious and intuitive minds. There are many proverbs concerning our heart and gut feelings: "I did it with heart," "You are always in my heart," "My heart is aching," "I have butterflies in my stomach," "The situation is lying heavily on my stomach," and "I have a gut feeling about that." Our hearts and abdomens are not only muscular but also neurological, endocrinological, and immunological organs. Our enteric nervous system has approximately 100,000 neurons; our hearts have some 40,000 neurons. They are independent and interdependent systems, just like our brains. They contribute to the autonomous function of the individual organs and, at the same time, they reflect our conscious and subconscious activity and therefore contribute to our feelings and thoughts. They habitually react reflexively to situations through intuition based on subconscious experiences and ancestral knowledge via our limbic system even before our frontal lobes have a chance to notice what is going on consciously.

Our heart has a magnetic field that transmits our emotions, which can be received by other animals and probably by human beings around us too. We experience feelings of compassion in our hearts, gut feelings in our abdomen, and rational thinking in our brains. We can contact our subconscious "heart intelligence" or "abdominal intelligence" by focusing on these areas and interpreting the information they give us in the form of feelings and emotions. Do we feel connected to another person or reserved about him? What kind of gut feeling does a situation give us? Is it inspiring, or do we have a bad feeling about it? Here our collective subconscious experience and that of our ancestors express themselves, and we can listen in to find help in decision-making. It isn't that we should solely base our decisions on these sensations but that we include them because they are valuable resources. We should also question them. Are they influencing us because of traumatic experiences in the past that don't apply to our situation today? Or are they giving us advice in a field in which we have no experience at all, and our subconscious is completely out of its range of competence? In any case, it is always helpful to take into rational account what our subconscious is trying to tell us about the situation we are facing by listening to our head, heart, and gut and by paying attention to the signals they are sending.

Listening to the "triad" according to Gabriela von Witzleben

Whenever we are in a situation in which we have difficulties deciding, we can reconnect to ourselves and bring harmony to our conflictive interior by asking our whole self to help us with the decision.

We imagine three circles on the ground: one as our head, one as our abdomen, and one as our heart. We step into each of these circles, focus our attention on the specific organ system in the triad, and ask each how it feels about our indecision. We can also let the triad members speak to one another about the topic since our brain is automatically connected to the other two organ systems (heart and abdomen). We bring our awareness to one part of the triad at a time. Each system tends to react with the following guiding principles:

- Brain: security

- Heart: connection

- Abdomen: autonomy

So, whenever we get into a situation where we need advice and to find new balance, we stop and bring our attention to our body using this reflection system. We can do this whenever we want to. We can, for example, make it a ritual to ask about the impending questions of the day in the shower. "What would be the best decision? What are your suggestions?" We may find a convincing compromise as we listen to our head, heart, and abdomen.

We reap what we sow.

Our attitude as a catalyst to attaining to our goals

As I have already mentioned, the attitude with which we meet our counterparts plays a key role in conflict resolution. It is essentially important to become conscious of our personal attitude and know its effects on our relationships. What basic attitude do we tend towards?

- A **submissive basic attitude**: Giving way—I want to please, to have harmony and peace.

- A **destructive basic attitude**: Force as its basis—I want to convince, to be right and win.

- Or is it our intention to meet our counterpart with: A **constructive basic attitude**: Collaboration and diplomacy—I want to understand using cognitive understanding and emotional empathy. I want to communicate what's important to me honestly and courteously. I want to respect myself and others using balanced justice and love. I hope to find a substantial compromise using the logic and creativity that all parties bring to the conflict, suggesting, at best, a new solution that goes beyond a compromise.

When we read about these different basic attitudes, we intuitively understand which one will bring more contentment, greater prospects, and more lasting success. So, let's check out our attitude and find out how we can integrate more collaboration and diplomacy into our lives. Our motto will be to:

Understand, communicate, respect, compromise, and resolve our conflicts creatively, bringing new projects and happiness.

"The Hedgehog Dilemma"

A family of hedgehogs got together in a bed of leaves under a bush to sleep at night. As it got colder, they drew together to give each other warmth. But because of their little prickly spines, they soon felt uncomfortable poking each other, so they moved apart again. Sleeping separately let the cold creep in again and forced the hedgehog family to snuggle together once more. Over time, they found the right distance to enjoy the cozy warmth of being together and, at the same time, found a comfortable distance for not poking each other.

- Retold after Nossrat Peseschkian (also used by A. Schopenhauer and S. Freud)

Recognizing other people's needs

Recognizing and considering the needs of others is an important aspect of maintaining a healthy relationship and building allegiances in our private and professional life. The needs for security, belonging, autonomy, and status are often vulnerable in relationships. When we infringe on them in a conversation, especially if our counterpart is particularly sensitive in one of these areas, our words can cause defensiveness or aggression and catapult the discussion from a calm dialogue to an emotional minefield. We might be able to manipulate and pressure someone into doing what we want them to do in the short run, but eventually, they will become reluctant to negotiate, bargain, or work with us again. Emotions play an outsized role in our negotiations and discussions, up to 80%. It is indispensable that our commitment to the other is truthful and authentic. We always act respectfully, accept differences in people, and acknowledge that they have the right to unique needs, values, and interests. We recognize that they may behave differently from what we expect and that we may not be in sync with them. Although many people build walls, our desire must be to build bridges to meet our fellow human beings. We can learn from one another and slowly develop from discussion to true dialogue. In professional and often also in private life, discussion is the predominant way of communicating. Perhaps we try to dominate, be right about everything, have better arguments, and naturally be the most popular. Talk-show-style discussions, which only scratch the surface of relationships, attract many viewers, but they do not help us grow in our personal or professional lives. When we engage in dialectic battles by trying to dominate and win the argument, we lose contact with our true goals and the needs we are seeking to fulfill. When our ongoing discussions fail to become a win-win solution with benefits for both sides, it is of no use to anyone; it's as if two parties of hens or cockerels exit with their heads held high, cackling pretentiously but with remorse and rancor hidden inside.

In a discussion, beneath the level of facts and numbers lies the relationship level, with its feelings and needs, wishes and desires, sympathy and antipathy, trust and distrust, and rivalry, which can lead to strong emotions depending on the individuals and conversational dynamics. In whatever conversation, private or professional, our gut feelings play an enormous role, and we will become frustrated, fearful, angry, or sad when our needs for security, relationship, autonomy, and respect aren't fulfilled.

"Treating people the way they are, we make them worse.
Treating them the way they can be, we make them better."
- Goethe

Our form of communication as a catalyst for attaining our goals

Barbara Fredrickson and Marcial Losada defined and investigated the Losada ratio, which describes the ratio of positive to negative feedback we must have to lead a well-functioning team. The quota of positive to negative feedback must be at least 2.9:1; otherwise, the team will be dissatisfied and not work well together. One might think the higher the ratio, the better, but above 13:1, there is insufficient direction, and the team's efficacy suffers. Just as a ship needs a tall mast with a big sail to catch the wind that propels it, it also needs a firm keel to stay on course. Above 13:1, the boat may topple or be blown aimlessly across the water. Positive feedback gives us energy and drive, but effusive compliments make us distrustful of the source. At a ratio beneath 2.9:1, we lack direction and motivation. An optimal ratio is around 5:1. The ratio of positive to negative feedback depends on the basic attitude with which we enter a conversation. It makes the difference between discussion and dialogue.

The more we communicate actively and constructively, the higher the probability that we will get what we desire. By being aware of our counterparts' attitudes and communication styles, we will be able to manage our situation more dynamically and ably and keep from being hurt.

Constructive and destructive attitudes can be further divided

- **Active constructive**: "Wow, that new suit really fits you well! You must wear that for our next date!" Nonverbal: constant eye contact, showing positive emotions

- **Passive constructive**: "Looks nice." Nonverbal: little to no emotions displayed

- **Passive-aggressive**: "I'm going on a short vacation this weekend." Nonverbal: hardly any eye contact, turns away

- **Active aggressive**: "That was expensive. I wonder how you can afford that?!" Nonverbal: showing negative emotions

"Nonviolence, our natural state of compassion when violence has subsided from the heart."
- Marshall B. Rosenberg

"What I want in my life is compassion, a flow between myself and others based on a mutual giving from the heart."
- Marshall B. Rosenberg

CHAPTER 2
NONVIOLENT COMMUNICATION IN PPT

A language of life and empathy

When, instead of requesting, we command or demand or are perceived as authoritarian or controlling, our counterpart will feel pressured, deprived of their autonomy, fear punishment, and become defensive. They will consequently resort to one of the reactions possible in such a situation: to rebel or to submit. If we intensify our authoritarian position with verbal force by using moralistic judgments ("Aren't you ashamed of what you are doing?") or comparisons ("Your colleagues are really doing it a lot better than you"), we are hurting our counterpart's need for esteem, connection, and respect. These tactics alienate them and burden them with guilt, shame, and smoldering feelings of anger and resentment. These feelings then contribute to a diminished disposition for responding to us out of goodwill and inner motivation, now and in the future. A request is perceived as a demand when our counterpart feels coerced and hears a threatening undertone. How people hear us isn't always in our hands, and what they hear is often distorted by their projections.

Nonetheless, we must try to make ourselves clear. If someone feels free to respond to our request based on their own values and needs, they will do so out of goodwill and inner motivation. When we request something, our counterpart can accept it or reject it with an empathic "no" out of free will. This request becomes an opportunity to raise their self-respect and self-esteem. They can fulfill the need for connection and contribute to life by participating autonomously and joyfully in this shared activity or enterprise. But this requires that we initiate a request instead of a demand so they can agree to participate of their own free will.

"There is a place beyond the fields of right and wrong;
I'll meet you there."
- Rumi

"The highest form of intelligence is observing without
evaluating."
- J. Krishnamurti

"When we hear people combine observation with evaluation,
we are apt to hear criticism."
- Marshall Rosenberg

In nonviolent communication, as in PPT, we want to separate observations from evaluations to convey a language of needs and not morals. Speaking the language of needs makes it possible to connect through a "language of life" as Marshall Rosenberg used to call it: "The concept of punishment assumes badness on behalf of people and that they have to be made to repent for what they have done." When we mix our observations with our evaluations, our requests become demands. When someone speaks evaluatively, this can evoke pleasant or unpleasant feelings in us. At the extreme, moralistic language can endanger the fulfillment of a need, and it causes fear, sadness, and frustration. We respond with anger and outrage, become defensive or aggressive, trying to force our counterparts to do what we expect them to do by judging, blaming, and naming.

For example:

"John, you are such a lazy slob! You always leave the dirty dishes in the sink." Indicting John as lazy or immoral will not motivate him to change his dishwashing behavior.

Manipulating someone through guilt is an ineffective tactic of coercion. The coercer tries to make the other person responsible for his own unfulfilled needs or frustrations. (For example, saying to a child, "It really hurts me to see that you don't do your homework.") Taking responsibility for other people's feelings can be mistaken for positive caring, such as children doing everything for their parents' happiness.

"Let's talk with one another instead of about one another."
- John F. Kennedy

General guidelines for communicating observations, feelings, and needs and for making requests

We can change the message to John by not diagnosing the cause (he's a "lazy slob"), staying in the present, and avoiding words like "always," trying to accurately convey the number of times we have observed a sink full of dirty dishes, indicating how we feel when we see the kitchen in that state, and making a positive request instead of a negative one. At the same time, we must understand that the technique without the inner attitude will not make the difference between a request and a demand.

1. **Observing**: What do we observe others saying or doing that is enriching our life or not?

2. **Feeling**: We state how we feel when we observe this action: Are we hurt, scared, joyful, amused, irritated, etc.?

3. **Needs**: We say which of our needs are connected to the feelings we have identified.

4. **Request**: We make a specific request.

Now we might reframe our request to John:

1. "John, when I get home and see the dirty dishes in the sink..."

2. "I feel frustrated because..."

3. "I need more order in our kitchen."

4. "Could you please clean up after eating?"

By explaining how we feel and what we need, we give the other person a chance to connect to us instead of alienating him with demands, moralistic condemnations, or defensiveness. We can then make a request he can fulfill out of compassion and understanding.

Anger

Anger dominates other emotions and therefore tends to be superficial, covering up many other emotions and the needs hidden beneath them. Although we might see our anger as disturbing, it is an important indicator of our frustrated or unfulfilled needs that require attention. Anger can mask underlying feelings of sadness and fear.

These feelings indicate that deep down, we believe our unattended need may not be fulfilled and that our longing for it is strong and sincere. When we express these subtler feelings lurking beneath our anger, we have a greater chance of connecting with our counterparts. We receive compassion and understanding, which can create the connectedness necessary for agreement and fulfillment of both parties' needs. Connection, understanding, and compassion are the keys to giving our counterpart a chance to express his feelings, and then he can reciprocate by fulfilling our needs. It is important first to experience our feelings, needs, and desires and then to have the language to express them. Our anger is the energy, that locked-in desire that can help us overcome the hindrances to fulfilling our needs. The greater the desire and the hindrances, the stronger the energy, and the more carefully we must manage it. But the result is always worthwhile when we can transcend our anger and use its energy. We must combine our intellectual and emotional intelligence to build relationships instead of destroying them to meet our goals. Once again, it is important to use the techniques with everyone's needs in mind and not simply be manipulative to get our own needs fulfilled.

As Marshall Rosenberg says, **the way I receive a message depends on myself alone**. I am the person who can decide actively on how to take a message. I am responsible (response-able).

Four ways to receive negative messages

There are four possibilities for receiving negative messages, according to Nonviolent Communication, the method Marshall Rosenberg has created.

1. **Take it personally** by hearing blame and criticism ("I'm such a lazy idiot. Why don't I do the dishes?")

2. **Blame the speaker** ("My partner really is a compulsive tyrant.")

3. **Sense our own feelings and needs** ("When I come home tired and frustrated, I don't have any energy left.")

4. **Sense others' feelings and needs** ("I can understand that he feels frustrated when he comes home and wants some order.")

How I react to something depends primarily on myself. If I am in a traffic jam, I may say: "Great! I am going to miss the boring presentation my boss gives on Mondays, and I can finish listening to my audiobook." Or I might say: "Shoot, I won't be able to see my favorite television show." Consider this situation: When we're standing in line for the cashier and a kid spills milk all over us, we might get mad, because in our mind, he is an insolent brat. But then suddenly, our attitude changes when we look directly at him and realize he is a disabled child who accidentally soiled our clothes. Another example: How do we react when we see a speedboat crashing into our own new boat and damaging it badly? But then, when we get closer to the offending craft, we see there is nobody inside. What new emotions arise?

So, we are never angry about what people do. **People's actions are only the stimulus for our anger**. The true cause of our anger lies in our own unfulfilled personal needs, which are hidden beneath the layer of blame and judgment (thinking) we want to hurl at our counterparts. Whenever we get angry and apply judgment based on rules, we assign fault and wrongdoing to the other without seeing our hidden needs. We rigidly try to coerce them into what we want them to do, applying our belief that the other deserves punishment. But when we are aware of our unfulfilled needs, we may get angry, but we then can choose to follow the path of connectedness instead of the one of coercion and punishment. Marshall Rosenberg says that when we judge others, these judgments are nothing more than "alienated expressions of our needs."

Suppose we want to bring a change to our relationships and experience more connectedness. In that case, we can act as follows: When someone does something that negatively touches a need of ours, we can experience and recognize this need and become aware of the feelings accompanying the event, such as frustration, anger, sadness, and fear. We can refrain from using moral judgment and indignation to manipulate our counterparts into doing what we want. Instead, we can express our subtler underlying feelings and needs so that they can understand and connect with us and find a common solution. This way, we can escape stepping into the spiral of verbal violence, which can escalate into physical violence. Remember that the person who uses force is powerless, and integrity is the difference between power and force.

The more we **truly listen** to other people, the more they will hear us. Listening intensely to the other, even if it takes time, can save time and emotional peril in the long run. When other people hurl criticism, insults, and verbal attacks at us, we can look behind these derogatory statements and consciously decide not to identify with them. We can look beyond the negative comments and realize that they are motivated by the speaker's unfulfilled needs and hurt feelings. We can take them as a gift to understand and give back to our counterparts in their pain. When we refrain from identifying with these intimidating judgments, we can see the other person as a human being counterattacking defensively to protect his needs. We have the possibility to open to ways of listening and connecting through empathy while still being true to ourselves. Two prerequisites are that we must be in an empowered state, and we must give the other person our time. When we empathize with somebody's *no* or his rejection, and we understand his underlying feelings and needs, it protects us from taking his judgments and deprecations personally. We can manage our emotions and needs by becoming conscious of them as they lie beneath the dominating violent thoughts and feelings we experience. Meanwhile we do not become judgmental of ourselves and do not go into self-flagellation. We become aware of our common humanity when we experience one another in our feelings and needs. We need time for empathic listening. And we are the ones who must take the first conscious step, because when our counterpart believes he is being blamed, he will not be able to listen to our pain. So, we must first hear him out before we send our message. We must make a conscious effort to step out of this vicious circle of blaming.

Two ways of using force

There are two ways of using force. One is the **protective use,** when trying to prevent injury or injustice, such as snatching a child's hand away from a hot cooking plate just before he touches it. The other is the **punitive use,** which makes people suffer for their perceived misdeeds. If we are to avoid the punitive use of force, we must transcend our anger. We must see beyond what we want or think we can accomplish with our fists or by using coercive verbal force in the form of comparisons, moral judgments, or insults. We try to retaliate when we believe that other people have caused our pain and deserve to be punished. However, suppose we become conscious of our feelings and needs and those of a fellow human being. In that case, we might be able to use the energy of anger and the accompanying feelings to explain how important an issue is to us and begin to see that the issue is perhaps just as important to our partner.

Listening unconditionally

When we really listen to who people are, what they are feeling and needing, and not their disparaging language, we don't see them as monsters anymore. When we listen unconditionally, we offer the other person a chance to look inside and understand themselves, feel understood, and make connections to themselves and to us. If we interrupt them, we may block the cathartic flow too soon. They may believe we are interested only in ourselves or in solving the problem. We may not hear the other yet unexpressed or more urgent desires they are harboring. When we have heard someone out, we see how their tension diminishes, and they begin to relax, and at this point, they are no longer compelled to speak. That is when we can look at a possible point of connection.

One way to listen better is to **paraphrase** what the other person is saying and to acknowledge the needs that are generating their feelings or requests. By paraphrasing, we show our counterpart our understanding and willingness to cooperate, thereby gaining their willingness to listen to us. Paraphrasing is repeating in our own words our understanding of what we have just heard: "Ahh, so you really don't have that much time to spend on..." We can also reflect on emotionally charged messages. But we should do so only when we believe it will provide better understanding and greater compassion. It is important to be aware of our tone of voice. We paraphrase with the aim of getting a *yes* confirming that we have understood:

"This project will never be finished with so much incompetence at work!"

"So, if I understand you correctly, you are afraid that the project will never end because they aren't doing their work well."

"Yes, exactly!"

Another way of signaling our understanding is to **address the feelings we perceive our counterpart is harboring**. For example:

"This teacher is really driving me nuts!"

"So, he really irritates you?"

Of course, we can only make presumptions, but even if our intuition is wrong, it signals to our partner that we are interested in what they are going through, giving them a chance to further explain. It is an effective way of creating bridges.

In a discussion, we must remember to give our counterpart the **time** they need to get in sync with us before we decide on our common goal and methods to achieve it. It is not helpful to pressure them verbally or through our body language; we must give them the **space** and time they need. We demonstrate positive body language while at the same time maintaining eye contact. If we pressure them, it will leave the impression that we are manipulative and hassling. When our counterpart gets into more explanation, we need to hear them before giving our point of view. Listening longer gives us a better chance of being heard. Often when people have something to say, they just want to be heard: "I don't want you to do anything. I just want you to listen." We should even listen to our counterpart's silence.

When we see no other way out of the discussion and the pain is too great, we can always **scream nonviolently**—"I just can't go on anymore at the moment"—and/or take a **time-out**. Another way to connect to ourselves and others is to stop and breathe, recognize our judgmental thoughts, connect to our needs, and then express our feelings and unmet needs. We can defuse our stress by listening to our feelings and needs, discerning between what we really need and what we believe we should do. We can defuse stress from others by using empathy to deeply understand them.

"Growth occurs through a meeting between two individuals who express themselves vulnerably and authentically in an 'I-Thou' relationship."
- Martin Buber

Strengthening our active listening capability

"The hearing that is only in the ears is one thing. The hearing of the understanding is another. But the hearing of the spirit is not limited to any one faculty, to the ears, or to the mind. Hence it demands the emptiness of all the faculties. And when all the faculties are empty, then the whole being listens. There is then a grasp of what is right there before you that can never be heard with the ear or understood with the mind."
- Zhuang-Zhuo

The **first five steps of conflict** resolution consist primarily of listening actively and compassionately: Compassionate and active listening means being completely present for the other person. We listen with all our faculties and try to understand profoundly with the intention of helping our counterparts. Compassionate listening entails empathy, feeling what the other person is feeling, observing intensely, and taking in all the details of the other person. It's about listening with dedication and love, making the other person the most important subject in the moment. Active listening consists of showing patience, recapitulating, paraphrasing, and asking about underlying needs and feelings. This is helpful, especially for making contact at the beginning of every conversation and also when the conversation becomes more complicated or escalates to an emotional level. If you want to be listened to, then listen to others. There is always something more to be heard that can lead to more clarity in a relationship. Hear the other person out. Use open questions, not closed ones—questions like who, what, how, what for, and where open the conversation. Closed questions shut down a conversation, but open questions launch it into a wide range of possibilities.

What isn't listening

Marshall Rosenberg quotes Holly Humphrey's list of common behaviors that prevent us from being sufficiently present or connecting empathically (as opposed to intellectually):

Advising:	"I think you should…", "Why didn't you…?"
One-upping:	"That's nothing; wait till you hear what happened to me."
Educating:	"This could turn into a positive experience for you if you just…"
Consoling:	"It wasn't your fault; you did the best you could."
Storytelling:	"That reminds me of the time…"
Shutting down:	"Cheer up. Don't feel so bad."
Sympathizing:	"Oh, you poor little thing…"
Interrogating:	"When did this begin?"
Explaining:	"I would have called, but…"
Correcting:	"That's not how it happened."

Active listening

Active listening instills a feeling for the momentary relationship, when we can focus and empathize to understand where the conversation is heading. When we are listening actively, we notice slight changes in the speaker's temper, pace of speech, intonation, gestures, and posture.

We can use the skill of active listening to calm a discussion and reconnect. When things get too difficult or aggressive, we can take a time-out, take a break, change the topic, or get something to eat or drink. When these strategies don't work, we might also get a mediator.

Let's practice listening actively and compassionately with someone in person or on the telephone. Or let's consciously use active listening during everyday discussions to help turn them into genuine dialogue.

Four techniques of listening and giving empathy

- **Silent and nonverbal listening**

Just to listen to the other with the greatest attentiveness.

- **Reflective listening**

Paraphrasing the contents: "So you are going to buy a car because you need a means of transportation."

- **Silent empathy**

Listen and guess the feelings and needs behind the other person's words and express them afterward. "Ah, so you are sad and need someone to talk to because your dad died a couple of days ago."

- **Guessing feelings and needs during the dialogue**

As in silent empathy but during the dialogue: "Ah, so you need someone to talk to," or "Oh, you feel sad because your cat died a couple of days ago."

- **Holding a need**

Stay together in the beauty of the need and hold it: "Let's just hold this need of yours together and feel how that feels."

"The best fighter never gets angry."
- Lao Tzu

Mourning and self-forgiveness

Frustration, anger, sadness, fear, disappointment, and *grief* are **natural emotions** that help us pursue our needs. Feeling *guilty* can be seen as reacting with sadness and frustration to not having complied with our inner set of values, and it can direct us towards the fulfillment of these. But when guilt is connected to the belief that punishment and reward are necessary, it can become toxic, causing us to deviate from life, creating depression and stagnation instead of helping us fulfill our own needs and values and those of others.

It is the same with *shame*. Shame is sensing one's own fault in the eyes of another. If it is devoid of self-esteem and misbalanced with notions of punishment or even self-flagellation. It also diverts us from fulfilling our values and needs. If punishment is our focus, we will not go through the period of mourning necessary to achieve true redemption.

When we sense true guilt and shame without the socially inculcated punitive aspects, we can **truly mourn** what we have done, **find self-forgiveness**, and make amends. We can ask ourselves:

- What was the good reason I wanted to do it?
- Which needs did I infringe on by doing so?
- Was I unable to act differently, or did I not want to act differently?
- Or maybe I was unable to want to act differently?

In any case, we can then understand ourselves and why we acted this way. We can mourn, forgive ourselves, and if we find there is a true necessity, also make amends. Self-forgiveness is an important aspect of self-compassion that can **hold the two parts of our motivation**: One is the way we acted given certain reasons, and the other is our regret for doing so and our wish that we might have acted differently. **Self-compassion** allows us to understand ourselves more completely and accept our ambiguities, and it shows us ways to fulfill our own needs and those of others in new ways. Without self-compassion, we fall into self-flagellation and depression. When we connect to our needs, we can let go of concepts and strategies we had once habitually used, and we open ourselves up to the chance to discover new ways to fulfill our needs. We can meet and embrace both needs and parts of ourselves, the one that acted in that way in the first place and the other that wishes we hadn't done so.

- Let's take an example from our life and hold two dissimilar needs, one in our right and the other in our left hand. Now let's feel a sense of care for both needs. We may do this exercise with someone else's needs and our own needs as well. Then we try to imagine a way to satisfy both. Often, when we become more aware of both needs, we can resourcefully find new ways of fulfilling them.

"If you want to build a ship, don't drum up the men to gather wood, divide the work, and give orders. Instead, teach them

to yearn for the vast and endless sea."
- Antoine de Saint-Exupéry

Fulfilling our inner motivation is the strongest reward

We may think it strange that reward can be negative, but if we do something solely for the reward of accomplishing the task, then we are not connected to ourselves or the task anymore. When motivated by an extrinsic reward, we lose our intrinsic motivation and forget our own needs. Whether it's an immediate or long-term reward, manipulating someone through rewards will not work in the long run. It will only lead to demotivation.

"The more you become a connoisseur of gratitude, the less you are a victim of resentment, depression, and despair. Gratitude will act as an elixir that will gradually dissolve the hard shell of your ego—your need to possess and control—and transform you into a generous being. The sense of gratitude produces true spiritual alchemy, makes us magnanimous large, large-souled."
- Sam Keen

Expressing our gratitude makes the best compliment

Compliments are positive judgments. Similar to rewards, they can be perceived as manipulative, especially when the one complimenting has an agenda, and an intent lurks behind them. But we have the choice of how we compliment. If we flatter someone's ego by telling him what a "great person" he is and what "extraordinary feats" he has accomplished, we risk being perceived as manipulative. Instead, if we compliment another person for giving us a wonderful, elating experience, we are **expressing our gratitude** by telling him how he has contributed to our lives, and we are celebrating his contribution. It is more effective to focus specifically on what the other person has done, how we have benefitted from it, and how thankful we are. Instead of "What a great lecture you gave today" or "What an excellent speaker you are," we might say, "I am so happy to have participated in your communication class today. It was very inspiring and has shown me new ways to help me connect with my family. It has given me the keys I've been looking for such a long time." We express this genuine gratitude not only by our words but also their congruence with our body language, posture, and gestures.

Our ability to **receive appreciation** is just as important as our capability to give it. We often ask ourselves if we are worthy of praise, or if the person offering it will expect something in return, putting us in their debt. Earning and deserving are central to our culture. We are not accustomed to simple giving and receiving. We have the chance to give back to the person who is expressing his appreciation by giving him the gift of receiving it empathically. When we demonstrate empathy, we can receive the compliment without conveying superiority or false humility. Genuine thankfulness enriches our life, whether we give it or receive it.

"Talking about the problem makes it worse. Talking about its solution makes the solution more probable."
- Steve de Shazer

Cognitively arrested alternatives as a basis for depression, resolving them as a basis for living

According to Ernest Becker, a Pulitzer Prize-winning social and cultural anthropologist, thinker, and writer, depression is often based on "cognitively arrested alternatives." Becker identifies those situations in which we can't decide on one of our viable options or pathways. We become frustrated by waffling continuously and slowly lose our energy and motivation. This dithering can reach an extreme, and we become completely paralyzed with indecision. It's as if we hear two voices, each beckoning us to follow. One is saying, for example: "I am such a stupid bum. I keep doing this boring, senseless job. It is such a waste of time, but the money is good." The other says, "Always these stupid, unrealistic ideas of finding an interesting job. My family needs food and not a dreamer at the table." In this example, we are conflicted about risking the family's financial security while we try to interview for a meaningful job. When we get stuck in this dilemma, we use derogatory speech about ourselves, and we close our eyes to all the other opportunities life is offering. If we phrase the question differently, our attitude becomes more inspiring: "I really want a job that gives me more satisfaction. I want to be part of the change in the world. At the same time, I want to take care of my family's needs. What alternatives do I have?"

We can find innovative solutions by using the following formula:

When A, I feel B because I need C; therefore, I now would like D.

"When I spend time at a job that doesn't give me professional satisfaction (a need), I feel frustrated and sad. Therefore, I want to find a new job that gives me fulfillment."

"When I imagine jobs that give me this satisfaction, I fear I will not be able to earn a living for my family. Therefore, I want to be sure that my family is financially secure."

We can then evaluate with our partner what the possibilities are and where the willingness lies to help each other find fulfillment and security. A solution could be, for example, to both find part-time jobs and thereby create space for a meaningful hobby.

Doing things out of our free will

When we focus on what we really want instead of what is wrong with ourselves and others, we can direct our attention to achieving new, stimulating goals for ourselves and with our fellow human beings.

We need to be conscious of why we are doing things and do them out of free will: When we "should" ourselves and others—for example, "You should do your homework now"—we give the impression that there is no choice, which blocks our profound sense of autonomy. **"Shoulding"** stimulates fear, guilt, and shame when we don't comply with the duties and obligations that we set for ourselves or others. The coercion and the negative feelings connected to it become the motivation for our decision-making instead of our free will and the desire to enrich and contribute to our lives. When we stop "shoulding," we can direct our energy towards creativity and play, responding out of our innate pleasure and enthusiasm, connecting compassionately and helping one another to contribute creatively to life.

Changing a "have to" into a "choose to"

Let's think about and make a list of the things we believe we must do. Now let's become conscious that we are doing them out of our own free will, that we have *chosen* to do them: "I choose to..." Then we express the reason we are doing them: "...because I want..."

Do we say, "I must study French now" or "I want to study French so I can have fun speaking to people during my vacation"?

Whenever we make choices, we can make them consciously, seeking to understand the reasons with the underlying needs: "I choose to... because I want..."

Saying no compassionately

"The Difficulty of Doing Things Right for Everyone"

A man and his son were walking along a street with their mule. After a while, the little boy tired, and his father urged him warmheartedly, "Why don't you get on the mule's back?" They continued on their way, the son astride the mule, chattering happily. But suddenly, a woman observed them and exclaimed, "Why is this spoiled little brat allowed to ride the mule while his poor old father has to walk?" So the boy dismounted, and his father took his turn riding the mule. But again, another person cried out, "What an uncaring father! How can the lazy man let his poor little boy walk while he rides the mule?!" But, just as soon as the father lifted his son up in front of him, a third critic looked and spat at them with rage, "How can they be so cruel?! All that weight—the mule's back is sagging. Look, it must be in pain!" So, they got off. But when they were walking along again, father and son hand in hand and the mule trotting along next to them, they heard someone laugh. "How stupid can one be? Two guys taking a mule for a walk?!" The father sighed, giving his son's hand a caring little squeeze, "Now you've seen that it's impossible to make everyone happy."

Retold after Nossrat Peseschkian (*Oriental Stories*, p. 148)

Saying no is an art, one that needs to be practiced when one wants to preserve one's relationship. Instead of simply saying no, one can simultaneously contribute to a counterpart's well-being. How do we do that?

1. We listen empathically to what the other person needs from us.

2. We appreciate what the other person expects or wants us to do.

3. We formulate our *no* response; we express the reason/need that is keeping us from saying yes and our feeling when we are saying no.

4. We help look for or suggest an alternative solution.

Examples:

When asked to clean the kitchen:

- "It's great that we both want the kitchen to be clean, but I'm sorry that I can't help you wash the dishes now because I am running late and already unnerved. What do you say I help you do them this evening?"

When asked to discuss a topic:

- "I am glad you want to discuss this topic; it is important to me as well. I must finish this task first, though, because the deadline is approaching, so I'm unhappy I can't help you now. Could we talk about it at lunch?"

Additional techniques for saying no:

- **Yes, if...:** Define the terms for a yes and ask for some time for reflection.

- **Help to self-help:** Offer some advice on solutions where your participation is not necessary. (What can the other person do to find help?)

- **Soft, decisive no:** "I understand your point of view. Please understand mine as well."

- **Hard, decisive no:** "You are wasting your time; I won't change my mind."

Remember that hard, decisive no's are a big strain on relationships and can seriously damage them.

If we are someone who always says yes automatically, then we must learn to ask for some time to reflect so we can decide if we really want to respond positively to the request. Sometimes our counterpart will try to maneuver us into a yes by using all kinds of tricks, but once we've explained why we said no, then we stick to our decision. Harmony is often mistaken for harmonizing.

It is important to state our limits. We must speak frankly and plainly; sometimes, we signal our willingness to discuss or negotiate when we aren't willing to do so. We must be clear about our boundaries and establish our limits clearly beforehand.

"If I'm ninety-eight percent perfect in anything I do, it's the two percent I've messed up I'll remember when I'm through."
- Marshall Rosenberg

See the glass as half full and not half empty. Focus on what you want and not on what you don't want.

More communication prerequisites and skills

Carmen Kauffmann, a talented and successful communication coach and friend of mine, teaches the following communication skills, which are essential for reaching our goals, especially in difficult situations and conflict.

Rhetoric and physical presence

Our rhetoric must be adequate for and adapted to the situation, and it should reflect our inner values and moral integrity. Apart from our goal and the message we send, how we express ourselves is just as important. We must choose our words carefully and use appropriate phrasing, metaphors, and quotes. Through regular practice, we can hone our communication skills and develop more spontaneity. When we are authentic and credible, we can touch our counterpart's soul and communicate our arguments in a logical, specific, and understandable way. We can combine ethos (ethics), pathos (emotions), and logic (intellect) to creatively make a point and convey our intentions. What we express physically must match our words: We are genuinely ourselves without pretense, physically and verbally present. We demonstrate our openness by smiling, keeping our hands visible on the table, our torso facing our counterpart, and maintaining an upright posture, whether seated or standing. We show our undivided attention through eye contact, active listening, and nodding our heads as an expression of our understanding.

How to be assertive and impose ourselves when necessary

When we try to assert ourselves forcefully against the will of another, we must be aware that we are putting the relationship at risk. The other person might become resentful, and their benevolence towards us could change. They could even become defensive or aggressive in the future, and we might gain a new enemy. Whenever we resort to force, we must be conscious that the stakes are high—does the situation justify our aggressive intervention? Perhaps, if our counterpart continuously imposes his will, and all other diplomatic attempts have failed. In this situation, we are acting out of self-defense. When someone constantly snubs us and repeatedly disregards previous agreements, continuing to yield to them is ridiculous. We must be able to defend our ground. It is a good rule to start out trusting in others, but when they abuse our trust, we need to be on guard and able to defend ourselves and our interests through measured responses. Many of us have learned to put the needs of others before our own, but we need to maintain a balance between our own needs and theirs. Occasionally, we must stand up for our rights, even if our tough position might provoke envy, jealousy, or anger. When we have the impression our counterpart might take advantage of us, we seek to find an inner stance of strength and resolve and to define reasonable limits within which we want to negotiate. Once we establish a just goal, we begin bargaining without compromising it.

Gaining a positive perspective on being assertive

Many of us have been taught to give way and be polite, and therefore we have a negative perspective on asserting ourselves. We can change this attitude by identifying good reasons for being assertive. We can practice changing our mindset by finding positive examples of assertiveness, such as:

- Asserting myself means finding freedom and doing the right thing.
- When I assert myself, I lead and take my life in my own hands.
- When I assert myself, I am just and reasonable.

We can take a moment and sit back to reflect on these perspectives and then look for other positive examples of assertiveness. We make a list of our examples and contemplate them regularly, for example, before going to bed, and so take in their veracity.

Gathering our assertiveness skills

Try to remember different demanding situations in which you asserted yourself against great odds. How did you do that? What was your strategy? What were the key ingredients to your success? Which strategies for self-assertion do you not like and why? What strategies of others do you see that are effective and that resonate with you? Which ones don't resonate? Now put them together and make a list.

Strong resolve through inner pictures

Entering a discussion with the right attitude and with strong inner pictures strengthens our resolve and assertiveness and gives us energy. To strengthen our resolve and motivation, we can:

a. Think about the inner pictures/ideas we often use when we want to assert ourselves in a discussion. Think of a true situation and become aware of the images that come to mind with all the colors, sounds, and smells accompanying them.

b. Imagine alternative, more powerful images that we might associate with such a situation that might be helpful. Rehearse and consolidate them in our minds.

Self-assertion in a weak position

Sometimes we are in a weaker position than our counterparts. Then we must channel all our resources to be able to assert ourselves. Here is a summary of what Carmen Kauffmann recommends:

- Make a step-by-step plan in which we first use soft methods without eschewing more pointed ones.
- Dig deeper when the cooperative approach isn't working.
- Ask what kind of support our counterpart needs to comply with the request.
- Make concrete proposals on how to reach the common goal.
- Ask for feedback on the progress.
- Make concrete deadlines.
- When applicable, escalate the problem to our superior.
- Convince our superior that this problem warrants his time.
- Consider the needs of our superior.
- The less time we have to solve this problem, the more concise we must be.
- Refer to the positive effects we can achieve, such as saving time or ensuring customer loyalty.
- Don't surprise our superior but ask if he has time. Show respect and never give the impression that we want to attack his decision-making authority.
- Offer prepared solutions that respect his tight schedule; he will be relieved when there is a workable solution at hand. After presenting the solution, let him decide.
- Always concentrate on the factual level of the conversation and forgo personal attacks.
- Use active listening.
- If you hear condescending generalizations, try to circle back to the concrete or specific matter at hand.

- And if nothing helps, then assert yourself boldly; we can't let others step on our toes the whole time. Don't try to produce the most original expressions. Say what comes to your mind because it is important to give an honest reply. Adopt an assertive posture, your hands on your hips, your chin upwards, and your shoulders forward while looking into your counterpart's eyes.

Preparing to respond with self-assertion in conflict

The conflict thermometer

To become more present, aware, and prepared for conflict, we can use the conflict thermometer. Draw a thermometer with a scale between 37 and 41.5 degrees Celsius, leaving ample space between the single degrees of temperature. For every line of temperature representing the heat of the conflict, write down the specific tactics you want to use for the specific situation. At lower degrees, you'll ignore the transgression or use more diplomatic strategies. The higher up the scale you go, the more heated the conflict. Here's where you must consciously moderate the discussion using de-escalating techniques. You might even need to take a break. When the temperature gets too hot, we reflexively defend ourselves and try to escape. Just like with fever, when our conflict thermometer reaches 42 degrees, the conflict can be deadly, and we fail to act consciously and conscientiously. This is when we are in danger of falling back on destructive behavior. Therefore, it is important to take effective measures before conflicts get too heated.

Conflict tension anchors

To illustrate the appropriate stress or tension for conflict situations, we can use conflict tension anchors. Draw an imaginary line of tension on the ground, extending from non-existent to maximum stress. We anchor each of the two extremes with firsthand experiences. The relaxed extreme may be represented by lying on the beach. The opposite extreme may be a high-stakes test. First, we experience each extreme and then locate the point on the line where the tension is right for us.

Three seats exercise

When we are preparing for an emotional discussion, we can use the three seats exercise to help find our stance:

We take three seats representing a neutral, a pleasant, and an unpleasant conversation and sit on each chair in turn to try to experience our feelings, needs, and posture in each.

When we sit in the unpleasant conversation seat, we can take the posture and the attitude of the pleasant seat and act as if the situation were pleasant, authentically representing our values and strengths at the same time. We can use this method to practice and prepare for the next unpleasant confrontation.

Conflict Tai Chi

The more pressure we are under, the more resolve we must show. When we experience pressure, we reflexively respond with counterpressure, or we might dodge the conflict or give way. To become more physically accustomed to dealing with pressure, we can practice conflict Tai Chi:

Practice physically with a partner. Stand with your hands against their hands, giving pressure, giving way, evading sideways. Use the memory of this experience as a physical anchor for building the necessary pressure in your next confrontation.

Sunflower of self-defense

For repetitive, uncontrollable conflict situations, we can use the sunflower of self-defense. If you repeatedly find yourself in situations where you are too paralyzed to react, it is time to create a repertoire of reactions that you can learn by heart and rehearse regularly until you learn to respond spontaneously. Draw a sunflower with five or six petals on which you write the specific verbal and physical reactions you want to use so you can remember them better.

Save what can be saved

We also must be prepared for the eventual situation when the conflict gets out of hand. It is essential to save whatever we can before the destruction is complete. We must use the emergency brakes to halt the escalation.

Carmen Kauffmann advises:

- Take a break.
- Lean back and take a few breaths; be conscious of your breathing, your heartbeat, and any other physical feelings.
- Extend your exhalations and be aware of the pause in breathing before you inhale again.
- Summarize what has been said: "If I understand you correctly..."
- Talk about your feelings.

- Describe what you believe is happening in the conversation at this moment.

- Resume the conversation later and ask for advice in the meanwhile.

- Simply keep talking without letting yourself be interrupted in the same manner as professionals do. This strategy should be a last resort because it isn't helpful in a constructive conversation. It merely demonstrates power. If somebody constantly disregards our invitation for a constructive conversation and abuses our friendliness by overpowering the conversation with a monologue, then we can resort to the same behavior in self-defense instead of giving the impression that we are malleable to their will.

"With life as short as a half-taken breath, don't plant anything but love."
- Rumi

General recommendations for a proficient dialog

Express what we want

It is important to be able to express what we want in our lives. We will be more successful if we use a positive approach and state what we want rather than what we don't. Conventional wisdom maintains, "You can catch more bees with honey than with vinegar." Let's speak in "I" messages instead of "you" messages as we often do. When we say, "You did this…" we are relating what happened and not saying what we want to be done, leaving the other person in defensive mode and clueless as to what we are expecting. "I" messages can be precise expressions of what we feel and want, so it's better to say, "I want…", "I would prefer…", "I would love…". At the same time, let's remember to ask rather than demand so our partner or counterpart will not feel obliged or coerced to do something. When we request, our counterpart maintains their autonomy—which we all defend because we all want free will. Let's practice making "I" statements instead of "you" statements by examining our habitual reactions in the past and changing them.

Solution, not problem language

When we express ourselves, we must use **solution and not problem language**. It is helpful to use positive verbiage, pointing to resources instead of deficiencies. The vision and inner attitude of seeing a glass as half full instead of half empty can change the outcome of our discussions and therefore of our entire project.

Win-win situations

Let's create win-win strategies so we can motivate our companions to cooperate to their own best advantage. All can benefit when we use the Harvard concept, a form of sharing in an intelligent way. For example, when there is only one orange, but two of us want it, we can fight over it. We can also cut it in half; then, each person gets half an orange. But another alternative is to discern what part of the orange each person really wants. One person might want the juice for drinking and the other the peel for making a cake. When we ask people what they really want, we might find clever solutions that satisfy both parties.

The "virtual relationship account"

In our culture, we learn that there is reciprocity, a giving and taking that should be in balance. Stephen Covey notes that every interaction we have with someone generates a positive or negative balance. Before we can take, we must invest; we can't simply take without having given before. Incurring a debt before contributing usually doesn't work and isn't received well. The fuller our relationship accounts are, and the more positive transactions that go back and forth, the happier and healthier our relationships will be. "We are all looking for appreciation, but only a few are capable of giving it." (Anonymous) All remarks we make have an effect on our relationship account, and consistent, authentic appreciation helps us cultivate our relationships. We shouldn't hesitate to invest continuously in our relationships, even if our painstaking initial investments are not reciprocated. We will benefit from these investments eventually. But of course, we shouldn't try to deliberately seek someone's appreciation. Let's check our relationship accounts with the people most important to us, looking at one where we have made good investments and another where we feel indebted. How did they get this way? What have we done, what are we currently doing, and what are we willing to do in the future for this relationship? Is there anything new we would like to try? Would it be worthwhile?

Carefully crafted questions guide the conversation

We try to lead in the direction of solutions instead of problems. We try to avoid questions like "Why?" when relating to the past: "Why did you do that?" "What was that for?" These kinds of questions lead to problem-oriented thinking, justifications, defensiveness, excuses, accusations, and counter-aggression. The other person can perceive them as accusations that force them to react defensively. We prefer looking toward the future with solution-oriented questions. "What can we do to manage this situation?" "What would be a satisfactory solution for you?"

And find out what the other person may need: "What is it you need?" "How do you feel about this?"

Never question our counterparts' motivations and interests

More importantly, we should not accuse the other person, saying something like "You are only looking for power; you never have the guts to risk anything." Guessing the intentions of another person is as unreliable as reading a horoscope. If we misread their intentions, our counterpart will feel attacked and will react defensively. Instead, we should offer convincing proposals without the ad hominem attacks. An example of a non-threatening proposal with a practical appeal is: "When you buy my car, you will save a lot of money since it has excellent fuel economy."

Humor

Humor works well for defusing a difficult situation, but we must take care not to tread on anyone's toes. The easiest way, without exaggerating or abusing it frequently, is to make fun of ourselves, using metaphors, aphorisms, or quotes while remembering to stay authentic.

When someone is continuously interrupting us

Let's not say, "Please let me finish what I was saying" in an angry or agitated voice. This will paradoxically give our counterpart even more attention. Instead, say in a calm, steady manner, "I would like to finish my thought..."

Communicating something embarrassing about others

If we must communicate something that could embarrass our counterpart, it's preferable to take him to the side and explain to him politely and honestly in private.

Misunderstandings

In everyday life, we have many misunderstandings. We must be careful not to criticize our counterpart for the false impression but simply make it clear that it was a misunderstanding.

The basic formula for convincing others about a plan

The **SMART formula** helps us concentrate on the basic pillars of planning projects and convincing others to commit enthusiastically. First, we must be **specific** in phrasing our goal concretely. Second, we describe **measurable** benchmarks that chart our progress and the eventual achievement of the goal. Third, we elicit the support of others by assuring them that the goal is **attainable**. Fourth, we convince others that the goal is **relevant** to our overall success. And last, we will fix a realistic deadline by which the project will be **terminated**.

Different methods for formulating our viewpoint concisely

- **Stating our arguments**

When we need others to commit to what we are saying, we have to formulate our viewpoint concisely.

1. *Viewpoint*: "I believe..." "In my opinion..."
2. *First Argument*: "Because..."
3. *Second Argument*: "Because..."
4. *Third argument*: "Because..."
5. *Consequence*: "Therefore, I propose..."

- **Three-sentence method for presenting concisely**

1. Description of the *situation*
2. Description of the *goal*
3. Determination of the *measures* to be taken.

- **Five-sentence method for presenting a more detailed description**

1. *Introduction* (Personal reference and reason for this occasion)
2. What is the situation? (Description of the *situation)*
3. What is wanted? (Definition of the *goal)*
4. How do we get there? (Description of the *measures* to be taken to get there)

5. What do I want from you? (*Request for commitment*)

Asserting our opinion against an opposing one

In difficult situations, we can introduce our argument against an opposing one in the following way:

- Take the *factual aspect* of the attack and verbalize it: "On the *one hand...*"

- Set your *argument against* this opinion: "On the *other hand...*"

- Then make a *counterproposal*: "Therefore/then..."

    For example, instead of:

- "If you don't follow my instructions, you will regret it!"

    You could say:

- "On the one hand, I can understand that you are putting all your hopes into the solution you are proposing; on the other hand, you should also listen to my constructive opinion. Then we can decide objectively which plan we shall use."

Celebrate our success

We shouldn't be afraid of self-praise. Self-marketing is an important instrument for demonstrating our capabilities.

Nossrat Peseschkian always offered a general recommendation about human interaction: **"If you want to get something out of a closed sack, you first must untie it."** It is the same with human beings. You must gain their trust and show them that your intentions will benefit them as well. Only then can you receive their cooperation for your goals. When we request, we must be very precise about it. The more precise we can be, the more probable that we will receive what we want. And as always, be careful what you wish for.

CHAPTER 3

IN-DEPTH UNDERSTANDING AND SOLVING INNER AND OUTER CONFLICTS TO RELEASE OUR FULL POTENTIAL AS INDIVIDUALS

Conflicts

Why is it that conflicts are so important in our lives? They provoke insecurity and emotional chaos and can even become destructive, especially when they escalate. Despite their negative repercussions, we can't avoid them. Conflicts are part of our life and tend to repeat if we don't solve them. Nonetheless, we can learn and grow from them.

"Love is like a glass that breaks if held too loose or too tight."
- Nossrat Peseschkian

Types of conflicts and their dynamics

We can differentiate between internal, social, and organizational conflict. *Internal conflicts* are conflicts among parts of the individual psyche, *social conflicts* are among individuals, and organizational conflicts are between different organizations. A *conflict* exists when at least two different parties with opposing interests and values both feel they are right and try to impose their opinion on the other. Conflicts can be *conscious* or *subconscious*. Individuals recognize that they are in conflict through signals such as tension, excitement, insecurity, anger, or fear. *Behaviors* of individuals in conflict include avoidance of eye contact, negative verbal expressions, masked friendliness, and insinuation of false facts. When teams are in conflict, members disregard instructions, ignore agreements, and mob colleagues. The tenor of the group can vacillate between escalated discussions and icy silences.

Dialogue on an issue level focuses on goals, methods, interests, and opinions and is based on a *positive or neutral emotional level* when it is conducted constructively. But when parties press, insist, and insult, verbally and nonverbally, communication deteriorates. Dialogue becomes a debate and descends to a *negative emotional level*, often with more damaging remarks. Then negative emotions begin to dominate our thinking, our perspective narrows or becomes distorted, facts bend, and we overrate the disturbing behavior of our opponent while trivializing our own misbehavior. When this happens, we regress to our limbic system, to our ancestral *fight-or-flight reactions*. We then have to find a way back to calmness and composure and move back up the evolutionary ladder, where we use our frontal lobes. In flight mode, we are possessed by fear, feel insulted and offended, fall silent, resort to evasive maneuvers, experience resignation, feel numb, lack physical sensations, and even experience paralysis and blackout. This can go as far as physically freezing or stopping, paralyzed, like a deer in headlights. In fight mode, we feel superior, arrogant, irritable, angry, and outraged.

Our intelligent reaction to conflict

Rather than regressing and turning to our instinctive reactions, we can learn to consciously put the brakes on our reflexes and become reflective and inquisitive the moment the irritants and the conflict signals appear. When we "veto" our reflexes, we can move up to our neocortex and perceive the situation, assess our feelings, needs, and values, and develop a strategy for reacting. This way, we learn to stop making an elephant out of a mosquito or a mountain out of a molehill.

Our attitude toward conflict

The integrative personality bases on a constructive basic attitude, collaboration, and diplomacy:

- I want to understand using **comprehension** and **empathy**.
- I want to communicate what's important to me using **honesty** and **courtesy.**

- I want to respect myself and my counterpart using balanced **justice** and **love** and find a substantial compromise using the knowledge, capabilities, emotional intelligence, logic, and creativity that all conflict parties can bring to a constructive dialogue. When I start respectfully, I have a chance of achieving more than compromise, and I can hope to find a new solution.

Hot and cold conflicts

We can distinguish between open hot conflicts and concealed cold conflicts. In *open hot conflicts*, the parties are overly motivated to achieve their aims; they literally explode in contact with one another, feel superior, look for direct confrontation, and want to convince by force. Those who adopt this stance in a conflict try to rally supporters to their point of view and think that rules are only hindrances. In *concealed cold conflicts,* on the other hand, the two parties are disappointed with one another because they have lost hope in finding a solution. They hinder and obstruct, talk ironically and sarcastically about each other, evade contact, and withdraw behind formalities, rules, and official channels.

Conflict resolution

Some people approach their conflicts by *imposing their will* through complete annihilation or subjugation, achieving what they want but leaving a devastated, intimidated, and reproachful counterpart who will tend to retaliate and have no further interest in collaboration. Another way to enter conflicts is with an *attitude of cooperation*, the most fruitful approach. One can come to a consensus or find a new solution by cooperating. Cooperation is possible when both parties respect differences, weigh individual interests, and work for a common solution. *Delegating one's conflict* to a higher power is another avenue for resolving conflict, especially when it appears unresolvable and is threatening to get out of control. The last solution is to *agree to disagree and separate*.

Preconditions for constructive conflict resolution are to respect each other and recognize one's own needs as well as the other person's needs by putting oneself in the other's shoes and trying to see the situation from their perspective. It is essential that one have a genuine interest in solving the situation while acknowledging that both parties should be ready to accept disappointment.

"You can stand on your standpoint, but you shouldn't stay sitting on it."
- Nossrat Peseschkian

When we are in a debate, it is important to stay calm, use "I" statements, remain empathic (or at least neutral), and see to it that our body language and what we are saying are in accord.

Always remember, conflicts are motivations for change, and they can promote innovation and creativity. When they are lived well, they promote diversity and tolerance and strengthen cooperation in groups. They can boost one's self-esteem and esteem of the other.

"Late Revenge"

After his trial, a man who had done many villainous things during his life was confined to a hole while the other villagers threw stones at him. The size of each stone was commensurate with the size of the grievance each villager had experienced at the hands of the man. As each stone pelted the man, he cried out in pain. Yet he accepted the stoning as fair punishment for his deeds until he saw a stone thrower whose face he didn't recognize. He asked, "How can it be that you are throwing a stone at me when I don't even know you?" The villager answered, "You may not remember me, but I will never forget the day you insulted me in front of my whole family!"

Retold after Nossrat Peseschkian (*Oriental Stories*, p. 152)

Conflict contents

It is important to define what we are looking for, how we want to get it, and the value we place on it. What we are looking for is our objective. Let's start with a concrete analogy. Our objective is to eat food. Whether we eat a sandwich on the run or sit down to a candlelit dinner, it is a basic need we all share. How we satisfy our need for food differs from individual to individual. The way we prepare food or the type of meal is based on our values. We can all agree that we regularly get hungry and want something to eat, but what we eat, how and where it is prepared, at what price, and with whom we eat it involves discussion and reflects the values we attribute to meals. We always have a need in common, with a personal objective and a strategy for satisfying this need, according to the ever-fluctuating value we place on meals.

Our very *basic needs* are *security*, *love*, and *autonomy*. These can be further differentiated and visualized on tables with *needs in reference to developmental stages*, as described in Maslow's Hierarchy of Needs or represented in Claire Graves' and Don Edward Beck's Spiral Dynamics ("The Emergent, Cyclical, Double-Helix Model of the Adult Biopsychosocial Systems"). In Maslow's Hierarchy of Needs, the foundational needs at the bottom of the pyramid include food, water, air, and sexuality, defined as the essentials for life. Then we require safety in the form of shelter and environment. After that, belonging to a group is crucial, and when this is fulfilled, the need for self-esteem emerges. When all these needs have been met, we seek self-realization and self-actualization. These fulfilled needs are manifested in everyday decisions. For instance, when we discuss the reasons for buying a car, we can see how people focus on these needs differently. Someone might say that for them, a car is important only for mobility and getting to work (autonomy/sustenance). Someone else may want a specific car for its external appearance and the attention he gets by driving it (love/belonging). Another person may be seeking a certain car for safety (security). And then another individual may desire a certain car because it gives him a feeling of power (self-esteem/autonomy), and still another person may want it because it has many of the attributes he wants to express in life (self-actualization). Other examples can be found by examining how our needs are fulfilled by our houses, jobs, hobbies, and friends.

Martin Seligman categorizes five activities that human beings enjoy doing for their own sake: **Positive Emotions, Engagement, Relationship, Meaning, and Accomplishment (PERMA)**. They can be seen as needs we seek to fulfill as well. Human beings are driven to fulfill an almost endless bouquet of needs.

Consider the long list of needs reflected in **Marshall Rosenberg's Inventory of Needs**:

CONNECTION: acceptance, affection, appreciation, belonging, cooperation, communication, closeness, community, companionship, compassion, consideration, consistency, empathy, inclusion, intimacy, love, mutuality, nurturing, respect/self-respect, safety, security, stability, support, to know and be known, to see and be seen, to understand and be understood, trust, warmth; PHYSICAL WELL-BEING: air, food, movement/exercise, rest/sleep, sexual expression, safety, shelter, touch, water; HONESTY: authenticity, integrity, presence; PLAY: joy, humor; PEACE: beauty, communion, ease, equality, harmony, inspiration, order; MEANING: awareness, celebration of life, challenge, clarity, competence, consciousness, contribution, creativity, discovery, efficacy, effectiveness, growth, hope, learning, mourning, participation, purpose, self-expression, stimulation, to matter understanding; AUTONOMY: choice, freedom, independence, space, spontaneity.

Nossrat Peseschkian's Four Dimensions of Life (body/work/social-life/spirituality) and his **actual capacities** (primary and secondary capabilities) encompass the whole spectrum of needs and goals delineated in Rosenberg's list. In addition, Peseschkian's dimensions and capabilities include the strategies we express in life and the values and emotional background tied to our goals and needs. The *basic capabilities* of *love* and *comprehension* are in themselves and in their differentiation from actual capacities based on human needs. For fulfilling these needs, we develop specific capabilities. They describe the way an individual connects in relationship with one another (actual capacities of love) and structures this relationship (actual capacities of comprehension), so he can achieve his objectives in his Four Dimensions of Life. The *primary* and *secondary capabilities* also develop value/emotional loads depending on positive or negative experiences and the conditioning on which their development is based. Peseschkian's paradigm encompasses the whole scope of human needs, capabilities, and values as well as the transcended forms of objectives and possible strategies for their expression.

"The Broken Vase"

A woman had betrayed her husband and was laden with remorse and sadness. When her husband came home, she felt overwhelmed and didn't know what to say. In her distraction, she accidentally knocked down an inexpensive vase. She began to weep bitterly when the vase shattered into thousands of fragments. Surprised by her reaction, her husband assured her, "But darling, this vase is of no value. Don't worry, tomorrow we will buy an even more beautiful one."

Retold after Nossrat Peseschkian (*Auf der Suche nach Sinn*, p. 21)

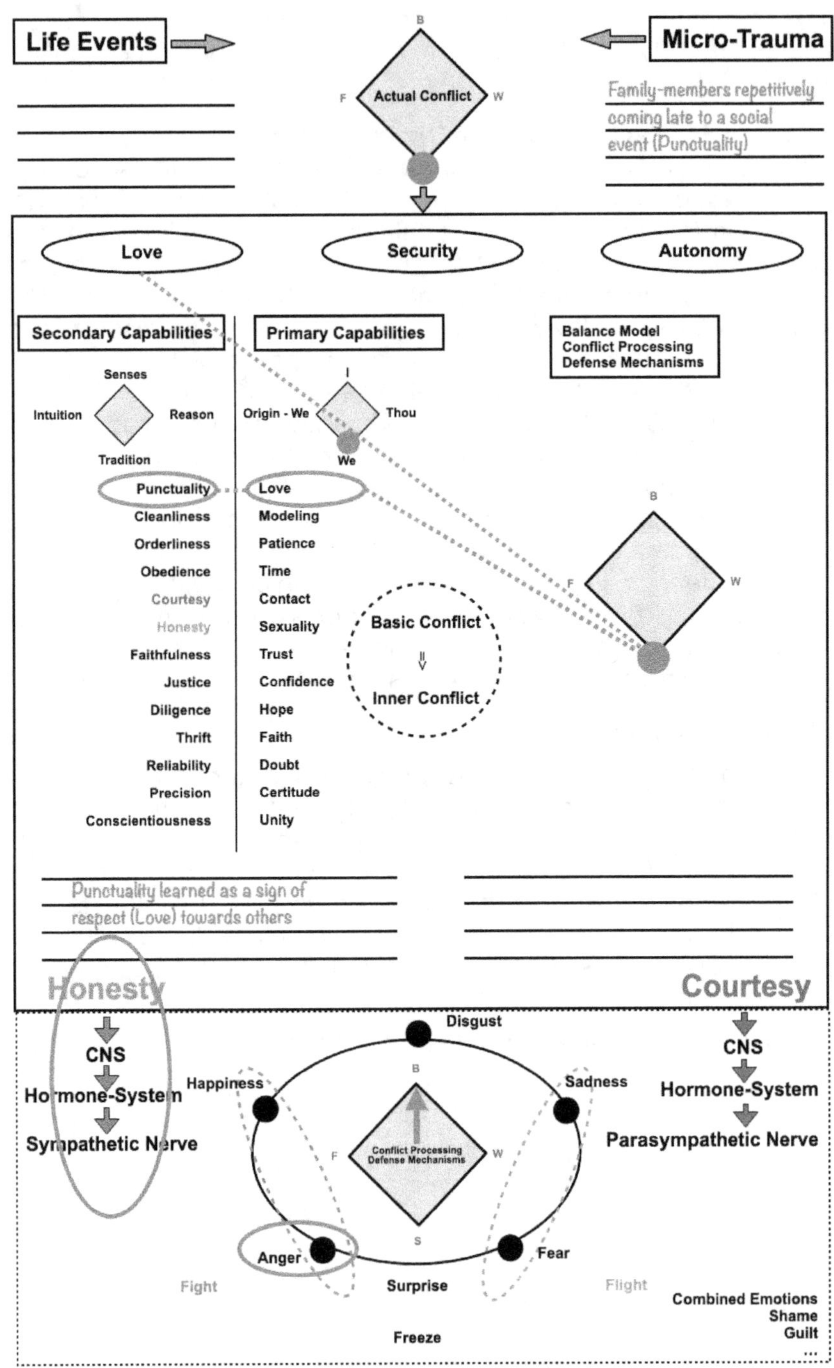

Introductive example of conflict dynamics

Conflict dynamics

As we will now discuss successively and in depth, in Positive Psychotherapy, we can distinguish between an **actual conflict**, which is an *acute* or *chronic-load situation* caused by *micro-* or *macro-trauma,* and the cause of the conflict with its *conflict content* (*objectives* and *behavior*) and *localization* within life (*Four Dimensions*). The **basic conflict** consists of the sub- or preconscious conflictive concepts for this situation within the personality structure acquired during childhood, with its *conflict content* (*objectives* and *behavior*) and *localization* (*Four Dimensions* and *Four Dimensions of role modeling and comprehension*). And the **inner conflict** is the resulting subconscious' seemingly irresolvable decompensation of the known strategies with internal (somatization) and external *escape* reactions within the Four Dimensions; they don't bring a solution to the situation but at least provide temporary relief or compensation. In the long run, the conflicts have to be solved or lead to helplessness, hopelessness, and further decompensation. So the inner conflict results from the actual conflict with its challenges touching the basic conflict and the lack of a solution through the prior known strategies/behavior patterns resulting in somatization and psychological compensation reactions with further helplessness and inner confusion. It may be a conflict on different levels of the conscious and subconscious, with the person consciously wanting something but subconsciously acting in the opposite direction, resulting in inner disharmony and failure to achieve his objectives. When the conflict is chronic, the person becomes symptomatic.

Introductive example of conflict dynamics

The repeated impunctuality of family members (*actual conflict*) at family gatherings meets one's punctuality concept learned as children (*basic concepts/conflict*) and leads to inner confusion and an outburst of anger and a headache (*inner conflict*).

The actual conflict

Theory

An actual conflict is an acute or chronic load situation caused by micro- or macro-trauma and the cause of the conflict with its conflict content: The objectives with their localization within the Four Dimensions of Life expression and behavior (actual capacities) to reach it.

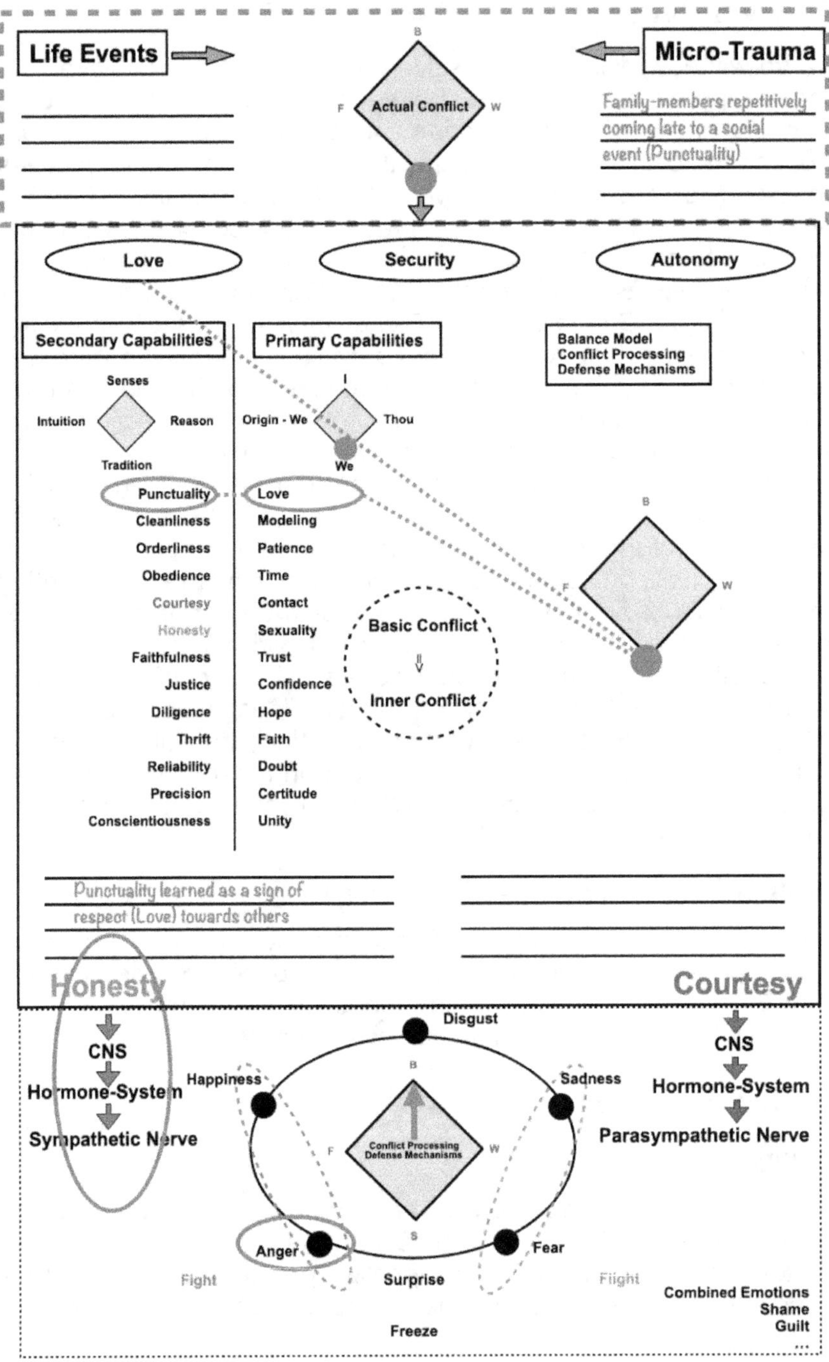

The actual conflict

Introductive example

Family members repeatedly come late to a planned social event. Impunctuality (behavior - actual capacity) is a micro-traumatic acute and chronic event happening at a family meeting (objective) within the social area (Four Dimensions).

Micro- and macro-trauma

Life as we know it continuously confronts us with conflicts that are based on trauma. Psychiatrists Thomas Holmes and Richard Rahe defined life events and their impact in 1967 by devising a stressor scale. Nossrat Peseschkian described what he called micro- and macro-traumas during the same time period. Macro-traumas or life events are strongly impacting incidents such as the death of someone close, disease, indebtedness, an accident, imprisonment, or divorce. Micro-traumas are all the small things that happen, such as minor arguments, running late, burnt food, flat tires, unsolicited advice, or misinterpreted intentions about taking turns cleaning the dishes, leaving the worn clothes thrown next to the bed for days, the little discussions we have on the phone with clients, or our boss nagging at us at work.

Micro- and macro-traumas refer to behaviors as described in the *actual capacities* or events happening within an area of the Four Dimensions that create conflicts.

Examples of micro- and macro-trauma as actual conflicts and how they affect our lives in the areas of behavior (actual capabilities) and life expression (Four Dimensions)

Micro-trauma

"A steady drop hollows a stone."

Micro-traumas within the actual capabilities

Within our own household, we can experience an actual conflict as micro-trauma in the form of a friend always coming late, "You're not punctual enough" (punctuality), our spouse leaving the dishes unwashed in the sink again and again, "You're not clean enough" (cleanliness), our son constantly leaving his dirty socks under the sofa, "You're not orderly enough" (orderliness and cleanliness), a friend never having time and missing appointments, "You don't spend enough time with me" (time and love), or our spouse lying to us, "You betrayed me" (honesty and trust).

We often use actual capacities to criticize our counterparts. Each one has opposite extremes:

Punctuality	=> fussy, pedantic	<=>	pokey, slow
Cleanliness	=> sterile	<=>	filthy/grimy
Orderliness	=> fixed, formal, framed	<=>	slovenly, sloppy, chaotic
Obedience	=> submissive, servile	<=>	mischievous, unreliable
Courtesy	=> artificial, hypocritical	<=>	rude
Honesty	=> lying	<=>	blunt, moral
Faithfulness	=> attached	<=>	disloyal
Justice	=> rigid	<=>	unfair
Thrift	=> wasteful, squandering	<=>	piggish, hoarding
Reliability	=> accurate, pedantic	<=>	irresponsible
Love	=> needy	<=>	aloof
Sexuality	=> frigid	<=>	desperate
Time	=> hectic, frazzled	<=>	slow, apathetic
Contact	=> superficial	<=>	reserved
Patience	=> permissive	<=>	impatient, anxious
Doubt	=> skeptical	<=>	gullible
Faith	=> pious	<=>	blasphemous, heretical

Micro-trauma within the Four Dimensions

We are hurt when someone criticizes us in any of the **Four Dimensions**.

- **Body:** "You look fat." "You shouldn't eat such high-calorie food." "You shouldn't eat junk food." "You reek of smoke and alcohol."

- **Achievement**: "Your profession is embarrassing." "What you've achieved up to now in life is ridiculous." "You can't even earn your way."

- **Social life:** "The people you hang out with are losers." "Your family is boring." "Knowing they are your parents makes me sick and wonder about you."

- **Spirituality:** "Your religion and your religious practice are blasphemous." "Your hobby of building model railways is childish and inadequate for an adult." "You should be more interested in news, culture... and not be so ignorant."

Macro-trauma

Macro-trauma within the actual capabilities

- Justice, Faithfulness, Love...: "My partner cheated on me after so many years of marriage. I lost my faith in men and love in general."

- Thrift, Reliability...: "My partner lost all our savings by gambling." "A friend deceived us badly by scamming us out of our money in a work partnership."

- Justice, Reliability, Honesty, Trust...: "Your betrayal caused me to lose my job and my money."

- Sexuality and Trust...: "I lost all interest in sex and my trust in men after being sexually abused."

- Hope, Confidence, Trust, Faith, Certitude ...: "When the earthquake hit our village, it devastated me."

Macro-trauma within the Four Dimensions

- **Body**: "The accident severely injured my legs, and I was hospitalized."

- **Work**: "I lost my job yesterday because our firm went bankrupt."

- **Social Life**: "My family died when they were buried by an earthquake."

- **Spirituality**: "I lost my faith when I heard our minister was accused of pedophilia."

Macro- and micro-trauma alike cause anger, fear, sadness, helplessness, hopelessness, and in the long run, even depression. The macro-traumas have an immediate impact, whereas the micro-traumas have a gradual impact.

When we look closely, we see many of the topics touch both the behavior or attitude we are showing and also how we are living or expressing our lives. To investigate them, we can look through the DAI or WIPPF and the Four Dimensions. The micro-traumas can add up to conflict outside or depression within or both. Macro-trauma can let the personality decompensate and fail to develop coping mechanisms immediately.

The basic conflict

Theory

As mentioned above, the basic conflict consists of the sub- or pre-conscious conflictive concepts that reside within the personality structure. These conflictive concepts were acquired during childhood and are no longer adequate.

Introductive example

As children, we were taught that punctuality was a sign of respect towards one another and especially family members. Those who were late were ridiculed and scolded.

As conflict content and conflictive concept, punctuality (behavior - actual capacity) is tightly linked to the experience of love/acceptance (actual capacity that becomes a subconscious objective) through educational conditioning (Four Dimensions of role modeling and comprehension) in the social context and especially family relationships (Four Dimensions - objective). As we've seen, Prof. Dr. Nossrat Peseschkian's inventories of behavioral expression, the WIPPF and the DAI, describe the basic capacities of love and comprehension in their differentiated form as actual capacities: the primary and secondary capabilities. He described these as an attempt to expand Freud's structural model of the psyche. The actual capacities are a differentiation of Freud's generalized idea of a self, which can suffer from a punishing and overstraining superego (thus from neurosis) into a self with separate areas of behavior with the potential for inner and outer conflict. These actual capabilities can be individually affected. We can have difficulties with one of the areas and no problems with another. We can be obsessive about cleanliness and simultaneously lax with punctuality. So, we go from a general perspective about a self with a punishing and overstraining superego to a very distinguished one discerning separate areas of behavior (primary and secondary capacities) with their problems and strengths. (Nossrat Peseschkian also conceived the Four Dimensions of Life as a differentiation of the "self-worth and feelings of inferiority" of Alfred Adler. Here a general concept of low self-esteem was differentiated into different areas of life in which one could develop a higher or lower amount of self-esteem.)

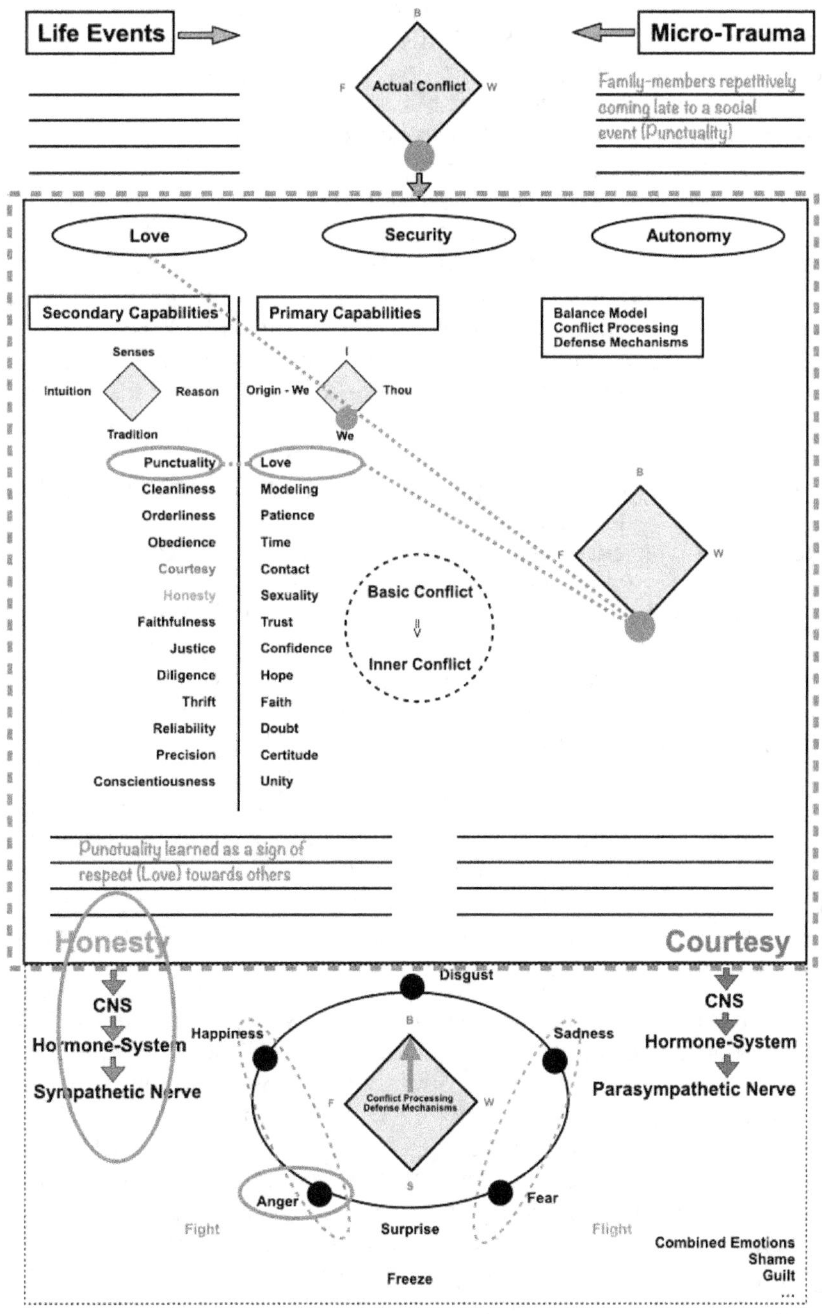

The basic conflict

Freud's structural model of the psyche consists of three interacting agents: the *id,* which is our drives and needs (preservation of the individual, species, and all the transcended ones), the *super-ego,* which is our inculcated values with their emotional load, and the *ego,* which integrates and manages the first two through our true capabilities. We can differentiate our actual capacities or our behavior in this threefold perspective: as needs, values, and capabilities. If we learned to express them by observing and imitating our parents, assuming our parents embodied them in a healthy way, we would have developed an equilibrated set of capabilities fitting our needs and values. If we learned them only through our parents' expectations, through conditioning by inculcating fear and hope as well as with *punishment and reward*our parents not being able to live them healthily themselves—they will manifest in us with a fearful, punishing, and overstraining superego and not in equilibrium with our needs and capabilities. *"Be worried, not that your children aren't obeying you but that they are watching you."* (Anonymous) Most of us have experienced education as a mixture of both. Education through punishment and reward manipulates us based on our three basic needs for *love, security,* and *autonomy* through conditioning by giving conditioned love, conditioned security, and conditioned autonomy. When we are repeatedly (micro-traumas) or harshly (macro-traumas) threatened with being deprived of these, it remains within ourselves as an emotional wound and will manifest itself directly as a basic conflict. Denying affection for not doing homework (conditioned love), denying a meal or locking children out for behaving badly (conditioned security), or taking away the car keys or making a youth stay in his room for an evening or a week (conditioned autonomy) are examples. The method behind it is always *fear*. When fear is connected to an objective or a strategy or behavior, it receives a negative attribute: Thrift becomes avarice, love becomes jealousy, and passion becomes obsession.

Fear itself is a healthy emotion, giving us the possibility to protect ourselves from danger. But if fear has been incorporated into a whole area of life, life loses its enchantment, and we don't have the verve to live up to our potential and can't see the beauty in things anymore. Punishment and reward are, in general, only of limited help in making someone do something, taking the focus away from the primary benefit of doing the thing and reducing it to evading punishment or achieving an external reward. Neither a paddling from the principal nor winning a trophy are effective motivators. If we explain the negative consequences or the positive results of an action, a person will learn its intrinsic value. A surprise gift of appreciation after a positive outcome can be a supplementary stimulus, but it shouldn't be the primary motivation.

Not only our behavior (primary and secondary capabilities) is subject to the experience we have with our parents and punishment and reward, but also the objectives we develop within our Four Dimensions of Life—the way we should take care of our health (body/health), what we should engage in professionally (work/achievement), what types of friends we should surround ourselves with (social life), and the faith we should follow (future/spirituality). We learn all these are learned through our socialization, a process through which our needs are differentiated and transcended, and we acquire goals with values and emotional loads.

The Four Dimensions of Role-Modeling

Object and self-representations are developed within the Four Dimensions of Role-Modeling, with which we have already gotten a bit acquainted. Within these four dimensions, we can see how our **I, You, We, and Origin We** relationships are formed:

Our "I" relationship—the relationship we have with ourselves, our self-perception, and our self-esteem—depends strongly on how we have experienced ourselves, how we were mirrored by our parents, our primary references, our siblings, and our grandparents. Did they love us, neglect us, or beat us? How did they show their love? How did they punish us? Did they use loving words, look at us lovingly, touch us tenderly, give us kisses and caresses, or did they neglect us or even hurt us verbally and physically? We discover our relationship with ourselves depending on how our needs are fulfilled as children. "Are we accepted or rejected?" is the key question. These primary experiences become a system of reference for later developments, our capability of developing self-worth and a stable "I," of binding and connecting to others, and a primary sense of basic trust. Our capability of self-expression and our drive to flourish can, at best, develop freely in a loving environment with admirable role models or, at worst, in a rigid or abusive environment in which our personality becomes neurotically overlaid with negative self-images and unreachable self-ideals. Through the experience with our parents, we may learn that we are worthy of going after our personal dreams, or maybe we have learned to despise ourselves and only fulfill the expectations of others through conditioned love, security, and autonomy.

The way we experience partnership, the **"You" relationship,** depends on how we experienced our parents' partnership. How did they live it? Were they in love, or did they have a marriage of convenience? Was one of them dependent on the other? Did they relate to one another through verbal and physical violence? How did they express their love or live their conflicts? What was their relationship to sexuality? Our parents' example influences the value we place upon partnership in life, how our drive for a partner is channeled, and how we should live in a partnership. Our parents' relationship impacts whether we think partnership is worthwhile or to be shunned. If we can be accepted in partnership and can accept others, what type of mutual treatment shall we expect? Our capabilities for an intimate relationship, togetherness, sharing, our choice in partnership and identity as couples, faithfulness, love, justice, solidarity, and rivalry are all derived from these experiences.

The social stamping of our "We" relationship capability depends on what the social life, the **"We" relationship** of our parents, was like. Were they sociable? Did they meet with friends or colleagues? Did they have friends of interest? Did they invite them over? Did they participate in clubs or political parties? What was the relationship to the greater family? Our parents' social profile is the basis of the expression of our need for social relationships. How should we live these relationships? How should we strive to find fulfillment in them? Is it worth having them at all, or who are we if we don't have outside social connections? Our social capabilities are shaped here—our need for social contacts, our ability to accept group norms, our hospitality, our emotional needs, and our capability to enter into contact with people of other origins. Role models are shaped in groups, and group identity gives support when group roles are accepted.

Our **"Origin We" relationship** consists of spirituality and worldview, passed down as social conditioning through our parents and close relationships. How did they live their spirituality with us? Did they have a particular worldview? Did they pray, read holy scriptures, go to temple, church, or mosque? Did they take us with them? What general worldview and picture of God did they have? Was it a benevolent or violent and punishing deity? Their beliefs are the origin of how we seek to make sense of our own lives. It is as if they inoculated us with a set of beliefs, ready answers to natural questions about our origin and eventual destination.

How we acquire capabilities and how we express our Four Dimensions of Life are formed not only through experience with our parents and primary reference persons, but we continue to form them later on in life through interaction with our close friends and social associations. What health and aesthetics concepts do we develop (body)? Which profession do we perceive suitable for us, how do we treat others, what is our role in a work hierarchy, which income can fulfill our aspirations (achievement/work)? The type of friends and family we want, how we treat them, how we live our social lives, what hobbies we like, what news information we prefer, what religion we follow, and our cultural preferences are all rooted in our various social contexts. Our form of conflict processing (escape reactions), what type of fear we are prone to, and the defense mechanisms for managing our fears are also formed through our social experience.

Nossrat Peseschkian discovered that there are **typical types of fear** connected to each of the four dimensions, such as vital anxiety to the body, fear of failure at work, anxiety related to social life, and existential fear about the future/spirituality. The human **defense mechanisms** we need for calming and managing our fears can also be associated with our fears. These include somatization, substance abuse, and bodily compulsiveness, rationalization, and intellectualization in terms of work; idealization, devaluation, identification, and projective identification in response to social life; and denial and splitting in reaction to future/spirituality issues. All of these fears and human defense mechanisms are also susceptible to being passed on from generation to generation.

Defense mechanisms

We can attribute even more defense mechanisms to the Four Dimensions:

Body/health

Mature

- *Suppression:* Consciously postponing paying attention to an emotion, thought, or need so individuals can cope with their present reality, combined with the ability to access, accept, and deal with these again during a later moment.

Immature

- *Somatization:* Reacting to and buffering uncomfortable feelings and stress caused by the inner or outside world that then manifest in the form of health issues when they become excessive.

- *Hypochondriasis:* Venting excessive fears as worries about one's health issues.

- *Conversion:* Venting an immense intra-psychic conflict as a physical symptom, such as becoming paralyzed, deaf, or blind, when it becomes overwhelming.

- *Substance abuse:* Escaping from emotions by using alcohol and drugs.

Achievement/work

Mature

- *Sublimation:* Transforming unhelpful emotions or instincts into healthy emotions or behaviors. For example, transforming aggression into a game by playing a heavy contact sport such as football or boxing.
- *Courage:* Confronting conflicts involving uncertainty, danger, fear, and pain.

Immature:

- *Rationalization:* Convincing oneself of one's excuses, that one has done nothing wrong, and that whatever one did was done for a good reason.
- *Intellectualization:* Gaining emotional distance from an experience by separating the emotion from the action, ideas, and intellectual aspects and then describing these in emotionally bland terms.
- *Reaction formation:* Converting unconscious beliefs, wishes, or impulses internally experienced as dangerous or unacceptable into their opposites and then exhibiting completely opposite behavior of what is truly wanted or felt.

Social life

Mature

- *Emotional self-regulation:* The ability to respond to the outer world and its demands with a range of situationally adequate emotions and socially tolerable behavior.
- *Emotional self-sufficiency:* The ability to be independent of the approval or disapproval of one's social environment.
- *Forgiveness:* The ability to let go of anger and resentment resulting from perceived offenses and not needing retribution or restitution.
- *Respect:* The ability and willingness to show consideration or appreciation. Respect can be a specific feeling of high regard for a person's qualities, feelings, actions, and conduct. Relationships and contacts built without establishing mutual respect are seldom sustainable in the long term.

- *Tolerance*: The ability to allow something one disapproves of.

- *Gratitude*: The ability to feel appreciation and thankfulness towards people, things, or events that appear in one's life. Gratitude is accompanied by happiness and wards off depression and stress.

- *Humility*: The ability to have a humble self-opinion that keeps one from over-evaluating oneself.

- *Mercy*: The ability to be compassionate and act accordingly in a position of power.

- *Altruism*: The ability to be of service and help others to contribute to their well-being.

Immature

- *Withdrawal:* The ability to remove oneself from situations and interactions when there is a threat of being reminded of painful feelings, thoughts, and experiences, therefore achieving temporary relief.

- *Introjection:* The ability to unconsciously identify with an idea or person to such a point that they become a part of oneself, thereby subconsciously assimilating their attributes.

- *Idealization and devaluation:* The ability to see more desirable qualities in persons than they really have and to use them as idols for worship and hope, or conversely, lowering them to a level where they don't present a threat to oneself anymore, thereby raising one's own self-value.

- *Identification:* The ability to unconsciously model oneself upon another person's character and behavior to escape punishment, such as a hostage does with his hostage taker.

- *Projection:* The ability to see one's own unacknowledged, unacceptable feelings, drives, and thoughts in another person, thereby experiencing them possessed by the other and not by oneself.

- *Projective identification:* The ability to let one's counterpart experience the precise feelings, drives, and thoughts projected onto him and make him react to them as one expects him to.

Spiritual life/future

Mature

- *Mindfulness:* The ability to focus one's complete attention, in a combination of curiosity and acceptance, on the experience of the present moment.

- *Moderation:* The ability to "reduce to the max," appreciating what is, not needing any excesses, and thereby staying within reasonable limits. It is the ability to exercise self-restraint on one's own feelings or desires without becoming compulsive.

- *Patience:* The ability to accept oneself, another person, or a situation the way it is.

- *Acceptance*: The ability to accept reality, the present moment as it is, without rancor or denial, and then taking reasonable action.

- *Anticipation*: The ability to look ahead and plan adequately for the future.

Immature

- *Wishful thinking*: The ability to bend one's perception of reality and look at the future more positively and opportunistically than is realistic, thereby relieving oneself of immediate discomfort.

- *Denial*: The ability to cut out a part of reality, of a threatening inner or outer conflict or situation that provokes unbearable anxiety and stress, and act as if it doesn't exist.

- *Undoing*: The ability to temporarily eliminate anxiety and stress caused by feelings, drives, thoughts, or behaviors that are perceived as threatening and unbearable, doing rituals that express exactly the reverse of the unacceptable, thereby symbolically nullifying the guilt-provoking thoughts, ideas, or feelings. For example, when one has had nasty thoughts about someone, one shouldn't have to eliminate the anxiety and stress they cause by them by acting overly nice towards them.

- *Splitting*: A primitive defense mechanism that allows oneself to split off impulses perceived both as desirable and harmful while at the same time leaving them unintegrated within one's self and then often projecting them onto others. Individuals experience relief by segregating experiences into all-good and all-bad, relieving themselves from the unbearable experience of ambiguity and ambivalence. Splitting can be combined with projecting when individuals attribute the qualities they unconsciously perceive and reject about themselves onto others.

- *Regression*: The ego's ability to find relief by temporarily regressing to an earlier stage of development and receiving attention and help with handling its unacceptable impulses. For example, regressing to helplessness by using whining to communicate one's need for support rather than using one's ability to speak with the appropriate level of maturity.

- *Dissociation*: The ability to drastically modify one's identity or character to avoid emotional distress. The ability to separate or postpone feelings that usually come with a situation or thought.

Attachment – differentiation – detachment

During childhood and adolescence, we progress through development from **attachment** to **differentiation** and then **detachment** in succession, dictated by our needs for **love**, **security,** and **autonomy**, which all exist in every stage but are predominant in one or the other. All the experiences we have, the pleasant as well as the unpleasant ones, drift from the conscious to the preconscious and then to the subconscious mind. Here they become inaccessible to consciousness but remain alive in our engagement with the outer world. With every subsequent contact and conflict, our emotionally laden experiences, values, and capabilities are challenged and express themselves.

We learned our goals and strategies for life as infants and children at an age when we couldn't understand what was helpful or harmful to us. We couldn't discern which strategies were empowering or which were limiting false beliefs because, at this age, our frontal lobes weren't yet functioning at their full potential. We simply assimilated everything our parents fed us—all the empowering but also all the limiting beliefs and experiences that sabotaged our conscious desires and goals. As children and young adults, we were prone to becoming emotionally handicapped with an inferiority complex, thereby acquiring further wounds. We were most obviously wounded by direct physical and verbal violence, such as ridicule. But we were wounded less obviously through opinions and criticism, which, at their best, were intended to be humorous and well-meaning but which we perceived as stinging and condescending. Of course, at the time, our learned behavior was an adequate reaction to the given situation; it was our life vest in a turbulent ocean. But the moment better ideas or solutions to our life questions open up before us, we have to seize them, just as we have to abandon our old life vest to be able to climb into a yacht when it comes by so we can sail the oceans of life in a new, sleek, fast, and modern vessel.

According to Freud, the I or the self can be described as the ego (the life-managing entity with its capabilities), the superego (the ambitions we have learned and acquired throughout life), and the id (our drives, which, in an extended interpretation, we can see as our needs). The ambitions of our superego should transcend our desires if we are in line with ourselves. If we have created life goals that deny and repress our needs, then we create **shadows** that torment us subconsciously. Inner critics can reinforce these shadows, which are the expression of our dominating values. Our inner critics tell us that what we are doing isn't only bad and shameful, but we have to feel guilty about our actions, and we should be punished. Our inner critics sometimes speak in the original, vehement, chastising tone of those who taught us our values. For example, we hear the voice of one of our parents telling us that we are worthless. Of course, all people have all the innate human values and capabilities, but if some of those values dominate and repress the others, we become ill. When we don't express one of our innate capabilities, letting it lie idle because we feel shy, we often find ourselves adoring that same capability in others. This is called our **golden shadow.** So, the objective is to get our aspirations in line and in balance with our needs. Our inner supporters are side by side with our inner critics as part of our superego. We need both the critic and the supporter. They must speak in moderate voices, communicating as mature adults so that both can be heard. When they are shouting, "You should do this" or "You shouldn't do that," we get out of balance.

When people talk about their ego, they are usually talking about their inner critic, who is guiding them according to an idealized self-image, dictating how they should or shouldn't be and what attributes and material objects they should have. When our ego or our inner critic, which is actually the criticizing part of our superego and not our true ego, tells us we are "a lousy speaker, not as good as the guy who presented before," it's not the best idea to ignore it, because repressing our inner critic will cause even more damage through rebellion in our subconscious. We must learn not to silence that voice but to assuage it so we can hear its message. We distance ourselves or we disidentify from it so that we can listen to its critical voice as well as the voices of our inner supporters, the positive side of our super-ego. After this adjustment, we hear, "Wow, this speaker is really good! I wish I could be as good as he is; I'm afraid I'll embarrass myself." We now also see how the initial message was overlaid by fear and the menace of punishment in our critic's voice. We must learn to calm our inner critic by confronting reality, relativizing our exaggerated beliefs, and allowing our inner supporters to speak. With time and effort, this will happen. When we have brought our critics and supporters into balance, a healthy reaction in the same circumstance would be that the inner critic tells us, "Wow, this competition is going to be quite difficult," while the inner supporter would balance our response with "Yeah, but we've got the stuff to make it, and anyway, competition is for fun, and if we lose against a good competitor, we can have a good time anyway." When our self is in harmony, we also like our self-image.

Taking an in-depth look at our **basic concepts/conflicts,** we see how the actual capabilities, the Four Dimensions of Role Modeling, and the Four Dimensions of Life expression (Balance Model) can evolve harmoniously or develop with conflict-potential through the way we learn to fulfill our needs and the way we adapt to our environment, as we are influenced by our experiences and conditioning with **love, security,** and **autonomy**. Our aspirations and behavior as adults are connected based on this learning process. We will not be learning if we continue to follow old models or faulty paradigms for happiness, such as the following:

- "I will be *loved* only through achieving, having a big house, being rich, finding good friends who accept me, or finding a great partner who accepts me."

- "I will be *secure* only if I find the best paying job after learning the best profession and marrying a rich spouse."

- "I will be *autonomous* only if I can get rid of the burdens my parents imposed on me, if I really excel in life, if I completely give my best—or maybe I simply can't be autonomous at all as my parents have always been telling me."

We can define the contents of the basic concept/conflict as a pre- or subconscious universal need/drive (**id**), that is expressed (it can also be suppressed through the expression of another need) through a conscious objective based on an ideal and overlaid with an emotional value/load (**superego**) as well as the strategy, through which it is sought to be achieved (provided by the **ego**). A basic concept/conflict is acquired in its greatest part in childhood but also through experiences later in life. A basic concept/conflict was, in an earlier time, a means of survival and adequacy. In later conflict-arousing situations, though, it doesn't meet the needs of the actual situation anymore. The capabilities or strategies the ego has at its disposition to fulfill the tug-of-war between the needs and the emotion-laden values no longer fulfill this task. So, the ego decompensates, and the individual starts somatizing and uses its other individual forms of conflict processing/escape reactions. This is what we call an **inner conflict**.

An important aspect of the basic conflict is also the *emotional load* our values must bear. This emotional load can be a direct wound, a pain inflicted in behavior (actual capacities), or life expression (Four Dimensions) and/or the conditioning caused by upbringing, connecting the ideal/value to a basic need such as love, security, and autonomy.

For example, we might have experienced conditioning by getting praise when keeping our room in order and getting good grades and being beaten when we left our room a mess or didn't bring home the expected grades. Or perhaps our parents gave us money and attention as an expression of their love only when we behaved according to their rules and showed high achievement. This kind of upbringing, where orderliness and achievement are linked with autonomy and love, given in the form of money and time, forges the personality for the future. We may have effectively learned to achieve love and autonomy at home with our parents, but when we grow up and live in a new environment, our strategy may not work anymore (except with people of the same education and then only in an unsatisfactory way). We may fall in love with another person who is appalled by our showing off our success and money, while they feel shortchanged because we are unable to give the closeness, emotional love, or presence they expect. As a reaction to their disapproval, we might start to brag even more about our achievements and invite the person we have a crush on to our luxuriously furnished house. But this only causes further irritation because our heartthrob experiences it as sterile and soulless. So, our efforts result in inner confusion and frustration. This experience may repeat itself again and again if the causes of the conflict aren't addressed.

The inner conflict

theory

The inner conflict occurs when a basic concept/conflict learned in childhood meets a series of micro-traumatic events or a major life event (macro-trauma). The ego doesn't have the resources and strategies to handle these events properly and resorts to somatization on the physical level and conflict-processing escape reactions on the external level.

Introductive example

Since we didn't learn a calm and reflective way of reacting to repeated situations of unpunctuality as children, when we are overstressed by repeated or massive situations of unpunctuality, we can't react in a controlled way, and we decompensate. This leads to verbal tirades and a headache as a flight reaction.

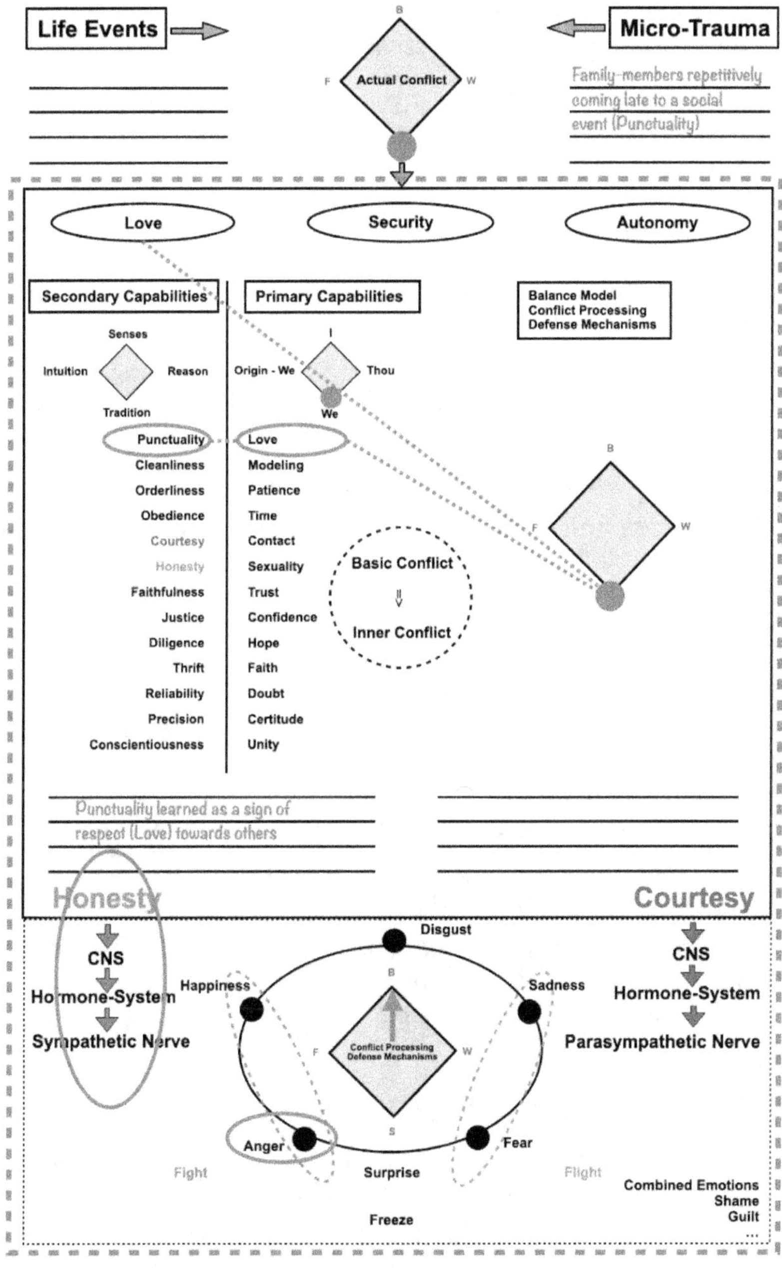

The inner conflict

The repeated unpunctuality (micro-trauma) of family members (actual conflict) meets our punctuality concepts learned as children (basic conflict) and leads to the decompensation of the ego and inner confusion with an outburst of anger and a headache (inner conflict—flight reaction within the Four Dimensions of Life).

In this situation, we react with honesty/candor since this is the key-conflict reaction strategy we acquired as children (see key-conflict further on).

The emotional level

When something, a positive or negative event, a micro- or macro-trauma, happens to us, we experience different emotions.

Both Dr. Paul Ekman and Traditional Chinese Medicine (TCM) have identified, as we will discuss shortly, some of the basic emotional signals our mind and body are sending us:

- *Happiness*: Arises when our need is fulfilled.

- *Surprise*: When something happens unexpectedly, and we haven't been able to evaluate, reflexively decide, and develop a further reaction to the situation yet. This occurs in animals as well and is known as the **freeze reaction**. By "freezing," an animal becomes immobile and quiet so as not to attract attention and hopefully escape its predator.

- *Anger*: It is the emotion that creates the energy (aggression, from Latin *aggredior,* to go forward; also, in a metaphoric sense, to fight for something) that helps us overcome the barrier between ourselves and the goal/need we want to reach.

- *Fear*: Something is menacing us and putting us in danger. We must protect ourselves and run.

- *Sadness*: We have lost something and must grieve so we can let go of it and find something new in due time.

- *Disgust*: Something is repulsive to us because it could harm us or even put us in danger.

Then there are **mixed feelings**. Here some examples:

- *Hope*: The apprehension of happiness, of achieving a goal for satisfying a need in the future; we might want to go after it.

- *Shame*: Our sense of disgust, fear, and other emotions in different blends as seen through the lens of an outside opinion. It shows us what we should do to stay in touch with others and get their approval.

- *Guilt*: The sense of sadness, fear, and anger directed toward oneself for having tried to satisfy a need/value that infringed on another need. It is based on our inner value system and shows the path to the right action.

All the listed feelings are important signals of what is going on within and around us, and we should take them seriously, treating them as friends. The messages behind them are of essential value for our self-regulation. Suppressing them makes us insensitive to chances and dangers lying ahead of or within us. Just as the physical disease of leprosy is dangerous because it takes away sensitivity and pain sensation, so too is our avoidance of sensitive issues and painful thoughts. By ignoring these mental signals, we risk injuring ourselves without noticing. If we experience very strong or painful emotions, we must uncover their origin. We must look at what our body and soul are telling us, where we are prone to injury, and where our inner conflicts might bring us harm.

All these emotions are essential signals that our needs are or are not being fulfilled. If we suppress our feelings, we suppress our needs and become sick. When our needs aren't fulfilled for an extended period, and the situation becomes chronic, anger becomes hatred and loathing, fear overflows into general anxiety and panic, disgust devolves into repulsion and bitterness, and sadness deteriorates into melancholy and misery. When ignored, these emotions become more intense and spill over into other areas of life. This spillover is called generalization. The essential task here is then to find new ways to fulfill our goals or create new ways to fulfill the needs underlying these goals. We may reconsider how important these goals are to satisfy our needs. Perhaps we have exaggerated their importance. Re-examining our goals might allow us to fulfill our needs in another way.

Happiness and anger are more closely aligned with the expression of honesty and the sympathetic nervous system. In comparison, sadness and fear are more expressions of politeness and the parasympathetic nervous system. These connections are depicted in the model of conflict reaction and were already known to the ancient Chinese, as we will describe further on. They also attributed different psychosomatic expressions of the body to each individual feeling.

When we enter conflict, our body is put into a state of alertness called stress. Stress is an important state of readiness to respond to the needs of a situation and prepare for action so the conflict can be solved. If the conflict isn't resolved sufficiently, and we stay in this state of alert with all the adrenalin, noradrenalin, cortisol, and blood sugar circulating in our blood over a long time, we tire and start somatizing. This can be demonstrated by looking at a cat's reaction in front of a dog. What does a cat usually do when it sees a dog? It gets ready to to either run away or claw the dog. The threatened feline arches its back, its fur stands on end, its pupils dilate, and its muscles tense, all to prepare for the next move. If we imagine these natural enemies, the dog and cat chained close to one another, we see that they will somatize. Over time, they will get backaches, hurting joints, loss of fur, and diarrhea. We have the same bodily reactions. If we are glued to our office, our clients and boss expecting too much of us, conflicts continuously arise on our daily agenda, and we too will soon have backaches, headaches, irritable bowels, sleeplessness, hair loss, and so forth. The longer we stay in this stressful state with our vegetative system at its peak, the more exhausted and physiologically damaged we become. Our stress finally manifests in functional and later even in organic diseases like dermatitis, hypertension, colitis, asthma, susceptibility to infection, and others because our immune system is out of balance.

When we look at Dr. Paul Ekman's work on universal human emotions, especially those he deemed the "primary emotions," and we compare them to the emotions described in TCM, we see that they are identical, with the exception of surprise. The Chinese have known these emotions for more than 2000 years and have already precisely observed the connection through somatization between certain emotions and specific organs. They understood that those emotions and the function of the organs had to be in balance with one another, which in Positive Psychotherapy, we would attribute to the good processing of conflicts. As Nossrat Peseschkian used to say, "A healthy person is not a person without problems but rather one who knows how to cope with them."

The relationships between organs and emotions in **TCM** are interesting in many ways because they also are described by some western proverbs, indicating that both cultures understood these universal truths.

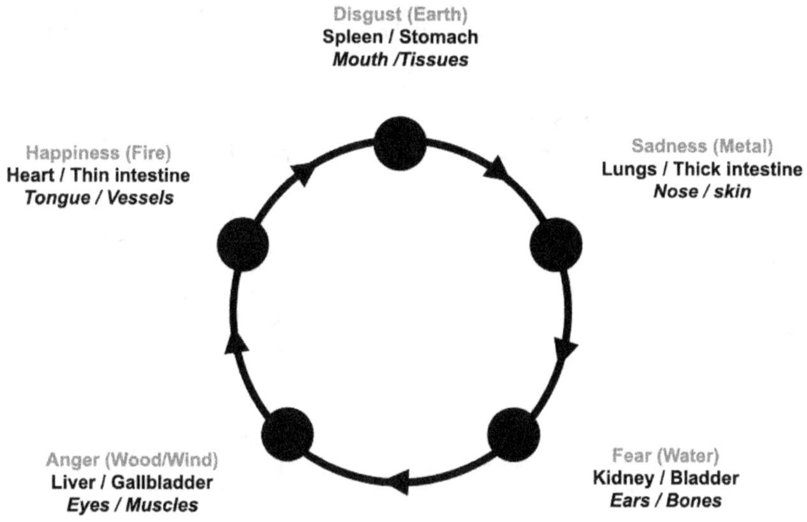

Happiness is connected to the heart and blood vessels; this is conveyed in an expression from German folk wisdom, "My heart jumps with joy." In medical practice, we have learned that too much excitement and joy are harmful. For instance, someone might die of a heart attack after winning the lottery. Disgust is connected to the stomach, spleen, and pancreas, and in German, we say, "This lies heavily on my stomach; I have to digest this." When something sad happens, we say, "I have to sigh deeply in sorrow, or grief is weighing on my intestine, or that goes under my skin." TCM sees lungs, large intestines, and skin as connected to sorrow. When we are frightened, "I might pee in my pants, and fear goes through my bones." In Chinese medicine, fear is connected to the kidneys, bladder, and bones. Finally, when angry, we say, "A louse crossed my liver, or this really makes my gallbladder overflow," and the corresponding TCM organs are the liver and gallbladder. We could continue the list, but it is evident that folk tradition has much wisdom with which we can work.

Another interesting coincidence pointing to an obvious truth is that the Chinese circle of transformational phases of emotions aligns perfectly with the conflict-processing scheme designed by Nossrat Peseschkian. Happiness and anger belong more to the honesty and sympathetic nerve expression, while sadness and fear to the courtesy and parasympathetic nerve expression.

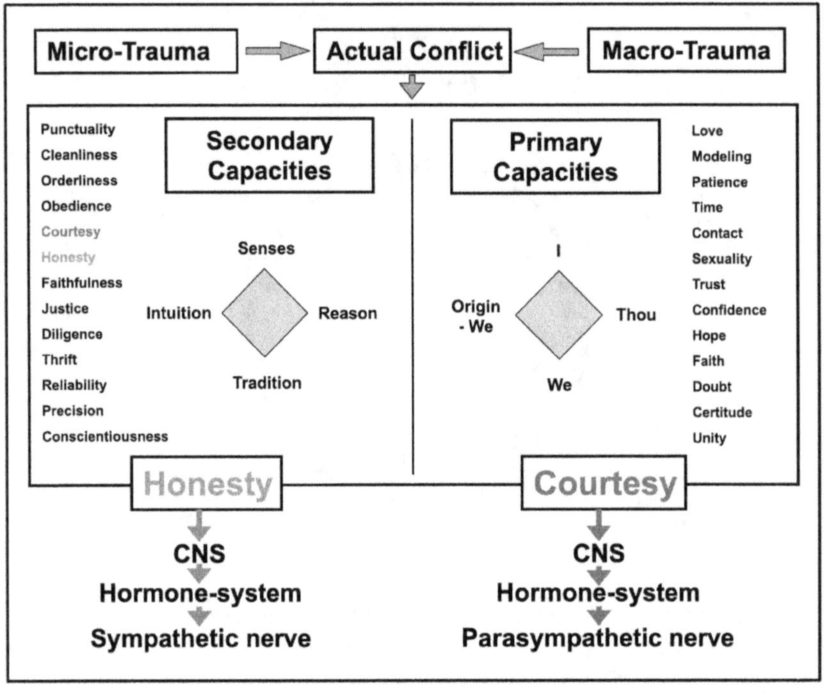
Micro-Trauma
Actual Conflict
Macro-Trauma
Secondary Capacities
Primary Capacities
Punctuality
Cleanliness
Orderliness
Obedience
Courtesy
Honesty
Faithfulness
Justice
Diligence
Thrift
Reliability
Precision
Conscientiousness
Senses
Intuition
Reason
Tradition
I
Origin - We
Thou
We
Love
Modeling
Patience
Time
Contact
Sexuality
Trust
Confidence
Hope
Faith
Doubt
Certitude
Unity
Honesty
Courtesy
CNS
Hormone-system
Sympathetic nerve
CNS
Hormone-system
Parasympathetic nerve

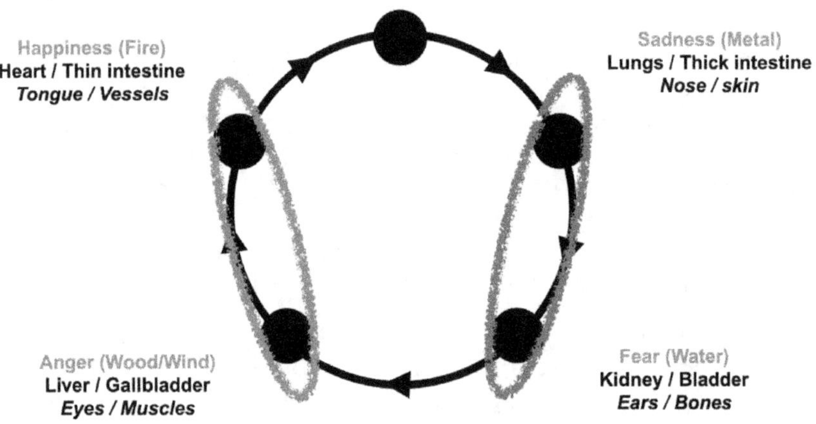
Disgust (Earth)
Spleen / Stomach
Mouth /Tissues
Happiness (Fire)
Heart / Thin intestine
Tongue / Vessels
Sadness (Metal)
Lungs / Thick intestine
Nose / skin
Anger (Wood/Wind)
Liver / Gallbladder
Eyes / Muscles
Fear (Water)
Kidney / Bladder
Ears / Bones

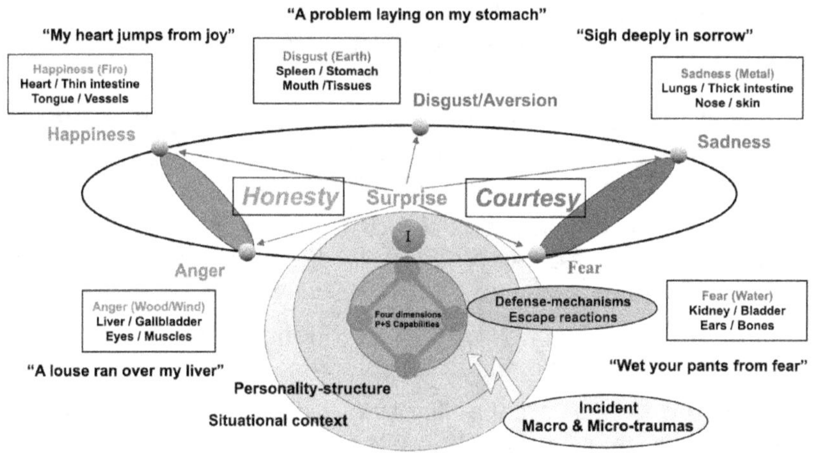

Exercises in psychosomatics

- What messages are our bodies sending us? What do we feel? What symptoms do we have? How can we interpret them? Write down the answers to these questions.

- We write a letter to our body, thanking it for its reactions and the messages it sends us. In turn, we can then evaluate these messages and see what habits we want to change so we will be in better health and in harmony.

Positive interpretation of diseases, symptoms, and emotions

Nossrat Peseschkian gave many examples of how we can interpret diseases and what they mean to us. We can reflect on what our body tells us and how this can influence our life when we listen to it. What could our symptoms mean? What is our body doing? In the following, we have a summary of interpretations:

- *Stress*: The ability to react to one's surroundings and to accommodate one's need for adaptation

- *Psychosomatic symptoms*: The ability to express through organic symptoms that, at the moment, there isn't a better way to communicate one's conflicts

- *Headache*: The capability to let conflicts occupy one's thoughts

- *Asthma*: The capability to make one's problems audible through bodily symptoms

- *Diarrhea/ulcerative colitis/Crohn's disease*: The capability to react with one's intestine to conflicts and discharge them in the same way one does with food
- *Adiposity/diabetes mellitus Type 2*: The ability to get satisfaction and a substitute for a lack of love and care through eating and to give oneself something good here and now
- *Cold and minor infectious diseases*: The capability to process the small matters of everyday life through the respiratory system and to achieve relief and care in this way
- *Dermatitis*: The capability to let emotional burdens crawl under one's skin and to signal one's problems
- *Sleeplessness*: The capability to get by with little sleep and to stay awake thinking about how to realize one's dreams
- *Hypertension*: The capability of resisting a permanent outer pressure by increasing one's inner pressure
- *Gastritis*: The capability to swallow or to ruminate on one's conflicts
- *Hyperthyroidism*: The capability to accelerate all processes of life and to mature
- *Loss of sight and hearing*: The capability to close down one's perception to the problems one does not want to hear and see
- *Heart attack*: The capability to take one's burdens to heart
- *Alcoholism*: The ability to make conflicts temporarily bearable, to create an illusion of inner warmth and security, to be able to accept one's personality and get rid of inhibitions and fear by using alcohol
- *Ambivalence*: The ability to keep putting a decision off and to not commit oneself
- *Fear*: The capability to avoid situations that are perceived as dangerous or difficult
- *Fear of solitude*: The need to be with others
- *Bed-wetting*: The capability of crying downwards
- *Depression*: The ability to react with deepest emotions to conflicts
- *Jealousy*: The ability to love without behaving in a way that would invoke reciprocal love
- *Existential fear*: The ability to care for one's future and not to abandon oneself to an illusory sense of security

- *Inertia*: The ability to evade responsibility and see to one's own needs

- *Fixations*: The ability to hold on to one's own perspectives and stance

- *Inhibition*: The ability to be careful about voicing one's opinion and to reflect on what one has heard

- *Masochism*: The ability to give one's partner the opportunity to enjoy

- *Narcissism*: The ability to love oneself and to experience one's supposed faults positively

- *Paranoia*: The ability to experience oneself as the hub of the world and its mysterious forces

- *Sadism*: The ability to take on the active role

- *Schizophrenia*: The ability to split off parts of the ego and to substitute a fantastic internal world for a dissatisfying environment or the capability to question everyday norms and to live at the edge of reality

- *Defiance*: The ability to say no

- *Impotence*: The ability to retreat from the sexual field of conflict

- *Frigidity*: The ability to say no with one's body

- *Premature ejaculation*: The ability to get to one's objective quickly

- *Kleptomania*: The ability to find something before someone else has lost it

- *Mania*: The ability to see a glass as half full, to experience oneself as powerful and able to overlook the trifles in life

- *Neglect*: The ability to ignore binding norms or to act contrary to them

- *Compulsive disorder*: The ability to do something with enormous precision, conscientiousness, and punctuality

- *Anorexia nervosa*: The ability to survive on few means; the capability to participate in the hunger of the world

- *Suicide*: The ability to question one's life and to change one's point of view.

Stress

Love it, change it, or leave it.

We will focus in detail on **stress** because it is so ubiquitous and often harmful. The pioneering research of endocrinologist Hans Selye indicates that stress arises when we experience a need for change. The stress level increases with the need for change, the tension between the perceived reality and what we feel should be. Physically, stress can be measured in heightened levels of hormones such as adrenalin, noradrenalin, and cortisol, as well as blood sugar and muscle tension, all of which are needed for taking action. Selye describes an **alarm reaction**, an **adaptation reaction**, and an **adaptation disorder**. These can also be defined as short-term, middle-term, and long-term stress. When we are surprised by a new situation, we go into alert mode, like when the neighborhood bully walks around the corner towards us or when a new boss criticizes us. However, in both instances, we experience **short-term stress**. When such occurrences happen regularly, we experience **middle-term stress,** and we have to find a solution or move on. When these activators occur on a regular basis, and we don't find a solution, it becomes **long-term stress** and can result in adaptation disorder.

Some of the best ways to cope with a stressful day are getting a physical workout afterward to get rid of the surplus energy and hormones, chatting with a friend to get rid of the inner tension, perhaps getting a massage, and finally turning it over to God or our spiritual entity. When we are experiencing middle-term stress, we can also use these stress relievers, but our primary work is to find a solution to the stressor. With long-term stressors, there is more urgency to make a decision on what to do before we lose even more energy and become apathetic in our indecisiveness. Even if we are indecisive, or we believe there isn't any solution to our problem or that anything we do will be wrong, we have to make a step in a new direction. Once we move, we can adjust the path along our way.

Taking conscious action instead of just reacting is important if we want to interfere with the vicious chain reaction that occurs when we experience chronic recurring stressors. As a first step, we must become aware of the fact that change is necessary and premeditate different actions we want to take. Then, as a second step, we must actively put a stop to it and willfully enact the change we have premeditated. This process can be difficult in extreme situations, but with attention and willpower, we can change habits and take hold of the course of our lives.

Escape reactions

To address our inner conflicts, we also have access to four typical **conflict-processing /escape reactions** on the behavioral plane. We use these behavioral reactions in different combinations according to our individual constitutions and situation. In the body area (*health/body*) next to the somatic expression of vital anxiety, restlessness, hypochondria, perceptual-, drive-, libido- and somatic-symptom disorders (SSDs), we also have behavioral reactions such as taking up substance abuse and risk-taking, such as motor racing, rock climbing, and other extreme sports. We can escape by working (*work/achievement*) intensely and losing sight of everything else, or by evading work with the fear of failure, concentration problems, and adaptation and stress disorders. We might escape into loneliness or companionship (*social life*), searching for relief with friends and other people or retreating into solitude but also taking it out on our close ones with social fear, affective disorders, and social behavioral disorders, withdrawal and dependency as its extreme form. We could escape into fantasy and spirituality (*future/spirituality*) with daydreaming, overly involving oneself in religious practice and denying reality, with existential fear, hopelessness, despair, senselessness of life, phobia, panic, and psychotic reactions arising in the long term.

The other side of the coin is that if we use these conflict-processing reactions wisely, we can **take refuge** in them because they are all resources. We can take refuge in sports and eating well to strengthen us (*body/health*). We can work intensely for our own accomplishments and self-esteem or earn supplementary money to realize a dream (*work/achievement*). We can also discuss our problems with friends or find some diversion and happiness in their company (*social life*). And we can plan a bright future while asking God for help (*future/spirituality*). The main thing is that we stay conscious of our problems and conflicts and use these refuge processes to help solve problems rather than to avoid them.

Example: Let's look at one family scenario to get a better understanding of conflict-processing reactions: A teacher observes that the child is always in a fantasy world (*escaping into fantasy*), and based on the teacher's observation, the parent acknowledges that the child has also started wetting the bed (*positive interpretation: crying downwards*). The counselor then discovers in a family setting that the whole conflictive situation started when the father began having difficulties with a new boss at work and worked harder and harder to comply with the requirements. The father began experiencing terrible stomach aches (*trying to digest the conflict*) and vent-ed to his wife, who then, in turn, developed headaches (*letting the difficulty pass through one's mind*) as well as backaches (*carrying the problems of the whole family on one's shoulders*).

"Fifty Years of Politeness"

An elderly couple sat together for breakfast one morning. The table was set with coffee, eggs, rolls, ham, and jam, as was the custom in the household. Today, after fifty years of marriage, *the wife thought,* I am going to take the tasty, crunchy top side of the roll. All these years, I have let him eat the part that I like most, but today I want it! *When he noticed his wife enjoying the top of the roll, her husband said, "Oh, my dear wife, how nice of you to give me the lower part for our fiftieth anniversary. All these years, I wanted you to have it since it is the tastiest part."*

Retold after Nossrat Peseschkian (*Oriental Stories*, p. 101)

The key conflict

Honesty and courtesy combine to create what Nossrat Peseschkian called the **key conflict**. Within all personalities, there is a type of switch for directing conflict energy outwards or inwards. Honesty is the capability to openly express our needs and conflict energy to the outside world, while courtesy is the ability to keep our needs to ourselves, politely not intruding into other people's lives. Courtesy allows us to prioritize the needs of others by confining conflict energy within ourselves. We need both honesty and courtesy, and when we use them in balance as strengths, we can express ourselves honestly and politely as an integral personality. If we are overly courteous, the consequence is many internal conflicts. Because we don't express our needs, we usually don't get what we want, and then we blame ourselves for not standing up for our needs. If we are overly honest, we inevitably create external conflicts, maybe seeming to get what we want at first, but that short-term gain tends to cause further conflicts in the long run. When the courteous person continuously keeps his needs to himself and the conflict energy inside, he acts like a dam on a river without an excess-water function. The water mounts up until the dam bursts, destroying the dam and causing enormous destruction downriver. The overly polite person's internal dam is likely to rupture suddenly; the damage he does to others and to himself, accompanied by all the guilt and self-recrimination, can be enormous and needs great amounts of inner and outer repair efforts afterward. Nossrat Peseschkian referred to an **ambiguous personality** as someone who tends to withhold his needs and conflict energy but then tends to explode regularly.

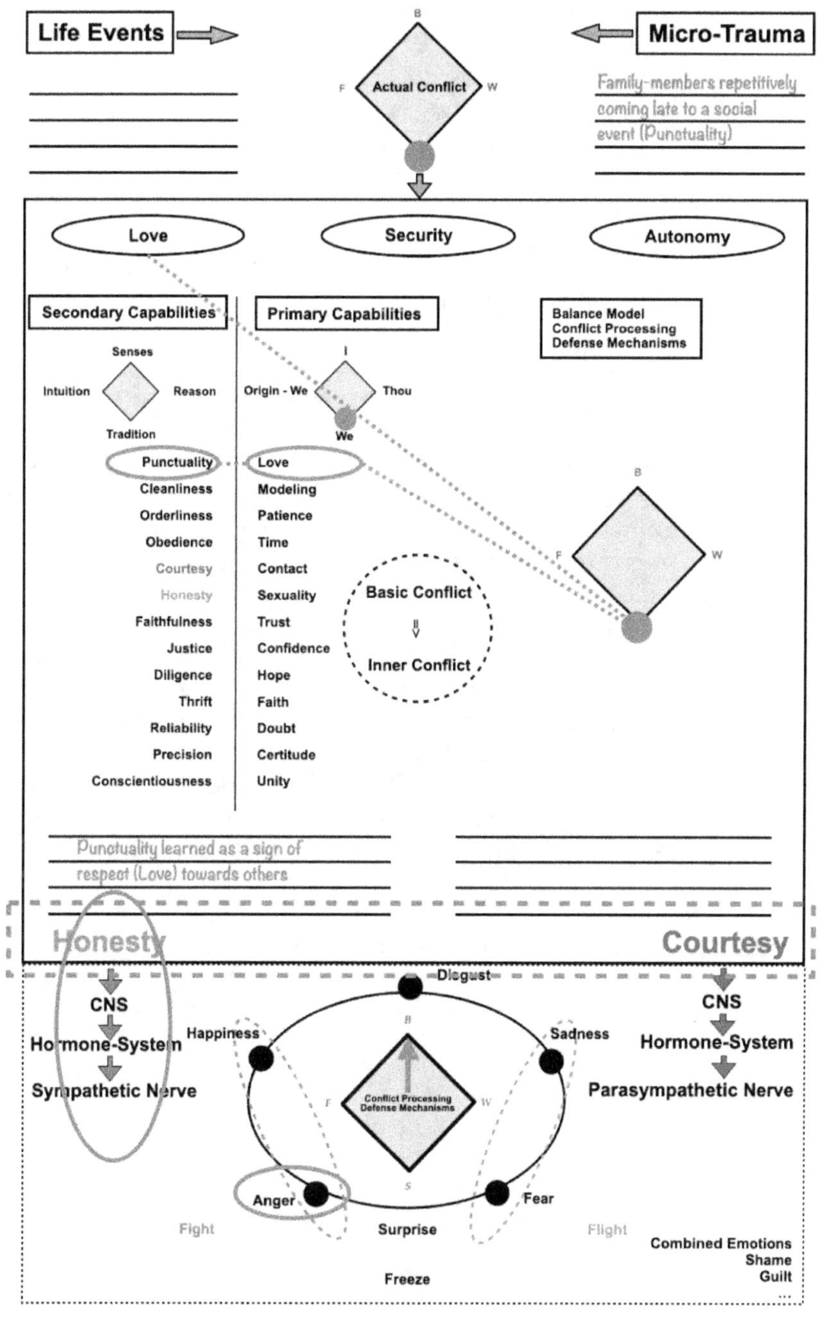

The key conflict

So, it is important to bring our key conflict into balance and make it a vital asset by expressing ourselves both courteously and honestly. When we balance respect for ourselves with respect for others, we create a connection or a working team where the needs of both sides are fulfilled.

Introductive example of key conflict

We react with open anger to the unpunctuality of our family members. As children, through genetics, for example, conditioning, or maybe as compulsive reactiveness, we learn to express ourselves with candor, often exploding in anger.

The second key conflict

Another essential conflict is the **conflict between love and justice**. It is essentially also the balance in the expression of the **primary personality** and **secondary personality**. The primary personality bases itself on connectedness and gives more importance to bonding and less to rules; relativizing and forgiving are always central in this belief system. The secondary personality, on the other hand, puts more emphasis on rules and their implementation than on maintaining a connection with another person. In its extreme, the secondary personality can be a law-and-order type with fundamentalist tendencies, whereas the primary personality tends to relativize and can be blinded by love. Instead of seeing justice as applying the laws, we can see justice more as "the ability to balance one's own interests with those of others," as Nossrat Peseschkian described this secondary capability. "Justice without love sees only performance and only compares. Love without justice loses control over reality. Learn to balance justice and love." When we learn to balance justice and love, we become a more integral personality, which also consists of a balance and unity of the other inner concepts.

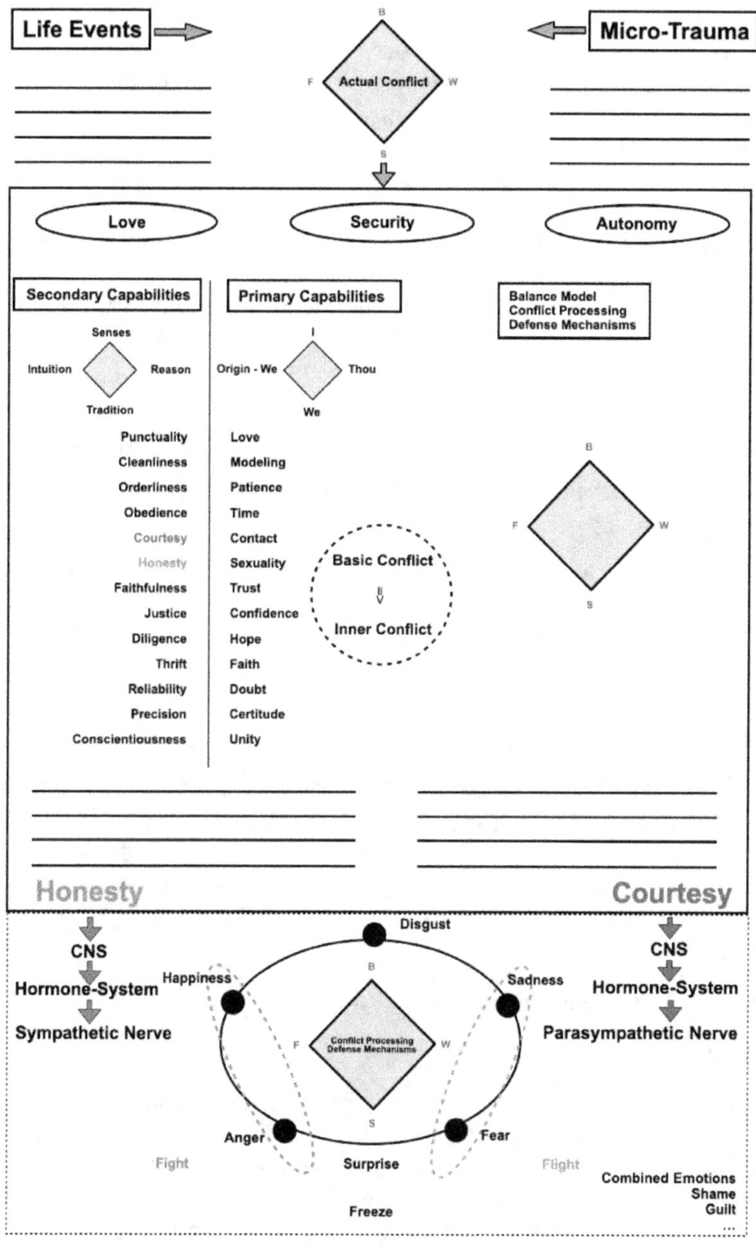

Blank conflict diagram

A short summary

An **actual conflict** is an acute- or chronic-load situation caused by micro- or macro-trauma, causing an **inner conflict** when it touches the **basic conflict** of a person because the individual's conflict-solving strategies cannot remedy the situation. The **actual conflict** is described through its *conflict content* (*behavior and objectives*) and *localization* within life (*Four Dimensions of Life*). The **basic conflict** is described through its *conflict content* (*behavior and objectives*) and *localization* within life (*Four Dimensions of Role Modeling* and *Four Dimensions of Life*), and the **inner conflict,** as the subconscious' decompensation of the ego which, in its futile efforts to resolve the conflict with its known strategies, has no other option than to resort to internal and external escape reactions as temporary compensatory mechanisms for reducing its inner tension.

"Not every death is tragic, not every marriage wonderful."
- Hamid Peseschkian and Arno Remmers

A life event is initially value-neutral and gets its unique individual value through individuality and personality. This means that how we react to a movie has very much to do with ourselves. The movie may touch one person and leave another completely bored.

Understanding through examples

Now let's get into some examples of conflicts and how they affect us. With these examples, we can systematically apply the schematic representation mentioned above and below. Let's start with some simple examples and try to recognize the conflict contents and dynamics, and then we will go deeper, all the way to describing whole cases.

Torn apart between two objectives

- **Example 1.**

Just imagine one is working hard to get a project done at work while having an appointment later with one's spouse and children. Time is running out for finishing the day's objectives, and the appointment time is near. Here are two competing *objectives and strategies:* 1. **Finishing the project:** *Diligence* and *conscientiousness* at work for getting one's project done, linked to *security* and sustenance, and 2. **Getting home to the family:** *Punctuality* for an appointment is linked to *love* and *time* with our family. Since one cannot meet both objectives, these two compete with one another. The more they are emotionally laden with conditioning through negative experiences, punishment, and reward or through positive experiences in the past, the greater the inner pressure becomes. As Nossrat Peseschkian always said, "Friction produces warmth."

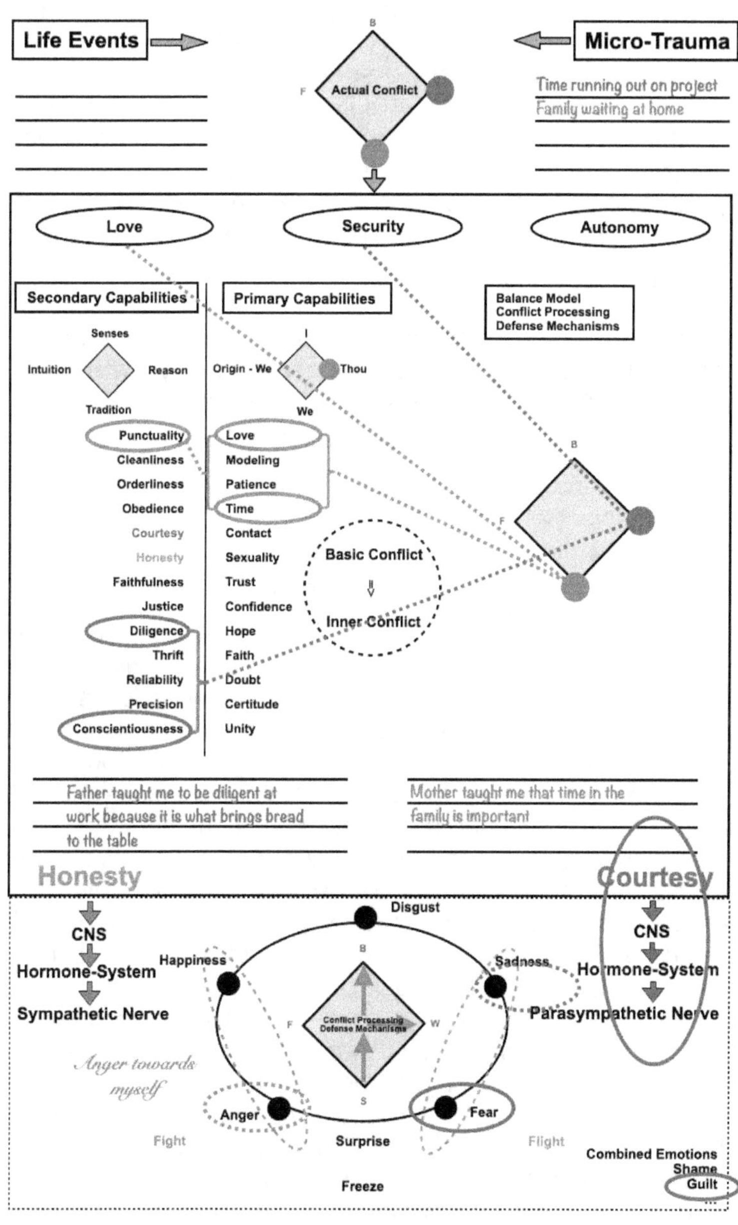

Place these competing objectives into our modified structure model of Freud and our conflict schemata to see the conflict in more detail:

A pre- or subconscious universal *need/drive* (*id*) is expressed through a conscious *objective* with its *ideal* and subconscious *emotional value/load* (*superego*) and *strategy* to reach it (provided by the *ego*), concurring with another pre- or subconscious universal *need/ drive* (*id*) expressed through a conscious *objective* with its *emotional value/load* (*superego*), which we seek to fulfill through a different *strategy* (provided by the *ego*). It is literally two parts of the personality on different levels of consciousness in rivalry with another, the fulfillment of the needs through the objectives and the strategy conflicting with one another, one need suppressing the other as a result, with energy produced through the conflict seeking an escape route.

Applied to the example

At work, when pressured by our unfinished project: *Objective* (*superego*): finish work diligently and conscientiously; *strategy* (*ego*): stay till it's done; *need* (*id*) for security and sustenance: earn the money to support the family.

On the other hand, we want to keep our commitment to our spouse and children: *Objective* (*superego*): spend time with our family; strategy (*ego*): leave the work for tomorrow and go home so we will find affection not face frustration and dissatisfaction; need (*id*) for love: tend the family.

Of course, our inner pressure mounts as we try to finish our work and time passes and our task still isn't finished. Although we sense pressure from our *need* for *sustenance* and *security* weighing stronger at the moment than that for *love/appreciation*, the other side competes forcefully the more it is neglected. The higher the inner pressure, the more *emotional load* has been given to the opposite *needs* and their irreconcilable *objectives* and the *strategies* for sufficing them and the longer the period these have not been working anymore. Depending on the set point of our *honesty-courtesy key conflict*, this pressure will lead to external aggression or more internal aggression, the latter resulting in depression. The *locations* of the *actual conflict* can be determined as conflicts between *social life* and *work* (*Four Dimensions*). The two active *basic conflicts* here are *diligence* and *conscientiousness* connected to *security* and *sustenance* (learned in the *work* area of the *Four Dimensions*) and *punctuality* connected to *time* and *love* (*basic capability love* differentiated into *time* and *love* learned in this case through the *I-Thou relationship*). Here the *inner conflict* is the futile competition between the two *basic concepts/conflicts*. The *inner conflict* results in strong emotional reactions. If it arises repeatedly or becomes permanent, it will lead to continued *escape reactions*, in this case, working harder and reducing social time with the family.

- **Example 2**

Another situation could be growing up in a very religious household where diversions, especially sexuality, are deemed inappropriate and evil. As a child, we suddenly discover we have a sexual drive and get into fierce conflict because we begin to believe we are evil or possessed by demons. Here our conditioned capability of *faith/religion* was without conflict as long as puberty and interest in sex hadn't developed. However, the moment emotional attraction and sexual drive arose, our *inner conflict* emerged.

Consider an explanation of this conflict by using our modified structure model and our conflict schemata: The *need* (*id*) for sex arises as an adolescent, and we feel the urge to go to bed with a partner as a *goal* (*superego*) defined by social exemplars and *strategy* (*ego*). At the same time, our belief systems tell us that we should be celibate as a *goal* (*superego*) and remain chaste as a *strategy* (*ego*) because sexuality is of the devil, an *emotional load* (*part of the superego*). Wanting to avoid going to hell becomes a *need* (*id*) for *security* and *love* (from God). The conflict would be located between *spirituality* and *body*. The *basic conflicts* rival one another—our need to express sexuality (*suppression/chastity*) and our *need* to live our faith. The *inner conflict* is the futile battle between the sexual drive and the personal faith. As the inner conflict continues through time, it manifests in our physical body as somatization and promotes further escape reactions, for example, avoiding people to whom we might be sexually attracted and social events where they might be present.

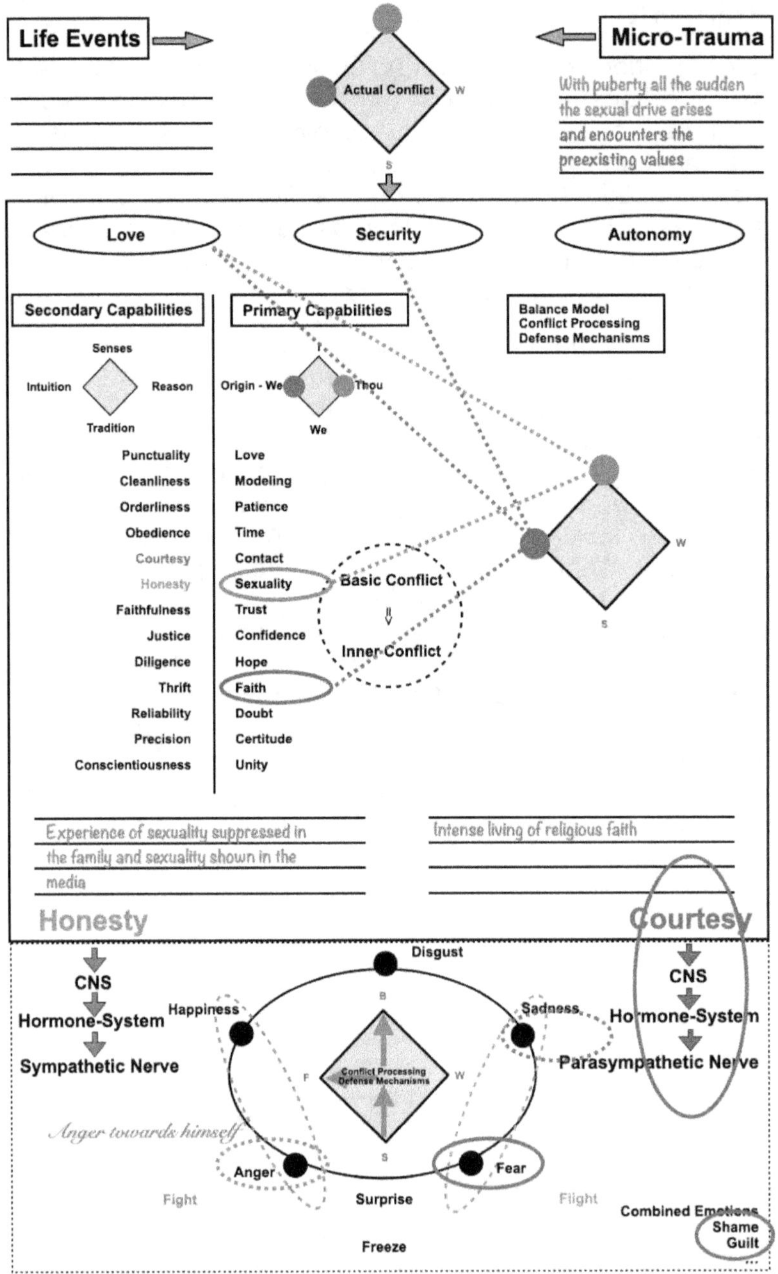

Life Events
Micro-Trauma
With puberty all the sudden the sexual drive arises and encounters the preexisting values
Actual Conflict
W
S
Love
Security
Autonomy
Secondary Capabilities
Primary Capabilities
Balance Model
Conflict Processing
Defense Mechanisms
Senses
Intuition
Reason
Tradition
Origin - We
Thou
We
Punctuality
Cleanliness
Orderliness
Obedience
Courtesy
Honesty
Faithfulness
Justice
Diligence
Thrift
Reliability
Precision
Conscientiousness
Love
Modeling
Patience
Time
Contact
Sexuality
Trust
Confidence
Hope
Faith
Doubt
Certitude
Unity
Basic Conflict
Inner Conflict
W
S
Experience of sexuality suppressed in the family and sexuality shown in the media
Intense living of religious faith
Honesty
Courtesy
CNS
Hormone-System
Sympathetic Nerve
CNS
Hormone-System
Parasympathetic Nerve
Disgust
B
Happiness
Sadness
Conflict Processing
Defense Mechanisms
F
W
Anger towards himself
Anger
Fear
S
Fight
Surprise
Flight
Combined Emotions
Shame
Guilt
Freeze

- **Example 3**

During the last year, a thirty-year-old woman noticed that she and her husband quarreled more about household tasks, and she wanted some time for herself. She had witnessed how her friends' husbands helped out at home. She thought it wasn't right that she did everything in the household while her husband simply rested, being pampered and doing whatever he wanted to do. They communicated less; her husband became irritable, worked longer hours, and didn't give her the attention she had enjoyed in the past. On the other hand, she became more engaged in her household and family work, felt lonelier and less loved each day, and often suffered hypertensive crises in the evening.

Actual conflict: There is a succession of *two actual conflicts in this situation*. The first is the continuous feeling of being treated unjustly, and the second is a reaction to her husband's reaction of withdrawing his attention and affection.

Basic conflict: In the first conflict situation, the *basic conflict* stemmed from the new concepts she had learned from her environment—how the household work should be shared respectfully (*justice – love*) and that she needed some space for self-realization, just as her husband had (*justice – autonomy*). These concepts contrasted with the ones she had learned during childhood, when her mother was always occupied with the household, and the division of labor between women in the home and men outside the home was clearly defined. The conflict situation arose as her perspective and values gradually changed.

The origin of the *second basic conflict* was that her mother had never had time to play with her as a child. To receive some *love* and *time* from her mother, she had to help her with the housework. Since this made her mother happier and emotionally warmer, she experienced the feeling of *acceptance (love),* and she adopted household chores as a strategy to receive *love*. Her husband withdrawing his affection (*love*) triggered the activation of this second—though older—*basic conflict*.

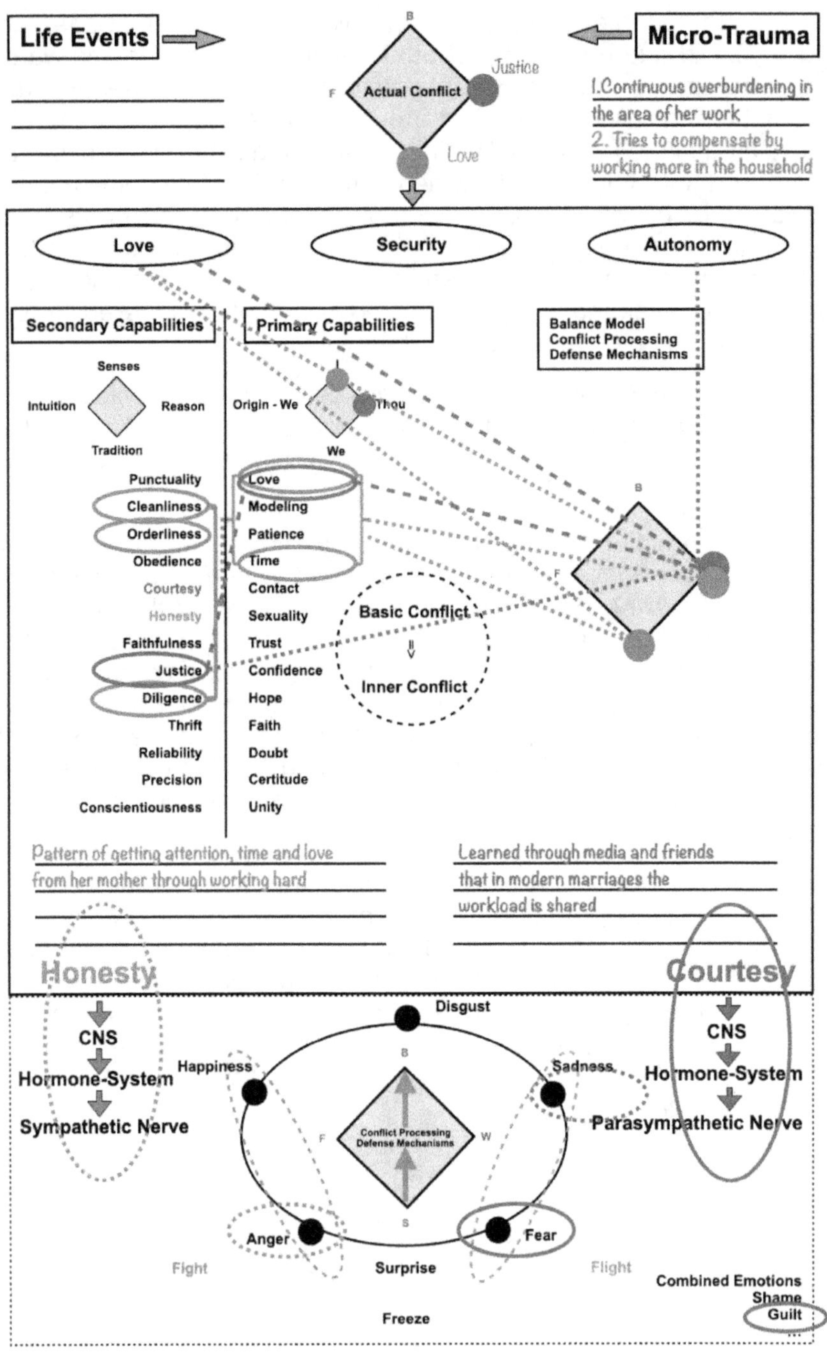
Life Events
Micro-Trauma
1. Continuous overburdening in the area of her work
2. Tries to compensate by working more in the household
B
Actual Conflict
Justice
F
Love
Love
Security
Autonomy
Secondary Capabilities
Primary Capabilities
Balance Model
Conflict Processing
Defense Mechanisms
Senses
Intuition
Reason
Tradition
Origin - We
Thou
We
Punctuality
Cleanliness
Orderliness
Obedience
Courtesy
Honesty
Faithfulness
Justice
Diligence
Thrift
Reliability
Precision
Conscientiousness
Love
Modeling
Patience
Time
Contact
Sexuality
Trust
Confidence
Hope
Faith
Doubt
Certitude
Unity
Basic Conflict
Inner Conflict
B
F
Pattern of getting attention, time and love
from her mother through working hard
Learned through media and friends
that in modern marriages the
workload is shared
Honesty
Courtesy
CNS
Hormone-System
Sympathetic Nerve
CNS
Hormone-System
Parasympathetic Nerve
Disgust
Happiness
Sadness
B
Conflict Processing
Defense Mechanisms
F
W
Anger
Fear
S
Fight
Surprise
Flight
Freeze
Combined Emotions
Shame
Guilt

Inner conflict: So, despite the woman's *courteous* personality, in the first conflict situation, the daily *micro-trauma* caused by unequally distributed household tasks and a need for more self-determination caused her to occasionally vent her anger with her husband. When her husband retreated and didn't give her attention anymore, she felt guilty, became anxious and sad, and unconsciously sought his *love* through *cleanliness* and *orderliness*. This pattern was contrary to her need for *justice*. Since she was preoccupied with cleaning, there was less possibility for the two to find time for one another or discuss their feelings, and so the situation worsened. Both felt personally rejected and escaped by working even more intensely. In the evening, the inner tension rose so high she often experienced hypertension.

Further examples of conflict dynamics

An example of **macro-trauma** can create an inner conflict: Imagine that a hurricane has demolished our house and town, our spouse and children have died, and we are the only ones left in our core family. Of course, our *trust* in life would be strongly impaired, our *faith* in God shaken, our *confidence* in ourselves as well. Our *hope* in the future would be diminished, and most of our other *primary* and *secondary capabilities* would also be affected. Next to the many inner wounds, the situation would create a feeling of helplessness and hopelessness. It would take us many years to heal and regain our previous emotional strength. The amount of time it would take us to recover from this trauma would depend on how our capacities had been affected previously in life.

Our needs for *safety, love,* and *autonomy (id)* would all be touched by the losses. We relied on the concept that nature/God protects us. That concept was shaken, just as our idea that we should have taken care of our family (*superego*), and our *capabilities* to manage the present state (*ego*) now appear to be insufficient. The *actual conflict* was the hurricane hitting our village with consequences within all of our Four Dimensions but especially in the areas of work and social life. The *basic conflict* is the apparently insufficient strength of our capability to provide for our livelihood (*secondary capacities* in the work area connected to *sustenance* and *autonomy*) and our ability to manage the grief of the loss of close ones (*primary capacities* in the *social life* area connected to *love*). Our *inner conflict* would express itself through different psychosomatic reactions. Perhaps we would start drinking, or in our hopelessness, depend on friends and temporarily abandon the idea of ever rebuilding our lives.

A **macro-trauma** on the **level of the actual capabilities**: Imagine we have almost finished a prestigious project but fail on the very last tests. Therefore, the whole scientific project is ruined, and our error costs us our job. This would obviously cause an adverse reaction in us. Our senses of *reliability, precision, diligence,* and *conscientiousness (secondary capabilities)* connected to our sense of *trust and respect (love) (primary capabilities)* are heavily affected, which themselves again are connected to our basic needs for *security* and *autonomy* and respectability (*love*). This applies within our work area. This major life event will remain deeply rooted in our memory.

So, we can understand the conflict contents and the intra-psychological dynamics illustrated in the examples above with the given concepts and diagrams. We also understand that conflict contents and dynamics remain very diverse, intricate, and intriguing.

- **Example 4: Introductory example of a patient**

A twenty-six-year-old apprentice teacher arrives for consultation, full of fear and visibly agitated, complaining about panic attacks, cold sweats, sleeplessness, and diarrhea. He says he has been suffering from colitis for a few months now. It had all started after the beginning of his apprenticeship a year ago. He has tried his very best, but his superior criticizes him and expects more and more. Since he is investing more time at work, he has less time at home now and gets into conflicts with his girlfriend. She generally understands him well and helps him calm down, but his fears of being unable to manage the work situation, his sense of insufficiency, and concerns about losing her make him well up in anger fits, and his panic attacks add stress to the relationship. He believes that if he isn't successful at his apprenticeship, he will probably never make it in life and will probably even lose his girlfriend. Most of his anger is directed at himself.

When asked about his Four Dimensions, he shared that he had found good resources in a healthy diet and sports. He has good friends, although he has seen them less in the past few months, yet he knows he can rely on them. He also has a profound spirituality that gives him strength in these difficult days. When relaying the past five years, he tells how he passed his teaching exam with good results. Before that, he had had several unstable relationships with women from whom he had separated, thinking they weren't the right match for him. Going into his family background, we discovered that his mother was very loving and had patience and time for him. She was always active, eating well, biking, and hiking; she worked as a teacher and was very fond of her job. She had good friends and was a spiritual woman as well, but she was often sad and frustrated because her husband never took time for her and the children and was too strict with them. She had fussed about this for years, but then she resigned herself to the situation because she didn't want to leave her children without a father, and the security of both parents was an important value to her. Still, he never was there for them, except as a breadwinner. Two years before his final school exams, the patient's mother finally divorced his father and left with the children. Because of her own experience, his mother always insisted: "Find the right person who really fits you!"

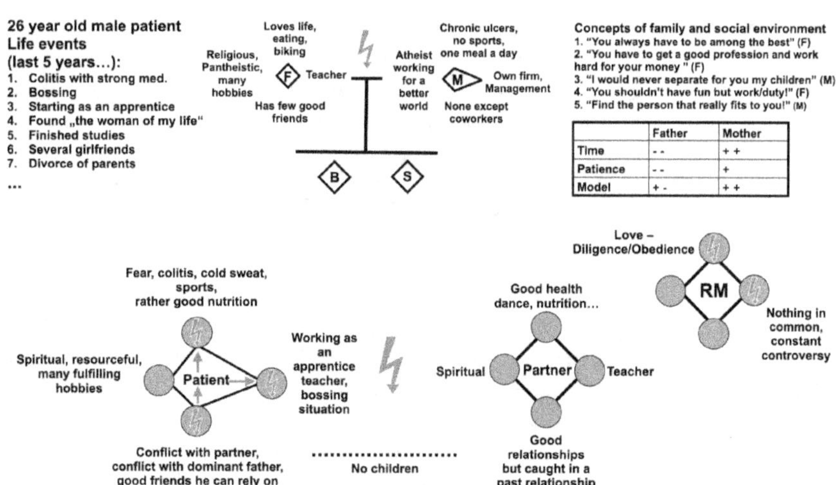

In contrast to his mother, the patient's father had never eaten well except at home; he skipped meals, had frequent ulcers and headaches, and never did sports. He worked "24/7," the patient related, and seldom went on a holiday with the family. When he did so, he usually took along some work to do. Despite all his devotion to his work, the father had never been really successful. Except for his coworkers, he had no friends and was an atheist. He believed in duty and in achievement and that one "always has to be among the best." Honor meant getting a profession and working hard for one's money; this was the only way mankind could find salvation. He never had time for his children except when they had achieved something exceptional. He was impatient and screamed often and never served as a model to the children as their mother had.

Looking at the Four Dimensions of Role Modeling, we find two major *basic conflicts* in this patient. He had adopted one of them through his father's education in the area of the *"I" relationship*. As a child, he received positive attention only when he was obedient or had accomplished something remarkable. On the other hand, when he erred, his father screamed at him so fiercely that it "scared the shit" out of him. Luckily, he had a mother from whom he received ample attention. The *second basic conflict* was in the area of the

"Thou" relationship. He had internalized the terrible relationship with his parents and vowed never to get into a relationship like theirs. He didn't want to find himself a "prisoner of such a marriage" in which he would quarrel with his partner about different convictions and interests day in and day out, yet not leaving each other. He really wanted to be "sure of marrying the right person" and be able to live his own interests (search for the perfect partner). This had led to changing girlfriends often. And now that he had found "the girl of his life" who had the same interests and many similar habits, he was afraid of losing her because he sometimes lost his temper, was very grumpy, and had panic attacks.

Of course, next to these two major *basic conflicts,* many more conflict contents and dynamics can be found within the case history and are interesting to analyze.

Looking at this case history, we see different *life events* cascading: the divorce of his parents, multiple girlfriends, graduation, finding "the woman of his dreams," and his apprenticeship. The unrealistic demands of his supervisor resulted in *micro-trauma* in the form of degradation, which brought him to decompensation. This conflict and its results then impacted his relationship with his girlfriend, causing conflict to arise between the two. Finally, the conflict manifested in the physical symptom of colitis.

His continuous search for the perfect partner—the one who would give him maximum opportunities to realize himself—inevitably brought repeated breakups and an increasing amount of insecurity to his self-worth and ability to maintain stable relationships. The disease, and the *macro-trauma* of his parents' divorce, repeatedly changing relationships, and the insecurity in a new apprenticeship touched the areas of *trust, confidence, hope, faith, doubt, certitude, unity*, and more. The colitis is strongly connected to the sense and need for *physical security*, the trauma within the relationships to family and partnership more to the *security in love*. The subsequent *micro-trauma* of harassment by a superior touches on the *basic conflict* inflicted by his relationship with his father. His *basic conflict* of trying to receive attention and appraisal (*love*) through *obedience* and *achievement* was triggered but futile and led to decompensation in the form of headaches and irritable bowel. His further conflict-coping reaction of working harder (*escape into work and retreat from social life*) didn't alleviate the conflict and meant that he saw his girlfriend and friends even less. With an *ambivalent honesty-courtesy* personality trait, his emotional outrage went mostly inwards. He blamed himself and felt shame and guilt. He escaped in loud fits that irritated his girlfriend and led to the next conflict. His memories of his parents' relationship and its consequences engrained in his mind, his mother's reactions, the divorce, and her sadness consciously and subconsciously led to further decompensation, making the colitis worse and eventually leading to panic attacks.

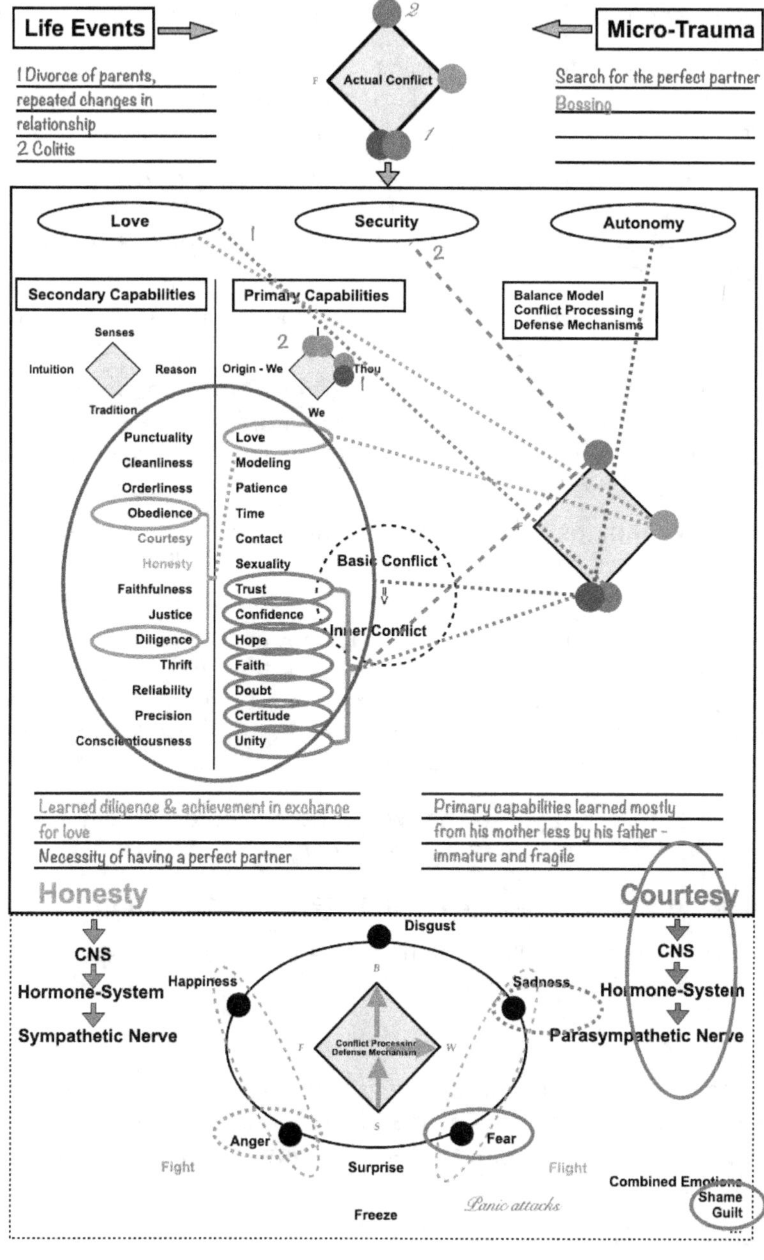

- **Further examples to analyze**

Here are some more examples we can analyze with our schemata in PPT. There are many more planes on which conflicts can be acted out. Here are just a few:

Imagine the following conflicting needs and values.

- One is the desire to travel and see the world, and the other is the belief that work is the most important. Work wins out in the end, so we stay at home working or mulling over our inner conflict.

- Another example of conflicting values is the enjoyment of food pitted against an exaggerated ideal body image. Since we don't feel accepted and loved because of our negative body image, we vomit our food after eating.

- Or we want to be thinner and lose weight, but we feel insecure around others and eat to keep a protective layer around us.

- We want to earn money and to express ourselves by living the life we want with a big house and an impressive car, but our parents in our childhood taught us that money and luxury are sinful and cause pain to others.

- We have the desire to find a life companion, but our parents' bad relationship is rooted in our subconscious, leading us to believe that relationships bring only pain.

- We are together with a beloved partner and want to feel close to them. At the same time, we experience their fragility and mortality. A superstitious fear of vindictive fate lurks in the back of our mind, that if we cherish something, it might be taken away and leave a great emptiness behind.

The difference between what we want to create and what we actually create depends on our inner conflicts.

Visualizing a conflict situation with the conflict diagram

We can visualize a conflict situation for an individual by applying our diagram in the following way:

1. *Actual conflict*

- What are the macro-traumatic or micro-traumatic events of the actual conflict? Where, in what dimensions, does the actual conflict affect the balance model, and what behavior or subject is touched?

2. *Basic conflict*

Actual capabilities (behavior):

- Do actual capabilities play a role in this event, and which ones?
- Are these my vulnerable, sensible, neuralgic actual capabilities? Are they my barking dog, my shadow self?

Dimension of role-modeling:

- How are my individual emotional areas developed? Do I see any deficits, such as, for example, missing self-esteem?
- Does the event touch one or more of the four emotional areas, and which ones? Is this the area in which I have a deficit?

Four Dimensions of Life expression (balance model):

- Which of the Four Dimensions is touched, and what is touched? A strategy or goal?
- Does the event touch an area that is especially important to me, and is it connected to my self-worth?
- Does it touch an area I've neglected, that I have never occupied myself with but now must engage?
- How balanced am I now? Do I have one-sidedness, burdens, deficits, stress, grief?
- What are my typical escape reactions? Am I using them here?
- Do I tend to use any defense mechanisms?

Learned behavior (actual capacities), strategies, and goals:

- Do any of the items above remind me of behavior, strategies, and goals that my parents or someone who has served as a model to me used?

The three primary needs

- Which primary needs have been touched on, and in which way? Are they especially sensible to me? Which emotional load is triggered? Where does it lie? Why is it so important to me?

Honesty and politeness

- Which capacity do I usually use? Which one am I expressing now?

3. ***Inner conflict and its expression***

- What are my emotional reactions?
- What are my escape reactions?

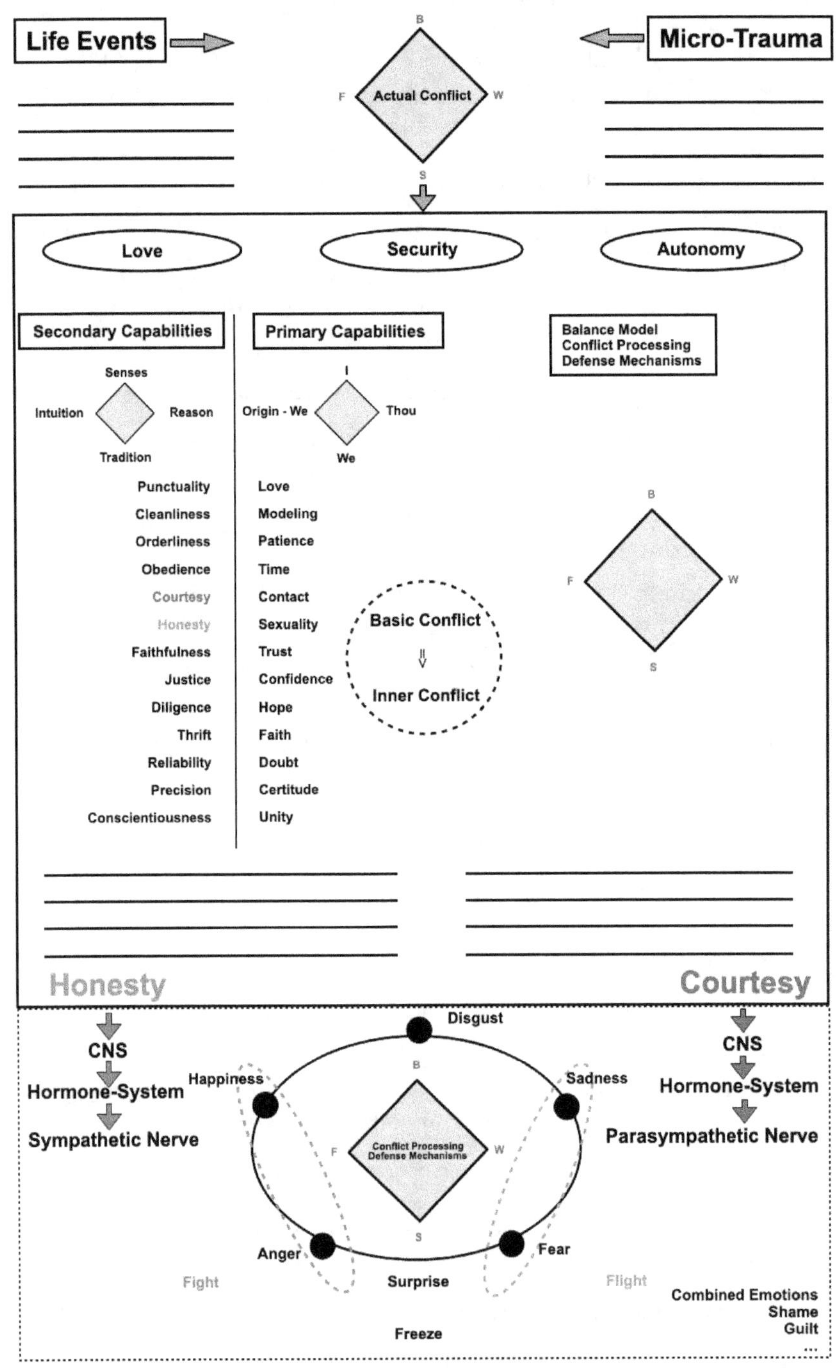

Blank conflict diagram

Inter- and intra-personal conflict

Intra- and inter-personal conflicts have many of the same components. There are always one or more conflictive topics with two or more protagonists fighting over them. In the intra-personal conflict, different personality parts collide; in the inter-personal conflict, individuals collide. In both cases, emotions arise, and with the rise of tension, a calm and rational elaboration of the conflict becomes impossible because the limbic system, with its archaic fight-or-flight reflexes, overrides the intuitive and rational insights of the prefrontal cortex. As the goal is always to have our needs fulfilled and our lives and personalities intrinsically connected, and since we are dependent on one another, it is best to work together to fulfill them.

*"If you work alone, you add; if you work
together, you multiply."
- Nossrat Peseschkian*

Working through our conflicts and finding creative solutions in the interest of all is essential because smoldering conflicts bring dissatisfaction, stagnation, and depression to all participants in the long run. To find our strengths, fortify them, and at the same time uncover our conflicts and elaborate solutions, we can systematically sort through our Four Dimensions of Life, the DAI, and WIPPF. We can use these instruments to evaluate how happy, indifferent, or unsatisfied we are with our own lives. Furthermore, we can take our Four Dimensions and actual capabilities and analyze where they are in harmony or conflict with those of our partner and children. By celebrating what we enjoy and take pride in and by working through our critical topics, we not only enrich our own lives but also those of our fellow humans.

Conflict management with the five steps of PPT

For working through our conflicts, we have the five therapeutic steps of conflict management in PPT.

Interpersonal conflicts

General procedure

Observation distancing and making an inventory

- We look systematically and thoroughly through our life and that of our partnership with the Four Dimensions of Life expression and the actual capabilities with the DAI or WIPPF to find the harmonious, the indifferent, and the conflictive areas. We can do this alone or with our partner. We remain empathetic to our partner.

Situational encouragement

- We look for the positive, harmonious aspects first and celebrate them.

Verbalization

- We look for the areas that we seem to be indifferent about and find interest in them.

- We look for the areas that create difficulties and apply the following questions:

    a. What are we unhappy with and why? What needs are relevant, and what feelings do we have about them?

    b. What are our memories and associations of personal life-defining experiences related to this topic? How did our parents fulfill and live these needs specifically, and how did we learn from them?

    c. What concerns our counterpart? What makes them unhappy? Why? What needs and feelings do they seem to have about these concerns or unsettling situations?

    d. What are our counterpart's memories and associations of life-defining experiences about this topic? How did their parents fulfill and live these needs specifically, and how did they learn from them?

    e. What are the positive interpretations of both sides?

    f. What compromises or, at best, new strategies could we find for meeting our needs more wholesomely?

Broadening of goals

- What new goals could we set for the future when we have liberated the conflict energy?

Interpersonal conflicts within the topics of our Four Dimensions of Life

We investigate our Four Dimensions and those of our partner or the person with whom we are having difficulties to reveal specific causes for our happiness, indifference, or discontentment: body, work, social life, and spirituality/cultural life.

By comparing our Four Dimensions, their contents, the energy we invest in each, and the satisfaction we receive side by side with those of our spouse or counterpart, we can systematically analyze where we are in harmony with each other, where we are indifferent about each other, and where there are definite conflicts. We can agree, disagree, or be indifferent to how we live our Four Dimensions, how we care for our health and our professional, social, and spiritual/cultural life. I may be very happy that my partner exercises and eats well, has a good-paying job with professional satisfaction, and that they have good friends and solid family ties. I can also be dissatisfied because they work long hours, do not devote time to spirituality, drink to calm down before bed, and never want to go to the movies together.

We look at the Four Dimensions of our partner and how they view our dimensions. Where are we in sync? What are the differences of little significance, and what are the ones that really matter to the point of making our skin crawl?

What needs are met, and how? With which strategies do we meet them together?

What needs aren't met? How do the strategies fulfill the needs differently? And how do they work contrary to each other?

Example

Let's look at an example of how to analyze our life and that of a partner concerning how our Four Dimensions complement one another and see how we can improve our relationship and benefit from each other.

Observation distancing and making an inventory

- We look systematically and thoroughly at our life and that of our partner with the Four Dimensions of Life expression and find the harmonious, the indifferent, and the conflictive areas. We mutually give ourselves empathy and encouragement for our efforts.

Situational encouragement

- We look for the positive, harmonious aspects first and celebrate them:

"In general, I am very happy with how we live our Four Dimensions and especially about how we live our family life."

Verbalization

- We look for the areas that we seem to be indifferent about and find interest in them:

"I've never really cared about his spirituality and his work. I could show some more interest in them."

- We look for the areas that create difficulties and apply the further questions:

"It really matters to me that we never take time for ourselves and that all our time is spent with our children. He says that the children are the most important thing in his life, and he doesn't need to go to the cinema or theater."

    a. What is it we are unhappy with and why? What needs are relevant, and what feelings do we have about them?

"I really love my family, and we have loads of fun together, but I also want to have some time with my partner. Because we always spend time together with our children, I get very frustrated because I also need quality time, love, and intimacy with my partner. I want to go to the movies, to a concert, go dancing, or have a private dinner with them." (time, fun, love, pleasure, autonomy)

    b. What are our memories and associations of personal life-defining experiences related to this topic? How did our parents fulfill and live these needs specifically, and how did we learn from them?

"I have always yearned to spend time with my partner. My parents always took a weekend off together, like two or three times a year, completely for themselves and to enjoy themselves as a couple. They loved concerts and theater."

    c. What concerns our counterpart? What makes them unhappy? Why? What needs and feelings do they seem to have about these concerns or unsettling situations?

"My partner always says that it is enough for him to be together with the children. He is happy going to the playground, playing games with them, and reading stories. He worries about what mischief they could be up to when they are not with us. He says their safety is what is most important to him." (Time, fun, love, pleasure, safety)

    d. What are our counterpart's memories and associations of life-defining experiences about this topic? How did their parents fulfill and live these needs specifically, and how did they learn from them?

"His parents always did everything with their children and had a very tight family life."

    e.   What are the positive interpretations of both sides?

"All of us spending time on the playground, playing games at home, and reading together is great fun. Doing something as adults together could also be great fun. We could share time, points of view, and wonderful new experiences. We just have to discover experiences that might be meaningful to both of us. Knowing that the children are safe is important as well."

    f.   What compromises or, at best, new strategies could be found for meeting our needs more wholesomely?

"We decide that having fun together as a family is still central to us both. It is important to be sure our children are doing well. For that, we can ask our parents to come over once in a while to take care of our kids. Then maybe we can take an afternoon or even a weekend off. We can recognize that we are seeking the same needs in different ways, and together we can find ways to bring balance to our life and maybe discover new ways of family life and life as a couple."

Broadening goals

- What new goals could we set for the future when we have liberated the conflict energy?

"After a nice evening discussing future plans, we found that simply going out to eat and maybe dancing afterward was a great change. We also discovered that hiking once or twice a year, as we did when we met, would help us meet our needs. We are happy to try these changes, and my husband is willing to trust others with the care of the children."

Inter-personal conflicts within the topics of the actual capabilities

As we have already seen in the earlier chapters, the actual capabilities are our bases of interaction and either our source of harmonious teamwork or conflict in working together. When we have different sets of actual capabilities that go hand in hand—different but supplementary—we can get along well with one another and excel in our work together. When this is not the case, we can investigate where our difficulties lie and find mutual ways to learn to compromise.

Now let's look at an example of how we can better understand the strengths of our actual capabilities and learn from the differences we may have so we can become a better team.

Example

Observation distancing and making an inventory

- We look systematically and thoroughly through our actual capabilities and those of our partner with the DAI or WIPPF. We find the areas of harmony, indifference, and conflict. We can do that alone or, even better, with our partner. We approach this discovery with empathy for ourselves and our partner.

Situational encouragement

- We look for the positive, harmonious aspects first and celebrate them.

"Looking into our everyday life, we agree on most topics like cleanliness, punctuality, and orderliness in the household. We are happy to inhabit such a home."

Verbalization

- We look for the areas we seem indifferent about and find interest in them.

"She is actually good at getting what she wants without making a great fuss. She has the capability to bring politeness and honesty together in a special way. I think I can learn from that."

- We look for the areas that create difficulties and ask questions.

"We usually get into fights about our finances; she likes to spend, and I prefer to save. But she usually persuades me to spend in the end."

   a. What is it we are unhappy with and why? What needs are relevant, and what feelings do we have about it?

"I really get upset when she spends our money at the spa and buys decorative items that aren't really necessary!" (thrift)

   b. What are our memories and associations of personal life-defining experiences related to this topic? How did our parents fulfill and live these needs specifically, and how did we learn from them?

"Both of my parents saved a part of their income. Hard times are inevitable, and one has to be prepared for them. Money spent on recreational pastimes is a waste. One must be financially prepared." (thrift, achievement, security)

c. What concerns our counterpart? What makes them unhappy? Why? What needs and feelings do they seem to have about these concerns or unsettling situations?

"She gets upset when I tell her to spend less so we can invest in the future. By spending now, she seems to be fulfilling her need for well-being, fun, and beauty, she tells me. She doesn't worry about the future. She says God has always provided for her, will continue providing, and that she never spends more than is in her account, which is true." (well-being, fun, faith, hope, confidence)

d. What are our counterpart's memories and associations of life-defining experiences about this topic? How did their parents fulfill and live these needs specifically, and how did they learn from them?

"Her parents have a beautifully decorated house, and her mother loves spending in the same way she does, and it is always pleasant to be In their home. But her parents argue about the same topics as we do."

e. What are the positive interpretations of both sides?

"She invests creatively in her well-being and our comfort at home. She is optimistic about the future. I can put aside funds for a rainy day."

f. What compromises or, at best, new strategies could be found for meeting our needs more wholesomely?

"I could actively participate in creative adventures with her, and we could decide together how we will finance them. We can also do some relaxing and wellness activities together that would really help us both."

Broadening goals

- What new goals could we set for the future when we have liberated the conflict energy?

"We had some wine together and talked things out. We now understand each other's needs for thrift and safety while we also see the needs for well-being, fun, beauty, love, and having an appealing home. We can plan, create, and enjoy together."

Intrapersonal conflicts

Just as we can get into conflict with the people we live and work with, we can have internal conflicts within different parts of our personality, personality traits, or beliefs. We can find the opposing conscious and preconscious aspects using the Four Dimensions of Life expression and the actual capabilities with the DAI or WIPPF. Let us look into ourselves and find out where we live in harmony with ourselves, where we may be indifferent towards some of our inner qualities, and where our conflictive areas lie. Our goal is to find healing.

General procedure

Observation distancing and making an inventory

- We look systematically and thoroughly through our life with the Four Dimensions of Life expression and the actual capabilities with the DAI or WIPPF to find the harmonious, the indifferent, and the conflictive areas. We give ourselves empathy for them.

Situational encouragement

- We look for the positive, harmonious aspects first and celebrate them.

Verbalization

- We look for the areas that we seem to be indifferent about and find interest in them.

- We look for the areas that create difficulties and apply the following questions:

    a. What part of us are we concerned and unhappy about? What needs are concerned, and what feelings do we have about them?

    b. What are our memories and associations with personal life-defining experiences about this topic? How did our parents fulfill and live these needs specifically, and how did we learn from them?

    c. What else are we concerned and unhappy about, why, and what needs and feelings do we seem to have about it?

    d. What are our memories and associations with personal life-defining experiences about this topic? How did our parents fulfill and live these needs specifically, and how did we learn from them?

    e. What are the positive interpretations of both sides?

    f. What compromises or, at best, new strategies could be found for meeting our needs more wholesomely?

Broadening goals

- What new goals could we set for the future when we have liberated the conflict energy?

Intra-personal conflicts within the topics of our Dimensions of Life expression

Let's look at an example of how to analyze our personal satisfaction with life and the conflicts we have within ourselves concerning the Four Dimensions. This internal investigation will teach us how different beliefs and aspects of our personalities can be integrated or brought into greater harmony with each other. Throughout life, we can progress in understanding ourselves better and learn to integrate the different capabilities we possess for healing.

Example:

Observation and distancing and making an inventory

- We look through our Four Dimensions of Life expressions for what we are happy or indifferent about and the ones we are discontented with: body, work, social life, and spirituality/cultural life. We give ourselves empathy for them.

Situational encouragement

- We look for the positive, harmonious aspects first and celebrate them.

"Looking at my Four Dimensions, I find many areas in the topics of body, health and family that make me happy and proud."

Verbalization

- We look for the areas that we seem to be indifferent about and find interest in them.

"I could examine or analyze my spirituality and give it more importance."

- We look for the areas that create difficulties and apply the following questions:

"In the area of work/achievement, I am not happy about my profession. While the work is satisfying, I am not earning enough to fulfill my dreams. Another thing that strikes me is that I keep spending everything I earn. I feel guilty about having money and living in relative luxury. These thoughts torment me."

a. What part of us are we concerned and unhappy about? What needs are concerned, and what feelings do we have about them?

"I am not earning as much as I want to, and what I earn, I spend right away, although I would like to buy a luxurious house with all the trappings of a mundane life. I really want to realize myself by living my dreams. I love seeing people live in luxury, and I want to do so too. I would like to share this with my friends. My strategy is to work hard at my job and try to save money, but the office I work at doesn't pay well." (money, beauty, self-actualization)

b. What are our memories and associations of personal life-defining experiences related to this topic? How did our parents fulfill and live these needs specifically, and how did we learn from them?

"My parents worked hard, thinking only of the welfare of their children. They continuously grumbled that money was hard to come by, and yet it slipped easily through their fingers."

c. What is another part of us we are concerned and unhappy about? What needs are concerned, and what feelings do we have about them?

"Because I feel a pull to live a saintly life of sacrifice, (thrift, faith, love for others/compassion), I spend my money on presents for the family and give them to the homeless and charitable organizations. So, in the end, I save hardly anything of the little I earn."

d. What are our memories and associations of personal life-defining experiences about this topic? How did our parents fulfill and live these needs specifically, and how did we learn from them?

"My parents taught me that it was immoral to live in luxury when other people had so little. They were regular churchgoers and praised St. Martin for sharing with the poor."

e. What are the positive interpretations of both sides?

"Living life in all its beauty and possibility enriches everyone emotionally and motivates others to do so too. Sharing what one has affords others the opportunity to participate."

f. What compromises or, at best, new strategies could be found for meeting our needs more wholesomely?

"I recognize that money is energy with which I can also help others. I can get a clear conscience and can balance my life by donating some and using some for myself. I recognize that I am undervaluing myself by continuing at my current job, so I can seek a better-paid position. I also recognize that my parents' situation was of a different time."

Broadening goals

> g. What new goals could we set for the future when we have liberated the conflict energy?

"I will have a great new job that is fun and pays well at the same time. I will use my money wisely, donate to good projects, and give some money to the homeless. I will find balance by living a modestly luxurious life."

Intra-personal conflicts within the topics of our actual capabilities

Now let's look at an example of how we can learn to understand and integrate differences we may have with certain actual capabilities, so we can become more harmonious people.

Example

Observation and distancing and making an inventory

- We look at the actual capacities of the DIA or WIPFF and see which attributes we value, which ones we are indifferent about, and which ones really irritate us. We give ourselves empathy for them.

Situational encouragement

- We look for the positive, harmonious aspects first and celebrate them:

"I was surprised to see that I am quite balanced in my capabilities."

Verbalization

- We look for the areas we seem indifferent about and find interest in them:

"I see that faith is not occupying much space in my life, and strengthening it could promote my well-being, so I want to give it a bit more attention."

- We look for the areas that create difficulties and apply the following questions:

"It really gets on my nerves that I am always late to work. People must think I really can't get myself together." (punctuality, reliability, trust, love)

    a.   What part of us are we concerned and unhappy about? What needs are concerned, and what feelings do we have about them?

"Timeliness demonstrates to my coworkers that I am reliable and trustworthy; I want my boss' appreciation rather than comments on my tardiness. But every morning, I can't resist dozing a bit longer before opening my eyes and getting ready for the day. Then I have to rush, and I arrive late." (punctuality, trust, reliability, love)

    b.   What are our memories and associations with personal life-defining experiences related to this topic? How did our parents fulfill and live these needs specifically, and how did we learn from them?

"My father put a lot of importance on punctuality and was consistently on time. As he said, punctuality is a sign of reliability and trustworthiness."

    c.   What is another part of us we are concerned and unhappy about? What needs are concerned, and what feelings do we have about them?

"I like going slow in the morning and getting up late. The bed is warm and comfortable. When I have to get up right away, I get grouchy." (pleasure, relaxation, comfort)

    d.   What are our memories and associations with personal life-defining experiences about this topic? How did our parents fulfill and live these needs specifically, and how did we learn from them?

"Getting up slowly and enjoying the morning with Mom in childhood was always grand. My mother's habits were just like mine. Leisure time was important."

    e.   What are the positive interpretations of both sides?

"Being on time and getting work done feels good and avoids problems with my supervisor and my team, and staying in bed a bit longer and having a wonderful coffee before leaving is great too."

    f.   What compromises or, at best, new strategies could be found for meeting our needs more wholesomely?

"I could simply go to bed a bit earlier and change my rhythm a bit instead of watching senseless television in the evening. That would give me some more time in the morning."

Broadening goals

- What new goals could we set for the future when we have liberated the conflict energy?

"I could see to it that my partner and I enjoy our evening more, maybe do some evening meditation and prayer together. I could also write a short diary about the positive things of the day. That way, we would get some creative, positive relaxation before going to bed earlier and have more time for one another in the morning as well."

CHAPTER 4
HAPPINESS AND THE ART OF USING OUR CREATIVITY, NETWORKING, AND MONEY AS ENERGY TO REALIZE OUR DREAMS

"The bird doesn't sing because it is happy; it's happy because it's singing."
- William James

Happiness

What is happiness? Some may say it is the sum of small things that make one happy. Aristotle writes, "Happiness is strived for because of its own innate value, whereas everything else is strived for because it makes us happy." He adds that we must practice our virtues to become happy and live fulfilled lives and also that happiness occurs "when all wishes are fulfilled, and none are left open."

Through science, we know that we can all find happiness, although some of us are genetically predisposed to feel stronger elation than others. Some of us may be in a fix and down at the moment; as healthy individuals, though, we have the potential to solve our problems and find a new way to fulfillment and well-being. **Happiness is feeling that we are living our lives in a way that our needs are being satisfied according to our values**. The whole range of our feelings is nothing more than a gauge to measure our well-being or to show us what we must do to find happiness and a fulfilled life. Pleasant feelings, such as happiness, show us our needs are fulfilled according to what we value in life, whereas unpleasant ones show us that these needs and values require more attention. Maslow uses his familiar pyramid to describe the needs we must satisfy to become happy and fulfilled. We all have various needs—physiological requirements, security, belongingness, self-esteem, and self-actualization—but each of us seeks to fulfill them in our own individual way. When we apply Nossrat Peseschkian's Four Dimensions of Life, we can see the full scope of these needs expressed through an individual's different purposes, objective acts, and life experiences, all of them lived within the areas of body/health, profession, social and cultural/spiritual life. Looking at the Four Dimensions of Life, we can compare them to the blossoming of a beautiful flower with its lush petals. The flower that has received the necessary nutrition and care expresses itself fully in its beauty. Each of our "life-flowers" is individually and culturally crafted by nature and can contribute to creating a wonderful bouquet. The beauty and variety in life lie within the different expressions of our needs, harmony within our tolerance, and mutual appreciation.

Each of us has different goals and strategies for reaching these goals, yet they are always rooted in the same universal needs. These needs are the basis upon which we can discover each other anew and from which we can create new common goals when we are in dissonance. "We can stand on our standpoint but shouldn't stay sitting upon it," as Nossrat Peseschkian said. To live a fulfilled life, sociologist Aaron Antonovsky tells us, we must be able to **understand, manage, and find meaning** within it. Dr. Peseschkian shows us we can find meaning when our parents provide a protected yet challenging access to life. They must give us the space and opportunity to learn to explore with our five senses and then teach us how to use our intellect to understand whatever we discover and encounter on our way. We also need them to pass on all their knowledge and wisdom to us so that we can one day become the creative architects of our lives. Nossrat Peseschkian calls the Four Dimensions—five senses, intellect, culture, and intuition/creativity of learning—our capabilities of comprehension. If we become able architects of our lives, refining our purpose and defining our talents, we will develop a sense of effectiveness with internal control-conviction, a deep sense of being the author of our lives and not being at the mercy of outer circumstances (external control-conviction). In his research, Martin Seligman has found that happiness arises when we experience pleasure, states of engagement/flow, and meaning. But he further described life fulfillment and flourishing as more transcendent goals, going beyond happiness and bestowing greater meaning. Flourishing for Seligman consists of **PERMA: Positive Emotions, Engagement, Relationships, Meaning, and Accomplishment,** five individual objectives that we humans seek for their own intrinsic value. All these are essential parts of Peseschkian's Four Dimensions of Life.

Peseschkian describes the world as a constant challenge through which we are regularly obliged to grow. Our **body, our environment, and the Zeitgeist** in which we live are continuously changing, and we must adapt to these changes. We must learn what our body can do and develop its capabilities as children, know how to express ourselves with our body as adults, and later accommodate ourselves to the problems it develops as we age. We have experienced many changes in our environment throughout the last century, including the development of radio, television, cars, computers, and cell phones; still, we must be open to the future. We also lived many changes of the Zeitgeist through rock-and-roll, the sixties student revolution, flower-power, the cold war, hip-hop, and other trends as time passed by. Current events such as climate change, immigration, gender studies, and many more are now impacting our lives and will further influence the Zeitgeist.

Everything is in a state of flux, which requires us to adapt. "Either you go with time, or you'll be gone with time," advises Peseschkian. Life is a continuous spiral of growth consisting of alternating phases of challenges in which we pursue purpose through physical and mental fatigue and find enjoyment through flow and phases of restoration, in which we seek pleasure through leisure. As Dr. Peseschkian said, it is a game of balance, finding equilibrium between effort and relaxation: "There is no elevator to happiness; you have to take the stairway" and "Who doesn't take time to take pleasure in life becomes unbearable." This recognition and acceptance results in healthy personal growth through a process of differentiation and integration, of transcending towards a continuously more complex, loving, whole, integral personality. Those who seek **"eudemonia"** or long-term happiness usually end up happier and more successful than those who seek hedonism or immediate gratification. The now familiar "marshmallow test" has demonstrated that children who can postpone gratification have a greater probability of becoming happy and successful. In Walter Mischel's Stanford University study, children were given a marshmallow and told to wait in a room for a few minutes by themselves. If they waited, they would then be given a second one. In the absence of a supervisor, some of them resisted and waited patiently, while others succumbed to the temptation of the sweet treat and ate it up. In the decades of the follow-up, it was found that those individuals who waited became happier and more successful. Those who couldn't wait tended to be less successful and more prone to drug use and unhappiness. Although in recent years the study has been criticized as flawed for various reasons, it remains a metaphor for the feats of successfully postponing gratification. It has been shown in adults that the ability to postpone gratification in a test with questions such as "You can have $20 now or $50 in half a year" correlates with the individual rate of postponing gratification (*Psychosomatic Bulletin & Review*; Kirby, 2009). Individuals that are able to wait on gratification more seldom become addicted to drugs (*Addiction;* Kirby & Petry, 2004) and are more rarely obese *(Frontiers in Behavioral Neuroscience*; Simmank et al., 2015). These individuals also differ in their brain structure, for example, by the fiber tracts that run between certain areas of the frontal lobes that are important for self-control and ones between deeper-lying regions that are important for reward-oriented learning (*Journal of Neuroscience*; Achtergerg et al., 2016)

There are different ways to find happiness, as Hindus, Buddhists, and other wisdom traditions show us. That of the never-ending pursuit of the satisfaction of our aspirations and desires in what they call **samsara**, the eternal cycle of existence, or finding it as an upwelling of joy within the calm of meditation as **nirvana**. We can learn to value both forms. Looking at life as a musical instrument, we can learn to play it and enjoy playing our tune. We can achieve eudemonia in the cycle of life by mindfully observing life, letting it inspire us and teach us new capabilities, and then joyfully realizing these new aspirations with our newly developed skills. Afterward, we can look back with gratitude, observe our creation, and aspire to something new. We can achieve this with consciousness and mindfulness, making our experience a contemplative act of enjoying life's beauty instead of just running through it. **Playing the "instrument of life"** is always an art of using the rules of the universe. We can, for example, cook and develop the art of using spices, paint and use the rules of light and colors to pleasing effect, play an instrument and use the laws of sound and rhythm, solve mathematical problems and fall in love with numbers, dance with rhythm and movement, or excel in any discipline of learning, using its laws and harmonies to play the instrument of our creation. We can also find happiness within, the inner peace that lies deep inside ourselves through meditation and calming our thoughts until they disappear. What remains is an ever-widening experience of what is, of suchness, of the I-am-ness of experiencing everything as one and experiencing consciousness as the basis of life. With practice, we can experience nirvana, the state of **inner peace expressed by a rising of the subtle feeling of elation.**

There are many **spiritual pathways to happiness**. First, we must understand that religion is a composition of tradition, ritual, mythology, life philosophy, values, and spirituality. Many of us have thrown the religion of our childhood overboard; we can't accept one or more of its components because they are out of date or unexplainable to our rational minds. We have, over time, come to distrust religion. Yet, it is important to recognize and differentiate the various parts of religion separately. We must see that our spirituality is our ability to connect to the all, to what is, and that our life philosophy is our knowledge and wisdom about life and that we must both develop continuously and cultivate as life unfolds. We can undogmatically interpret mythology, rituals, and tradition and find individual meanings within them while we move away from orthodoxy in the direction of openness toward life. It is important to understand that throughout human evolution, all religious traditions, with their wisdom and experience, have been in the process of coming and going, evolving and re-creating themselves. We ourselves can participate in this process and continuously seek wisdom and spirituality in life. We can create new wisdom and find new depth in spirituality, allow it to mature, and then pass it on. Peseschkian said that religion is like a colorful lantern with the flame of spirituality glowing from within. There are an endless number of religious lamps within this world, each one different from all the others, and there will be an endless number to come.

The **happiness formula** based on research by Sonja Lyubomirsky, Ed Diener, and Martin Seligman demonstrates that 40% of our happiness is defined by our personal happiness set-point, only 7-12% by our conditions of living, and 50% by our voluntary activities. Our set-point is partly psychosocial and partly genetic (5HTT is the happiness gene with a longer, more robust, or shorter strand). The voluntary activities that contribute the most to our happiness are meaning, doing something for the good of others, and creativity, creating something proactively in our Four Dimensions of Life. Pleasure and consumption have high peaks but rapid falloffs. Research has also found that our happiness can be effectively altered through medication, psychotherapy, and meditation.

Daniel Kahneman, in his book *Thinking Fast and Slow* posits another theory. Kahneman claims that 70% of our perception of life satisfaction is due to our mood, which is in itself highly influenced by the connectedness we experience with the world, the gratification of our basic needs, and the freedom we have to express ourselves. The other 30% is due to **the way we evaluate life** or how we experience ourselves achieving our purpose. This shows that the harsher an environment becomes, the more difficult it is to remain high-spirited. On the other hand, there are some people who can elevate their level of contentment through purpose far above that of the way we are usually influenced by mood. This ability heightens their resilience and lets them remain more committed and serene in difficult times. One heroic example is the Nazi resistor Dietrich Bonhoeffer who was imprisoned in a concentration camp and hanged just as WWII ended. His spiritual conviction had fueled his endurance and let him give himself to his quest, his purpose of helping others and overcoming national socialism. In this way, he was a model for others.

Money and **power** are often misinterpreted as evil, and a good person is often seen as someone who doesn't have or use them. But both depend on the character of the individual wielding them and simply expose this person's nature to plain view for all. We can do evil or good deeds using power and money. We can egoistically use them to benefit only ourselves or use them altruistically, seeing the "all" in "all"-truistic and including ourselves. Research has shown that happiness grows exponentially with income to the point that sustenance is reached. Then the curve flattens rapidly, and no big differences can be measured anymore. It is important that our income can provide life's necessities. From there on, money helps us express our values and helps us achieve our individual goals. Money, though, can become a source of unhappiness if we chase after it solely for its own sake, losing contact with our resources and the beauty of life. If we have a good sense of self-effectiveness and a balanced sense of power, we can move ahead toward our goals and shape our lives. Science has also shown that freedom is a prerequisite to happiness, and in authoritarian countries, where one cannot effectively express oneself, the level of happiness is lower than in countries permitting individual expression.

The rider on the elephant. The rider represents the rational, the elephant the emotional. One must train the elephant well; otherwise, when temptation or fear arises, the elephant will always be stronger than the rider.

Creativity as a true expression of positum

Psychologist Mihály Csíkszentmihályi asserts that to be successfully creative, one must have had **intense exposure** to the specific field one operates in creatively during childhood as well as having developed a **talent** for it. Furthermore, one needs the **support** of people who will accept and validate this talent and creativity. People with talent often integrate **contrasting traits** that allow them to utilize a wider scope of characteristics than average humans do. Some have both the capability to fantasize and operate scientifically, which makes their inventions both creative and practical. Some are extroverted and introverted at the same time, effective ambiverts. They can work alone for days and then, when necessary, connect and communicate ideas. These capabilities lead to efficient work and the promotion of their ideas. They show pride and self-assurance, backed by their belief in the existence and proof of their creation while also demonstrating humility. Ambition and aggressiveness are necessary for getting ahead in the field of creativity, as well as selflessness, cooperation, and peacefulness. Creative people have a good dose of all. Psychological androgyny is another frequent trait of creative people, which means they combine the assertiveness, self-confidence, toughness, rigidity, and dominance of the masculine and submissiveness, nurturing, sensitivity, family orientation, and attention to the environment of the feminine. This way, with both ends of the spectrum, they have double the repertoire of opportunities. They are feminine and masculine at the same time, but in addition, they have **cross-gender traits**. To be creative, one must be rebellious, iconoclastic, and independent, going beyond the boundaries of the known. But at the same time, one must have traditional knowledge and know their domain and the rules. A creative person values the past for creating novelty that leads to improvement. One must function along life's rules. Creative people certainly are different, but not so different that others cannot relate to them. Wanting to be different is not a motive for creative work. Wanting to be different arises from negative impulses and leads to frustration. Only a positive objective can lead to genuine creative output. Innovation is not a safe or secure undertaking. One must be passionate and objective, attached and detached simultaneously. Creative people incorporate yin and yang by accepting criticism and simultaneously attaching it to their projects. Suffering, pain, and enjoyment accompany the goal- and process-orientation. These opposing traits are usually difficult to find in the same person, but without the personality of opposites, often, new ideas will not be recognized.

"Creativity is about working at the ends of both sides of polarities with the capability of anticipating the right idea and committing to it."
- M. Csíkszentmihályi

The process of creativity

According to Csíkszentmihályi, the process of creativity consists of different stages. Beginning with intense preparation, becoming immersed in issues with curiosity, then a time of incubation with changes and maturation happening in the subconscious, then a sudden *aha!* effect, and the creative new idea appears seemingly from nowhere. This *aha* moment is followed by periods of evaluation and self-criticism and finally, a strenuous elaboration phase that brings the whole creative project to perfection.

When we investigate success, we see that speed and IQ are highly correlated: Martin Seligman, in his book *Flourish,* from which the following information is drawn, describes fast automatic components and slow voluntary components. The speed of thought with which a task can be done reflects how much of that task is automatic and how much skill or knowledge is relevant to this specific task. Going slowly allows our executive functions to take over. Executive functions consist of focusing and ignoring distractions, remembering and using new information, planning action, revising the plan, and inhibiting fast, impulsive thoughts and actions. Unlike the underlying skill of knowledge, the executive functions of planning, checking our work, calling up memories, and creativity are slow processes. When more components are automatic, acquired earlier by speed and deliberate practice, the more time we have left over to use our slow process for the voluntary heavy lifting and hence better outcomes. The sheer amount of time we spend on a task multiplies how much skill we have for achieving our goal: *Achievement* is *skills* x *effort*. Time invested also directly impacts knowledge acquisition: The more time we spend on the task, the more knowledge we'll acquire.

There are often several paths to a goal. By some, you arrive quickly, by others slowly, and some paths turn out to be dead ends. Deciding which path to take is the slow process we call planning. The invention of new paths requires creativity. Our rate of learning is how fast we can deposit new information into our memory bank of automatic knowledge. The faster our rate of learning, which is not the same as our speed of thought about the task, the more knowledge we can accumulate for each unit of time that we devote to the task and the more time we have for the slow executive process. Effort is the amount of time we spend on the task. The main character determinants of how much time we devote to the task are our self-discipline and our grit. Genius is primarily the result of deliberate practice rather than a God-given trait, and self-discipline is the character trait that engenders deliberate practice. IQ and self-discipline do not correlate significantly, and self-discipline out-predicts IQ for academic success by a factor of two. From what is known from research, girls are more self-disciplined, and women's self-discipline does not decrease throughout life, but after college, many women are burdened by cultural factors and expectations that decrease their accomplishments. Since grit is a determining factor for success and consists of self-discipline and passion, it out-predicts IQ as a contributor to success by a factor of 50. More education is consistent with more grit, as is age; older people usually have more grit than younger people. The bell curve to success shows that the hours applied to a task multiply our progress toward the goal. So, we learn that success depends on practice, practice, practice. Our real leverage is the effort we expend to realize our goals.

Whenever we desire inspiration, we can do the following:

- As **beginners**, we stay open to whatever appears in our lives and meet it without prejudice and preconditions. Our professional mind is then ready to contribute its knowledge. When we meet things directly with our professional minds, we are often biased and miss opportunities and potential. But when we use our beginner's and professional minds in tandem, we can become truly creative.

- We can **associate with inspirational friends** and colleagues, those who live their interests and visions as we do while exuding enthusiasm and creativity. Together we can have uplifting and inspiring conversations bolstered by the wonderful exchange of positive energy. We can always make new friends and acquaintances by talking to strangers wherever we find an opportunity, like on a train, waiting in line, or in a café or shop. These conversations are fun and reveal surprises when we discover the adventurous stories and experiences of the astonishing people that surround us.

- **Networking** with those who share our interests to develop our creativity is just as important as our personal capabilities and communication skills. A creative person needs a group of experienced people in the domain in which he is creative, those who know the value of the novelty he is creating. If he remains without a resonating body, his efforts will often be in vain. Therefore, it is important to create a network of similarly oriented people who resonate with one's ideas so we can disseminate them more broadly. Depending on our field, we may have networks of companies, teachers, philosophers, sports groups, medical academicians, and so forth.

- When we **daydream**, we listen to our buried intuitions, fantasies, and desires. We can regularly take a few minutes to reflect on what we tend to daydream about. This is a relaxing and motivating form of creativity.

- In dark moments of crisis, focusing **on the positive** and keeping our goals in mind is helpful. Envisioning our future motivates us and gives us the power to stay solution-orientated instead of problem-oriented or playing the blame game, which brings all of us down. Instead of asking why something has happened to us, we ask what happened and what we can learn from it, make out of it, and have already made of it.

- By regularly **giving and taking graciously,** we increase the pleasure in our own and the lives of others. When we give something wholeheartedly every day, we receive gratitude in the form of grace. When someone gives us a present, we receive it wholeheartedly and return our gratitude. We can receive other people's gratitude in the same way we receive a gift.

"The Treasure of Knowledge"

A farmer's consistently reliable tractor broke down one day, and he couldn't get the engine to turn over. He tried every trick he knew, but the engine wouldn't make a sound. So finally, he decided to call a mechanic. When the mechanic arrived, he opened the hood, looked inside for a moment, took a hammer, and gave the motor a whack. When the farmer tried the ignition again, the motor revved up immediately. Happily, the farmer asked what the repair cost was. But when he heard that the price was 100 toman (Iranian currency), his smile turned into a frown. "How can it be that hitting the motor with a hammer cost 100 toman?" he asked. The mechanic replied, "Oh no, hitting the motor with the hammer only cost one toman, but knowing where to hit it cost 99."

- Retold after Nossrat Peseschkian (*Oriental Stories*, p. 10)

Money as life energy and an expression of our values

"You are rich when you feel rich" means that, to a certain degree, our happiness is independent of our money. But at the same time, money is energy that we can use creatively to express our individual values and can contribute enormously to our self-expression and satisfaction. Money is value-neutral. The idea that "evil" people use money in "evil" ways and "good" people use money in "good" ways illustrates that we are the ones who attribute our values to it.

Positive Psychology has shown that increasing income increases how positively we view our life circumstances but that our mood isn't influenced very much by our income at all. So, while our overall satisfaction with life rises with our income, our mood or spirit is raised mostly by an increase in satisfaction with our surroundings, which gives us more room for self-expression. Therefore, the deduction that happiness goes up with income reveals only part of the picture. The rate of satisfaction grows proportionally to our income only to the point that it surpasses the level of our basic needs, our basic security net. Once it reaches that point, the rate of satisfaction rises less with our increase in income. Since income has a limited correlation to life satisfaction, looking at satisfaction with Nossrat Peseschkian's Dimensions of Life expression or with Martin Seligman's PERMA can reveal more meaningful and deeper insights. Although these studies let us recognize the limits of the power of money, we also understand how money essentially contributes to our freedom.

We all need money, first to support ourselves but then also to realize our dreams and goals. We don't just want to survive but to thrive in life. We want to be wealthy materially, energetically, and psychologically, offering our capabilities and products with good spirit to improve our customers' health and well-being and contribute to our communal happiness. We should always remember that "time is money," and when our life has become a constant quest for money, we lose precious time in which we could be happy. We can pursue happiness in a better way than making more money—money shouldn't become our goal, but simply a means to our more meaningful goals. We can use money in our quest for truth, to create beauty, or to do good for others. When we think this way, money becomes an excellent friend to help us create what we dream of for the improvement of all. Instead of recklessly throwing our money away on things we don't truly value, we can invest in our future, in a more beautiful life. We evaluate how much we must earn and how we can earn it with smart and ethical methods so we can purchase what we aspire to. Money is currency, and currency is energy through which we can achieve what we value. Starting with high-spiritedness and gratitude for what we already have and where we already are, we surround ourselves and collaborate with creative, inspiring people who can contribute to our ideas and goals and support our vision of using money resourcefully. We throw the phrase "I can't" out of our vocabulary and set out to get what we want, doing whatever is needed and becoming who we must become, with a positive vision of money as a tool and resource for creating the life we desire.

Our relationship with money and the way we earn it are equally important. Earning money shouldn't drain our energy. We must find honor in our work and then must cherish money as a necessary asset to be used wisely and ethically, knowing that its value depends on the intentions of the people using it. Good people do good things with money; greedy people do greedy things. When we put effort into earning it, respect it, and are grateful for it, we create a profitable relationship for the benefit of all.

Mental strategies for wealth consciousness

We live in a world of abundance. We must be aware of our own abundance and realize that up to the present, we have had more than we needed. We lose energy and motivation by focusing on what we don't have and creating despair. Whenever we focus with gratitude on the abundance in our lives, we create a power pack of resilient energy which enables us to progress toward our goals. We will recognize all the opportunities before us, have the vigor to take the chances necessary to move forward, and have the open-mindedness to make the personal connections we need for success. Some of us were born affluent, others with fewer financial resources, but successful people, whatever their origins, have a common mindset. They believe in themselves and what they do. What's more, they take action to realize their aspirations. Our mindset is the key to our financial success and a fulfilled life. We must live our lives authentically, standing tall and dispensing our gifts.

Having money entails some obligations. Life is a give-and-take; the more we receive, the more we must share. Refraining from making money doesn't make others richer, but acquiring wealth and distributing it to others can enrich others' lives. We can be truly proud of ourselves whenever we contribute to others. If we act responsibly and ethically, we realize that having negative feelings about money is a waste of time. Having money and letting it flow according to what we value is a blessing because it is one of our tools to create more of what we cherish and share with others. If we really have a strong drive to do charitable work, we can do so, but we can also dedicate a part of our work time to charitable work without compromising our other goals.

Creating a positive mindset about money

One of the best things we can do to **make this world a better world is to work on ourselves**. Of course, we are already perfect just the way we are, but we can always continue on our inner path of growth. This is what we call **excellence**. Not to believe we are the best or must be the best, but to be grateful for what is and, at the same time, continue growing. Would we rather live in a world of happy, fulfilled, and nurtured people who aspire to be the best they can be, or do we prefer a world where people cower in shame, are fearful of risks, and hold themselves back? Which life gives us more energy?

To create a better life, we must investigate and understand what we need and want and then create the means to get it. We must be clear and honest with ourselves. Do we want to live an isolated life as a hermit, or are there any desires lurking within ourselves waiting to be fulfilled? We want to learn to understand and express, not to repress. We want to discover what desires will contribute to a grand life using our potential and talents. We must find out what we really want to do and why we are doing it and make concrete plans by estimating the amount of money we need to earn to realize our dream. Then we must get started without hesitation. Once we walk our talk, we create the motivation we need to persevere. Keeping the grand picture of what we want to achieve with all its benefits as an emotional vision gives us the drive to overcome obstacles and helps us continue as proactive, optimistic believers on our path to success. "Vague goals make vague lives, so we aim high, go steady and far." (Anonymous) The big five for success, according to Michael Bohne, psychiatrist and inventor of Process and Embodiment Psychology, are first knowing our talent and what we love doing, second finding our personal niche market where we can expand, third striving for it, fourth being ready for success and being able to believe in ourselves, and last having the guts to fail so we can get up again.

To be financially successful, we need to be high-spirited and believe in ourselves and our capabilities but also to believe in the **worthiness of what we produce**. Since money is nothing more than the buying power attributed to it, it is important to believe in our product and not undersell it.

"I worked for menial pay only to learn, dismayed, that any wage I asked of life, life would have willingly paid."
- Anonymous

The same product of the same quality, such as a purse, can be sold at $50 or $5000. We must investigate its market worth and sell it at the just price. Otherwise, we will always be the losers, either by selling under value or by selling over value and losing our clients. If our product doesn't achieve the expected benefit, we must change our product, service, or profession.

To stay fit and able to channel our energies into our economic success, it is important to **keep physically and mentally in shape**.

We must take care of our Four Dimensions, maintaining our physical health, fostering our social connections and our spiritual fulfillment, and getting help from inspirational advisors, mentors, and friends.

- **A positive mindset about money**

To create a **positive mindset** about money and heal our relationship with it, we write down all the derogatory phrases that come to mind and then find corresponding positive truths. "I hate money because it makes people unhappy." On the positive side of the coin, "Money is energy and contributes to fulfilling my desires and creating a better world." Money doesn't mean anything on its own. The qualities we attribute to money give it its importance and meaning.

- **The money envelope**

We can create a money envelope to heighten our motivation and resolve to achieve monetary success. We write on the front of an envelope: "Universe/God, please keep this envelope always full in the way you consider it right." On the back, we draw a star with as many points as we wish there to be areas from which we will receive income. Then we put some bills or a beautiful coin as a talisman into it, as well as a feeling of abundance. The intention and consciousness we put into the envelope will become our willpower, the energy we emanate, and what we attract. If we put money in with the energy of abundance, then we'll receive abundance. We keep this envelope in mind and mentally connect with it from time to time.

The people with the most luck in life are usually those who think most positively and design their life and apply themselves to it.

"A true decision can be measured by the fact that we have taken a new action. If there is no action, it's because we haven't really decided."
- Tony Robbins

Magic appears when we act.

CHAPTER 5
SETTING OUT TOWARDS OUR GOALS IN LIFE AND MASTERING CRISES ON THE WAY

"God will not have his work made manifest by cowards."
- Ralph Waldo Emerson

Setting worthy goals and planning how to get there

Earlier, we did exercises for discovering ourselves and planning our life. Now we want to get into the details of planning and realizing specific worthy goals and habits that will help us achieve our master plan.

1. What is it we want? What would we like to achieve? Let's give our goal a specific name and describe it precisely.

2. Why do we want to achieve this goal, and how important is it to us?

3. How will we reward ourselves for achieving this goal, and what other advantages will we accomplish by getting it?

4. How will we feel about achieving this goal? Let's give a detailed description.

5. What will we have to do to achieve the goal?

6. What obstacles might we meet on our way?

7. What could help us on our way? Are there more resources at hand?

8. Who could help us?

9. What small action will we begin today to get ourselves moving on the road to our objective?

10. What will we do tomorrow to get closer to our goal?

11. And next week?

12. And the following month?

13. What daily habits will help us to achieve our objective? (Read, eat healthily, sleep well, have great sex, further our skills, talk to inspiring friends, be mindful and grateful, meditate, pray...?)

14. What habit do we want to get rid of because it demotivates us, harms us, or simply slows us down and keeps us from getting to our objective?

15. What capability would help us get to our objective?

16. What else do we need to achieve our goal?

17. What will we tell ourselves when an obstacle appears? What will we do? Whom will we ask for help?

18. How will we know that we've arrived at our goal? Does any sensation let us know? Let's try to describe it. How do we measure our success?

19. How will we celebrate our achievements? What reward will we give ourselves? How will we tell the story? What will we tell ourselves about it?

"About the courage to take a test"

The king's sage adviser died, and he had to find a worthy replacement, so he devised a challenge to reveal the ablest among the contestants. He told the palace carpenters to build a huge wooden door with a big and sturdy lock built into it. Then he called anyone who considered himself wise to try to open it. The first contestant came and looked from afar but was so impressed by the size and strength of the door and lock that he didn't dare come closer. He only shook his head and turned away. The next competitor came and inspected the lock a bit closer, but he was too intimidated by this daunting construction to give it a try. Then came a third elderly, almost frail-looking man. He looked at the lock closely, touched it, rattled it a bit, and then handily opened it to the surprise of all. This contestant had noticed that the door wasn't locked but simply closed, and it easily swung open to his touch. So the king announced, "I see you not only have the wits but also the courage to give it a try! You shall become my new royal adviser."

Retold after Nossrat Peseschkian (*Oriental Stories*, p. 3)

Jumping into the unknown and learning by doing on our way to excellence

Once we have decided what we want to go after, getting started and then getting to the finish line can still be a major issue for us. Trying to be perfect and believing we must know everything before we even begin a project and start learning from it gets in our way of finishing what we set out to do. Time and again, we believe we are too unqualified and inexperienced for a project, but this is often just our subconscious fear, keeping us from trying determinedly to succeed. Therefore, we search for excuses so we don't have to get on that scary path toward realizing our dreams. Instead of wasting our time and energy obsessing about our lack of skill or believing we are frauds, we could instead throw ourselves into the new adventure and trust that we know more than we think we do. We can remember that the things we like are usually those we are good at, and when we are passionate about something, and we have the right pressure behind us to get it done, there will be no way around being successful. When we stop preparing ourselves and start working and letting necessity teach us, we will be surprised how fast we can learn and how much fun it can be.

"If you're serious about changing your life, you'll find a way. If you're not, you'll find an excuse."
- Jen Sincero

The **Pareto principle** shows us that perfectionism is an obstacle. The 80/20 rule demonstrates that 80% of the results can be achieved with 20% effort. The remaining 20% of the results need 80% effort. We get more things done well if we work with concentration but with moderate effort. What we achieve will also be highly appreciated, since when we don't overdo things, we'll get more done. The small differences between semi-perfect and perfect are hardly noticeable. Challenging ourselves a little by sticking to the nearly perfect instead of the overly perfect and seeing what results we will achieve can be a great game. We can have fun and get into this adventure with the spirit of young children and see what we can get away with. We learn to recognize that what we have is good enough, even if we didn't initially see its quality. In the beginning, we might feel pressured by doing less, but in the long run, we will have a more pleasurable, relaxed, and successful life.

Another important aspect of carrying through a project is **analyzing our difficulties and our weak points**, those impediments that often cause us to quit. We can search and find the causes of our dwindling energy and inclination to abandon the project, and we can prepare for the event so the next time, we can work through it. If we have been chastising ourselves for procrastination, but our projects have always worked out well for us anyway, we should ask if some level of procrastination is an asset. If so, why change a helpful habit? By accepting our procrastination, we loosen up and stop feeling guilty and wasting time reproaching ourselves. We can use the liberated time for other things we value. But if the procrastination is not serving us well, and we simply need more motivation, making a promise to a person we value can give us that extra drive and heighten our resolve to complete the project.

"If you are looking for a helping hand, look for it at the end of your own arm."
- Nossrat Peseschkian

Self-motivation and grit for pushing through to our goals

Our self-motivation and grit are key elements needed for progress toward our goals. Grit is the quality that helps us find a way through or around impending challenges and maintain our stamina in times of crisis. Consider the flame of a candle that is sustained by a strong wick and fueled by high-quality wax as a metaphor for our **motivation** and **willpower**. If either one is weak, the flame will be weak. Our willpower is a question of training and regular practice. Our motivation depends strongly on our emotional and cognitive filters or on our perspective and our intentional goals. Luckily, we have the mental tools to regulate our frame of mind. We can influence our convictions, attitudes, and goals, which are key to our self-motivation, by selecting clear goals and analyzing and modifying our convictions and attitudes. The higher we set the goals, the higher our self-motivation and the more energy we will have to exert. We call these mountaintop aspirations our **motivational goals**. We don't necessarily have to attain them, but they get us going and give us direction and drive. We must also have confidence in ourselves. Take a marathon runner who collapses just over the finish line. Had the finish line been 100 meters farther, he would have made it there too. We usually set our goals lower than what we can reach, stay in our comfort zones, and miss out on the elation of remarkable achievements. We must train our willingness to bear risks; otherwise, exceptional chances and possibilities for success will pass us by. Stereotypically, life within the comfort zone is legs up, TV on, brain off. We might better take our inspiration from Henry David Thoreau, who, in 1845, left the comforts of his home for a spartan and isolated cottage on Walden Pond, transforming his views of the world—both without and within.

When we ask ourselves what we have achieved in life, what crises we have surmounted, and what we are proud of, we find that our assessment is based on all we have achieved outside our comfort zone. Progress is usually possible only outside of our comfort zone. The more we have worked to get to our goal, the prouder we are of it. We are reluctant to leave our comfort zones because change brings about uncertainty, risk, fear, and maybe failure. But is failure always to be avoided? *Nothing is as successful as a failure.* Instead of making our children feel that they have failed when they get a bad grade, we can show them that maybe it wasn't what they were expecting, but they can learn from the experience; it is a sign that they must do something different. Problems are opportunities; a problem is something to be solved. We have the tools to exercise our cognitive, emotional, and willing capabilities when we are confronted with a problem. Two German sayings capture this idea: "Glück macht süchtig; Unglück tüchtig" / "Fortune gets you addicted; misfortune makes you laborious" and "Um einen Diamanten zu erhalten braucht man viel Druck" / "To get a diamond, one needs much pressure."

Are you giving your best toward what you value? What is important to you? Usually, it is health, family, relationship, work, continued education, and self-realization. We need to be motivated by a reason so strong that it moves us internally and forces us out of our comfort zone. Only with all our energy do we get all the success. We human beings tend to be consistent. When we have decided, we stick to it. So, let's find a meaningful commitment and be surprised about our consistency.

One of the biggest errors we can make is to say that outer circumstances are demotivating us. This means we can't do anything and are powerless since we are not in control of external factors. We must remember while we cannot control all circumstances, we can control our perception and interpretation. We can adjust our **victim attitude** and adopt the attitude of a **proactive optimist**. We can remember to act consciously and not just react unconsciously. We can fortify our self-empowerment. When we act, we become aware of how our response heightens our sense of self-esteem.

Our motivation, positivity, and action all contribute to a **psychological placebo effect**. Our belief in ourselves and that good results will appear with time and effort lead us to increasingly engaged thinking and acting. Our body will always adjust itself energetically to our future challenges, as we have experienced before; we intrinsically know it will supply us with the necessary energy at the given moment if we use it wisely. We amplify the placebo effect by thinking with commitment. *What can I do? What more can I do?* We make self-motivation a decision. Socrates said the following about success: "If you want something as much as you want air when you are drowning, then you will have success." Self-motivation isn't a personal characteristic; it is the result of a process of several steps, which can be learned. It is the capability to conceive of an effort, to begin, and to follow it through without external encouragement. We must be so excited about our plans that we can't be stopped. We must exude enthusiasm to a point that outside observers realize how serious we are. We build the conviction it will work and know with certainty that we will give all we can, and we will make it through to the end. To do so, there is no way around practicing our training standards regularly and committing to it again and again. We empower ourselves and begin to live the life in which we give our best every day. Living with a zest for our goal and the grit to see it through, we can get where we want to go.

"God, give us the grace to accept with serenity the things that cannot be changed, courage to change the things that should be changed, and the wisdom to distinguish the one from the other."
- Reinhold Niebuhr

Distinguishing where we are effective and where all effort is in vain

We must distinguish where we want to apply our zest for action because it is useful only in the **areas in which we really have influence**. There is the area of **0%**—that of God and the universe—then the "you" sphere (influences that are **external** to ourselves), which amounts to **0.1–99.9%** and is highly variable. Then there is the **100%**, which is me. Here I can really make a difference that gives me the highest dividend. So, we must dedicate ourselves to projects that really lie in our hands.

	100% Influence	0,1-99% Influence	0% Influence
Important			
Important & Urgent			
Unimportant			

- **Areas-of-influence exercise:** We make a list of all the themes occupying our mind and assign them to these three spheres. We prioritize them according to the influence we have on them and the importance and urgency they have for us. We mark the action that is important to us, is urgent, and on which we have an influence, and we get started immediately. When we have categorized and prioritized what is important and where we can really make a difference by working on it, we commit to 100% for the time necessary. With time, our challenge gets easier and easier to follow through as our successes add to our self-esteem account. We make a promise, keep it, and follow through. We adjust our settings and mental filters. When we are convinced that performance is worthwhile, then it is easier for us to start our personal projects.

"There is only a small corner of the universe you can be certain of improving, and that's your own self."
- Aldous Huxley

Acting and creating traction in our sphere of influence: When we do the things others don't like doing, we can call it practicing the **tai chi of willpower** for daily life. If we can be the person who does the things that others don't like doing, what will we be able to do, and where will we be after a year of such effort and practice? What popularity level may we have reached? What will we have learned from the process? Let's get into doing whatever we must do without reservation and prejudice, with a beginner's mind, and then do it mindfully. Everything we do can become our tai chi exercise. Entering our practice mindfully without reservation will strengthen our resilience and resolve since we no longer waste time avoiding and complaining.

"Desire is the key to motivation, but it's determination and commitment to an unrelenting pursuit of your goal—a commitment to excellence—that will enable you to attain the success you seek."
- Mario Andretti

Some tips on how to overcome reluctance to begin work and then carry through

- We plan to do things for a brief period, working on a small portion, which makes it easier in the beginning.

- Once we have begun, we will probably notice that we get carried away, and we can continue working with much less effort.

- Dividing a large project into small portions makes it easier to begin and to continue. We can call this making a "spoon list." With this approach, we enjoy every spoonful, and if we eat more than a spoonful, it is all the better.

- We can also make a promise to someone who is important to us that we will complete our project. Bringing someone else in on our plans obliges us to carry them out. We should also take breaks so we don't lose our enthusiasm.

- Finally, we are motivated to continue if we envision our future outcome when we have successfully finished our project, and we imagine all the benefits we will accrue.

"Productivity is never an accident. It is always the result of a commitment to excellence, intelligent planning, and focused effort."
- Paul J. Meyer

Practice getting out of our routine and comfort zone

- Change routes to work occasionally.
- Dress up in a different style than we usually wear.
- Get color or style advice.
- Say no when we mean it.

- Get involved in discussions in which we usually wouldn't participate.

- Ask a coworker with a contrary opinion how he sees a specific issue.

- Invite three experts on a certain matter to a meeting or a lunch/dinner.

- Contact clients who didn't buy from us to find out what would have to change for them to do so.

- Make a presentation on a topic.

"The cow and the watering pot"

A farmer once had a cow he loved very much. She was really all the world to him because she produced so much milk and therefore contributed to his modest income. He took care of her, giving her the best hay, fodder, and fresh water every day. One day, he thought his beloved cow really deserved a new watering pot. So, he went to the city and bought an expensive one. Back home in his stable, he filled the watering pot and led his cow to drink. But oh my, when the cow bent to drink, her horns got trapped in the new pot. She battled against it but couldn't set herself free. Even with the farmer's help, the pot was still stuck, and the cow became more furious by the minute. The farmer panicked because he was fearful of losing the expensive watering pot. So, he took an ax and chopped off the cow's head. As the head fell, the watering pot broke, and the farmer began to cry.

– Retold after Nossrat Peseschkian (*33 und eine Form der Partnerschaft*, p.65)

Strong decision-making and consistency, even when we fail at reaching our goals

Until we commit to action, we lose time by waffling back and forth. But once we have decided and we truly commit, we can make great strides toward our destination. **Deciding upon and committing** to one's goals are essential to becoming happy and successful in life. This means we get clear about what we want and then push ourselves in pursuit of our goals with **enthusiasm** and **dedication**, no matter which challenges we must overcome on our way. And since there is no goal without obstacles, it is of greatest importance to have decided and committed to one's objectives. This commitment prevents us from quitting after a halfhearted try when the road gets rougher. Our decision and commitment must be reinforced by our unshakable desire to achieve our goal, the belief in ourselves, the realization that this goal is our destiny, and the knowledge that we will always have support from our friends. We will see new opportunities and make new friends on the way. So, if we commit to our vision with determination, even when we experience setbacks and must enter unknown waters, we can carry on steadfastly and not abandon the ship.

"Success consists of going from failure to failure without loss of enthusiasm."
- Winston Churchill

We all fail temporarily on our missions, but it isn't the end of the game if we pick ourselves up and get moving again, as have many successful people such as Michael Jordan, Steven Spielberg, Thomas Edison, Soichiro Honda, and Ludwig van Beethoven. Reading the biographies of spectacular people such as these can inspire us.

We fail only when we abandon our rendezvous with providence. Everything else is learning and gaining experience. Our solid commitment tunes out inner and outer critics who tell us we are incapable, we will never learn, or our goal is unreachable. To make our greatest impact in life, we must be honest with ourselves and follow our authentic desires and talents. Colin Kaepernick, an American football player who made headlines for kneeling during the national anthem, tells us how he did just that in the series *Colin in Black & White,* relating his unforgettable story of hardheaded commitment to becoming a quarterback against all odds. His belief in his talent and his profound desire to develop it propelled him toward his destination.

Successful people are decisive. **Deciding means making a choice and ceasing internal negotiations**. Less decisive people are paralyzed by self-doubt and fear they'll make the wrong decision. Successful people reflect and then decide quickly, confident that they are on the right track. When we hesitate and take too much time deciding, we torture ourselves. We lose our freedom by waffling back and forth, never getting anywhere and maybe even losing valuable opportunities for growth. This indecisiveness is known as **cognitively arrested alternatives** and can also lead to depression. Therefore, we should take to heart that decision is freedom and indecision torture.

- We can **practice effective decision-making** by selecting a menu item after reading carefully and then deciding within two or three minutes. Once we decide what to eat, we can't change our minds or obsess that there might be something tastier on the menu. We eat what we ordered, and if we don't like it, know that we can change our order the next time we come to the restaurant. We can do the same with selecting products in a store or online. Our objective in speeding up our decision-making is to learn to trust our intuition more and more. For everyday articles, we give ourselves twenty minutes to search online and then stay with the decision. With every decision, we give ourselves a deadline within a sensible amount of time. The more we practice, the better and faster we become. The more we know and experience, the faster our decision-making will be. We practice tuning into our intuition and trusting ourselves. We trust that we'll know in time when the decisions are tough. We have learned how to make intuitive and informed decisions! We don't waver or let our indecisiveness and excuses weaken our resolve or waste our time. Instead, we believe in ourselves and our innate abilities to make good choices on our personal path in life. We know we will find what is right for us, even when it means making the best of any decision we make. An arrow that remains in its quiver hasn't the slightest chance of hitting its mark.

Managing the most precious asset in the world

A common excuse is that we don't have enough time. However, if something urgent comes up, like misplacing our cell phone or car keys, we suddenly have more than enough time to look through our whole house and car. If we are frittering away our time, disrespecting it, acting like it isn't important, then we will have difficulty finding time for the important things in our life. We must **show time our due respect** and give our family, friends, and goals the time they merit. When we **make appointments** and **keep track** of them in our calendars, then we will develop a good relationship with time, and managing it becomes a capability. Another way to make good use of time is to **focus** and prioritize by shutting off all distractions such as social media and the newsfeed. We can manage our large projects without feeling overwhelmed by their enormity if we **chunk** them into manageable pieces that we can work through and then **celebrate** one after the other. When we look at the list of single tasks, the whole project looks more manageable. We can also divide our time into manageable chunks. We don't dread working the whole day if we plan hour-long sessions. We can create more time-consciousness by minding our thoughts and speech too. We can redirect our thinking and talk about how busy we are by focusing on what we enjoy about our projects. It's up to us to recognize that we are living a wonderful, engaging life full of interesting activities and that we can also take time to relax and bring ourselves into balance and flow with it. **Prioritizing** is another time-management tool. We ask ourselves, what is urgent and must be done right away and what can wait? What is important and what less so? We can set the **unimportant and not urgent** tasks aside. The **unimportant and urgent** ones we can delegate, and then we can work on the **important but not urgent ones** since they are usually part of our life goals. The **important, urgent** ones will rise to the surface and demand our attention, so we must handle them with the urgency they demand. Using this **prioritization plan** and delegation, we can effectively and efficiently make progress toward our goals. So, let's eliminate or delegate what we can and dedicate ourselves to what is important in our lives. The shorter the list, the better we feel. And let's always remember that we'll never get everything done and will never be able to do everything alone. Sharing tasks and responsibilities and believing that we aren't the only ones capable of the job helps us advance more quickly toward our goal. We need to stop thinking in extremes. We are neither heroic if we do the task alone nor unlovable if we ask for help.

If we obsessively **preoccupy ourselves with other people's needs**, they'll be happy and constantly ask for more, but we will get nowhere in achieving our own goals. We must each decide how to spend our time. **When we're tired and need a break**, we should take time off. We can return with renewed energy and enthusiasm and work through our tasks more efficiently than when we are exhausted. We don't want to work solely for others; rather, we want to live a fun and meaningful life together with others. When we wake up one day at the end of life and find out we didn't take time to enjoy ourselves or do something meaningful, always at the mercy of what we believed we had to do, we'll realize that something went wrong. If I concentrate only on **what I want**, I will live an egoistic life. If I focus only on **what I believe I should do**, I become duty-bound and rigid. If I let the situation dictate what **I must do,** I may eventually end up as a pessimistic conformist. But if I **combine my desires with meaning and necessity**, I will live a full life. We must make it our priority to have more fun and be more inspired, meaningful, smarter, and relaxed by finding a balance between what we believe we should do, what we want, and what is necessary.

"Coming together is a beginning, staying together is progress, and working together is success."
- Henry Ford

"One finger cannot lift a pebble."
- Hopi proverb

Strong and effective as a team

In his book *The Selfish Gene,* Richard Dawkins describes the **individual as the sole unit of natural selection**. In their *multilevel selection theory,* David Sloan Wilson and Elliot Sober, on the other hand, postulate that there are **different levels of selection, of which the group is also one.** We, as human beings, do not have great natural weaponry, armor, strengths, or speed. One of the things that differentiates us from animals is our ability to reason, plan, and work together. Altruism and compassion are created by our brain's neural network, and those qualities have been favored by natural selection. Human survival depends on our collective abilities and our ability to join with others in pursuing a goal. The **cohesiveness and social resilience** of a group matters. Neuroscientist John Caccioppo says, "Loneliness is such a disabling condition that it compels the belief that the pursuit of relationships is a rock-bottom fundamental to human well-being." The human brain isn't so much a physical problem-solver but a social problem-solver. Our massive frontal cortex is continuously using its billions of connections to simulate social situations and to choose the best course of action. Key components of social resilience are empathy and the capacity to create and sustain positive social relationships, which are essential to being successful in society.

- To **reinforce your belief in your individual power combined with teamwork**, write down a page of memories about a time when you were of value to others working in a team.

"A heart that does what it recommends is truly a good heart."
- Goethe

Five steps for managing challenges in life

When we are caught in a crisis, our thoughts circle around a seemingly unresolvable matter, and we see no way out but to focus intensely on our problem and complain about it. Hence it is important to proactively break out of our maladaptive rumination and crisis dynamics so we can resolve our fixation and its symptoms. We can apply Peseschkian's five steps of conflict resolution.

1. **Distancing**: Our first step in PPT is to say STOP and take a step back to clear our minds. We observe our circling thoughts and become aware of what is happening.

2. **Making an inventory:** We then start to systematically brainstorm, dig into, and analyze the conflict with all its positive and negative aspects, and we write these aspects down.

3. **Situational encouragement**: Once we have a wider perspective and better understanding, we can focus on the encouraging aspects of the problem and our life situation. Then we celebrate the stabilizing resources we discovered. Instead of neglecting them and taking account of only "the more important things" as we have done before, we now engage all our resources to regain energy and motivation.

4. **Verbalization:** After revitalizing ourselves, we now analyze our challenges and develop an understanding of how we can manage the crisis. We identify the relevant tasks and formulate some solutions and the best pathways to reach them.

5. **Broadening of goals**: Since motivation is essential to crisis mastery, we look for a "life-after-crisis" design and visualize it.

Balance in life as a resource in difficult times

As we have previously seen, Peseschkian noticed that when people get into conflict, there are four typical reactions according to individual dispositions. These four reactions can be all characterized as a form of escape. Some people escape from disease or risk behavior through somatization or substance abuse. Others escape into achievement by working excessively long hours, or they refrain from work by failing work expectations or quitting the job. Others escape into loneliness, withdrawing from friends or companionship or, alternatively, they excessively seek consolation or distraction from friends. Some escape into fantasy with daydreaming, religious fervor, and other rituals, or they reject spirituality completely.

Here is a simple example: Just think of someone who has conflicts at work, trying to work harder and harder to please her boss and at the same time neglecting her friends and family. The conflict precipitates headaches, backaches, and eventually sleeplessness and panic attacks. As her symptoms multiply, she loses her optimism for the future. With time, her body feels like she is driving with a pulled emergency brake **(the "hand-brake phenomenon")**. At her work, she will have the impression of having an insurmountable mountain in front of her **(the "mountain phenomenon")**, and in her social life, she will have the sensation of being separated from others by a glass wall **(the "glass-wall phenomenon")**, and in her spiritual life, she sees her future as if through dark glasses **(the "dark-glasses phenomenon")**. If all these phenomena are present at the same time, we recognize depression.

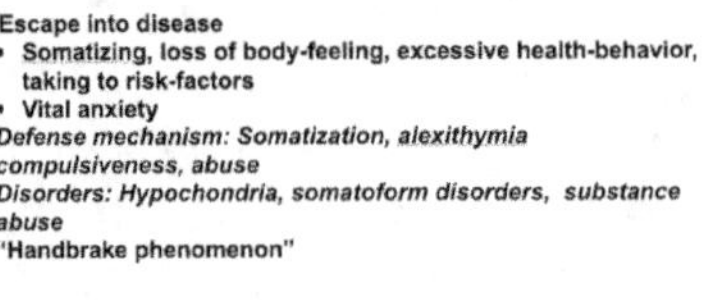

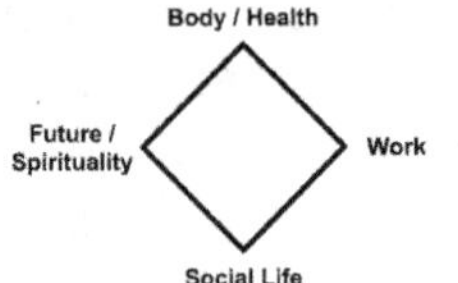

Escape reactions: Four forms of conflict processing as a description of disorders

It is good to have strong dimensions through which we can fortify ourselves and find consolation. This is different from the act of escaping into them. It means having friends and family to talk with, who can empathize and understand and help us solve our problems. We need to be able to find support in our spirituality and seek new ways to solve our problems and forge new creative plans. If we have cultivated the four dimensions, we will cultivate strong health that will see us through the difficulties with, at most, a headache. It is important to use these conflict-processing strategies consciously so we can progress and solve problems where they originate instead of avoiding them and escaping into other dimensions. If we don't, the imbalance will become chronic, and we will get sick.

Facing our problems means we assume responsibility for ourselves; we don't allow others to decide what course we should take. We can create our personal resilience by finding balance and flexibility within ourselves. Life isn't always a piece of cake; we are always faced with challenges. But by taking responsibility for and empowering ourselves and staying solution-oriented through awareness, acceptance, focus, and acting, we can live a happier, more successful, and fulfilled life. If things get to be too much, we can always reduce our load. If we don't overburden ourselves, we can get back to a manageable level. When we empower ourselves, we are operating as proactive optimists. We will be like a Weeble, the toy doll that you knock over, but it always comes back up again. So, when some circumstance knocks us down, let's simply right ourselves by using the energy of the fall to pop back up. Setbacks are feedback, not failure; they teach us how to do things differently, that we must get ourselves together again, draw a new and more detailed map of the situation we want to resolve, and find a new and inspiring way to reach our goal. We must keep our goal in mind while looking for ways over, under, around, or through our difficulties.

We shouldn't stay fixated on the problem, continually butting our heads against it like a bird trying to fly out a closed window while there is an open door nearby. Always remember: It's not about putting on rose-colored glasses but about our **clear view** and **strong attitude**! We don't simply make a wish, put it out to the universe, and expect that our problems will magically disappear, and our wishes will be fulfilled. We actively open our eyes, search for possibilities, and seize them with a proactive, optimistic attitude. If one door closes, three others will open. We must notice them and take responsibility for ourselves.

If one path doesn't work for us, we must try another. If our goal doesn't suit us anymore, we must try to find a new one.

"The pessimist always sees the problem in the opportunity: the optimist the opportunity in the problem."
- Nossrat Peseschkian

For a **pessimist**, problems are here to stay, and they dominate everything. A pessimist also believes he is to blame and he is the problem. For an **optimist**, the problem is temporary, and he will get over it. Optimists realize that problems are a part of life, a single aspect of a rich and wonderful existence. Let's not be like the monkey that closes its eyes and ears and doesn't use its mouth or hands and feet to get what it wants or where it wants to go. The ability to respond to problems is in our hands.

Balance in life is the key to our outer resilience. Keeping our four dimensions of life balanced is essential. These are the practiced resources that strengthen our resilience—living them intensely and consciously leads to fulfillment.

Who walks in the rhythm of his life never gets tired. Another part of the principle of balance is finding our equilibrium between **process-orientation** and **goal-orientation**. If we take only our path as our goal, meandering around and getting lost, we might be missing the sense of our life and feel lost and sad. On the other hand, if we work ourselves to death, we might die without having lived and fall into despair. We always have a choice. With process orientation, we can be on a path toward our life goals and enjoy every step of the way. We must find our personal balance between the two. So, let's take time for introspection to build our confidence and allow time to compliment the people we know.

We can make it a habit at the end of the day to assess. We can look at what we can be proud of, where we can do better, and how we can become more in balance with ourselves and life. Our self-improvement is essential for growing and keeping balance in life and, at the same time, our ability to lead. To become stronger, more resilient, and in balance with life, we can learn from strong leaders, who are self-confident and, at the same time, humane and resting within themselves. Let's be reminded that the way we treat others will always affect our personal success. When we make it a habit to help others and compliment them on their successes, we know that we are forging friendships and partnerships that will be pillars of our well-being and future success.

"Nobody knows what he is able to do until he tries it."
- Publius Strauss

Self-esteem and self-control

Having healthy self-esteem means we can look in the mirror and affirm our reflection. We can also accept our individuality with all its capabilities, personality traits, feelings, and needs. We accept and love who we are with all our quirks and challenges. We must give ourselves the same kind of importance we give others and not disregard our own needs.

Self-esteem means we acknowledge both our strengths and weaknesses. High self-esteem doesn't mean that we ignore or repress our idiosyncrasies but that we are conscious of them and accept them. When we are confident, we can have open, forthright relationships with our fellow human beings. Our sense of self-esteem is a sort of **psychological immune system** that defends us from outer attacks and humiliations and gives us faith in ourselves in times of crisis. People with healthy self-esteem have an armor against unjustified insults; unkind remarks just bounce off them, while someone with low self-esteem lets these poisonous arrows go straight to their heart. Having true self-esteem means to value ourselves and by doing so, being able to value others. A person of worth does not have to belittle others to feel bigger.

"Beliefs have the power to create and the power to destroy. Humans have the fantastic ability to take whatever experiences they have in their lives and give them a sense that consumes them or literally saves their lives."
- Anthony Robbins

What we think of ourselves, who we believe we are, is only a figment of our mind, created at a given moment in time. It is only an incomplete image of our true self. Most of us believe we are as limited as our internal image, that nothing can change and will ever change. Whatever we believe about ourselves is what we have perceived and isn't the whole picture. Who or what instilled these beliefs? Many people and multiple experiences have contributed to our self-image—our family, culture, whoever and whatever surrounded us, and all the experiences we have gone through on our way. Usually, we were taught with the best intentions. But not everything taught with the best intention is the best for our growth. Along with all our abilities, we have also absorbed all the individual and collective fears and insecurities that limit us. Many of these fears and insecurities were unique to their time and no longer seem relevant. Without even being aware and noticing, we've made them ours. Our parents probably loved us dearly, so they tried to protect us as best they could, admonishing us and transmitting to us all their fears of what might harm us. They conveyed their **potentiating beliefs**—ideas that help us believe in our capabilities and realize ourselves, as well as their **limiting beliefs**—the ideas that make us feel insecure and incapable and that repress our inner potential.

"Convictions are more dangerous enemies of truth than lies."
- Nietzsche

Consider the following story, a parable about beliefs that were helpful to us at the time we acquired them, but that we continue carrying around with us later, long after they have lost their value:

A man, walking on a journey, arrives at a wide and deep river he cannot wade across. Frustrated but not despairing, he continues walking along the riverside, where he discovers a canoe that enables him to reach the other bank. Elated to have made the crossing, he decides to portage the watercraft. He continues over mountains, deserts, and wide prairies for years, all the time carrying the heavy canoe on his shoulders. Although it has become a burden, he continues to shoulder it, because he remembers that the vessel had once been a lifesaver.
- Retold after an Indian story

A healthy inner dialogue for sustaining self-worth

"A mistake becomes a truth when the whole world believes in it."
- Mahatma Gandhi

If we really want to make our dreams come true, we must have a clear vision of how we will attain them. We must start believing in ourselves beforehand and do so by steadfastly going back to the vision of ourselves as a strong and able personality who has a **vision** of a more prosperous life. With **strong motivation**, we can overcome any limiting subconscious beliefs. Yet, subconscious limiting beliefs are very obstinate; they are the old life-vest that served us in the past. If we want to let go of these life-vests and swim toward our goals, we must have the courage to dive in and swim unaided.

The more we can envision the way we want to be and where we want to go, the faster we will get there. Initial progress may seem slow, but it is exponential. We can compare the process to ice on the windowpane in wintertime, which starts to form slowly and then spreads rapidly. A prerequisite for success is to envision beforehand and experience the power, capabilities, and creativity of changing our thinking and opening ourselves to the myriad possibilities before us, allowing them to show us the way. All we need is the faith to change. We know the direction we are sailing, and we can become "Peloponnesian sailors," jumping from island to island, from subgoal to subgoal towards our destiny.

We need **steadfast determination** to make this journey. If we resolve to keep an attitude of openness and internal power and high spirits, we will find our way. As Albert Einstein put it: "The world as we know it is a process of our thinking. It cannot be changed without changing our thinking." So take hold of our steering wheel or our mind. Even if it means "Fake it till we make it." We will see the results when we audaciously resolve to give our best and maintain a good attitude.

We can work on our brighter future by immediately **changing little things**. Then the big changes will arrive more easily—many just seem to fall into place. One of the things we can do is to improve our environment by making our house or our office more inviting day by day. It is important to start right away and to act continuously so we can see the progress persistent action produces. It is important that we don't just try to try. No, rather than try, we must just do it! If we try doing something, simply trying will always be in the back of our head, not the obstinate decision, "I will do it." If we act, we can refer to trying in the past tense: "I tried and succeeded."

"The most effective way to do something is simply to do it."
- Amelia Earhart

So, when we get start on a project, we start with the hardheaded decision to succeed, not just an indecisive wavering attitude of trying. This will make a big difference in our outcome and make success even more imperative. If, in any case, we don't succeed, we can always look back on it as a wholehearted attempt.

Our **everyday self-talk** creates our reality. When we want to change our behavior, we first must change our inner monologues. Once we've created **new mantras** and have gotten into the energy work, the feeling of engraining them into our subconscious, we can act. We also practice habitually focusing on the good, doing the things we love to do, and making the effort to go forward so we don't fall back into our habits.

We continuously strive to **improve our routines** by regularly adapting them to new ideas and trying to do something new every day. This way, we will continuously grow and be amazed by the new realities we discover along our path.

When we ask ourselves who we are, we don't focus on any of the limiting beliefs that keep us from living a happy, fulfilled, and peaceful life. Essentially, we are wonderful beings who go far beyond our own limited visions. We have more depth and capabilities than we alone can recognize.

It's important to be conscious of how we speak to ourselves and others. The **power of language** is immense; changing it will change our lives. If our thoughts revolve around being tired all day, and we continuously tell ourselves and others around us that we are tired, how could we be anything but tired? If we open our eyes to life and change our self-talk, repeating the words "I feel great, rested, bursting with energy, and ready to embrace my new day," we will see a change in attitude immediately. Within a short period of time, our whole life situation can appear different. Through the repetitive use of **emotional images**, we can produce the positive feelings we associate with these images, although initially, our state of mind may have been negative. We can actively decide to discover ourselves and mold a more generous vision of ourselves, which we then confirm with affirmations. Through repeated autosuggestion, these **affirmations** strengthen our positive stance.

To eliminate negative emotional habits, we can learn to lean into new equilibrating ones. When we are afraid, we can say, "I am confident." When we feel tired, we can say, "I am full of energy." We can influence our whole life through the images we create and the language of our inner dialogue. It is always important to listen to ourselves to determine what we need. If we change our self-talk and bring it in line with the vision of how we want to live and with the genuine person we are, we change our false inner beliefs. If we confront our reality with a more positive vision of ourselves, our false inner beliefs will fade into the background.

"It doesn't matter if you believe you'll make it or not, you will always be right."
- Henry Ford

At the same time, we must broaden our perspectives and abandon our limiting tunnel vision. **We should distinguish between characterizing our misdeeds as personal flaws, inherent parts of our being, and see them instead for what they are: temporary acts**. Rather than saying, "I'm stupid," one should say, "I behaved stupidly." We can criticize our acts but not our being. In the same way, we should not tell our children, "You are lazy." It is preferable to say, "You are acting a bit lazy today." We **shouldn't label** our kids because these labels can evolve into lifelong limiting and destructive beliefs. It is important to be just as lovable to ourselves as we are to our children. When we notice that we are pinning some negative attribute on ourselves, we can focus on a particular action instead: Rather than condemn ourselves for forgetting a parent's birthday, we can say, "Oops, I forgot Mom's birthday yesterday, but I will make amends and make it up to her with a nice compliment and a song, and then we'll have an evening at the restaurant she loves." We can **change from negative speech about ourselves to talking nicely to ourselves**.

An important rule for affirming self-talk is to **never generalize**. When we believe something is a rule, we eliminate all other possibilities. Instead, we can adopt a beginner's mind, observing each situation as a unique opportunity for good. We can revise a generalization, "Money is bad," into "Money is energy, with which I can do good things." Or convert "Love makes me suffer" into "The right love will make me happy." Or turn "Religion is for fanatics or the ignorant" into "Spirituality is my connection to life and the universe, and it gives me power." Or "All women are the same" into "The right person is out there, and I'll find her with time."

We can also respond to requests more responsibly by saying **"I don't want to" instead of "I can't"** because the first response gives us more autonomy. When we say, "I can't," we express an inability to comply with an obligation, whereas when we say, "I don't want to," we personally make the decision. We can also change "I have to" or "I must" into "I have the chance to" and "I will." Saying "I must" implies an obligation, and we humans prefer choices.

Another way to achieve positive self-talk is to **externalize**. Expressing that something negative exists externally and not internally is very healthy as well. Rather than saying, "My thoughts depress me," one can say, "There are so many thoughts rushing through my mind that I feel sad."

We decide to be responsible people by **taking care of ourselves**. It usually isn't difficult to do this now and then, but it's difficult to make it a habit. It's similar to bringing order to our office—it may not be big a task in the beginning, but making a habit of orderliness is. Once it becomes a habit, though, it feels easy again. Our lives, like Rome, weren't built in a day, but day by day and belief by belief, our thoughts can resonate within us word by word as repetitive thought-trains.

We can do a **daily analysis of our thoughts** to find out what is significantly affecting and altering our lives at the given moment. We are usually in automatic mode and don't reflect on our thoughts. Little changes in our thought stream can generate big differences. Consider the "butterfly effect" theory, which describes how a butterfly flapping its wings can cause a typhoon on the other side of the world.

Our conscious thoughts can impact our behaviors and lifestyle. To create lasting personal health habits, we begin with our thoughts. With **positive self-talk**, we begin to open ourselves up to new paths and possibilities, a whole new world. The converse is true as well. If our inner critic dominates, we close off the world. The words we use against ourselves are like an infection, a virus that we caught somewhere and that we carry around. We repeat phrases that are harming us, such as "Oh, you're such an idiot! You'll never amount to anything" or "Ahh, you've screwed up again; you'll never make a relationship work."

We can reflect on the reversed versions of these negative inner dialogues and look at ourselves from a different angle or a different situation and then create a new positive inner mantra. We can let go of our old refrain of self-fulfilling prophecies and create a new frame of mind: "I am intelligent and creative. I will surely find my individual path!" "I've made my best friends happy, and I can surely make my partner happy." "I may have messed up, but I will try until I succeed."

The five big developmental blockages

According to the psychiatrist Dr. Michael Bohne, these are the "five developmental blockages" that keep us from becoming mature, achieving our goals, and having strong self-esteem. The **big five** are:

1. **Blaming myself**: "I am an idiot; I am always the cause of problems." This is the best way of conserving inner pain.

2. **Blaming others**: "You were always the cause of my pain, and you should have treated me better." It may feel good to be righteous, and we want to get justice or even vengeance, but this keeps us imprisoned if we don't and can't.

3. **Expectations of others**: "You should help me on this project." This surely seems logical and plausible, but what happens if they simply don't do what we expect them to? We become addicted to the support of others.

4. **Everyday life regression**: "When I talk to my boss, I somehow feel like a small child." We shrink to a younger age and feel smaller, even though we are mature adults. This is a trance phenomenon.

5. **Dysfunctional loyalties**: "I have to study and work in this profession to continue the family tradition." When we do what others expect us to do—maybe our mother or father or grandparents—we disrespect our own desires.

We all have situations in which we suddenly feel insecure, weak, incapable, smaller, and younger than we are. We blame ourselves and others for our problems and expect others to resolve them (but they never do); we act loyally to others but are often disloyal to ourselves. These blockages come up in different situations and context and with different people. The thoughts, feelings, physical sensations, and self-sabotaging blocks rob us of our energy and weigh us down. Anger and bitterness sustain depression and undermine well-being. The stories we have around some topics are often just our own fictional accounts, and they can be rewritten. They are like chronic infections we do not treat.

Although our inner blockages and unhealthy strategies keep us from being happy and flourishing, we gain unconsciously from them and the stories we tell ourselves about them. That's why we keep them rather than discard them. We made them into habits for some positive reasons, hidden in the past, and we continue benefiting by telling false stories about them because we don't know any better or so we don't have to become conscious and admit they might not be true. If we become sick and depressed, lose our job, fail in a relationship, or our plans go up in fumes, we must get up again, roll up our sleeves, meet people, and risk getting hurt and failing again. There is no way around it.

Regarding Bohne's second blockage, it is cozy in the position of a victim, blaming others for our failures and not having to commit ourselves. As victims, we overly rely on others' compassion, attention, and help. We often don't notice it, but the indirect rewards of continuously going in circles with our stories often blind us and keep us from finding the right direction.

We can change our attitude through the thoughts and language we use about ourselves and others. We can take responsibility for our lives and care more for ourselves. We can discard our old stories.

If we think any one or more of these blockages are adversely affecting our own maturity levels, we can examine them.

Creating self-esteem by changing our false beliefs with a modification of Michael Bohne's Process and Embodiment Psychology

What are the stories that keep circling in our heads, that keep us down and keep us from developing?

1. We brainstorm freely and write about our **"self-esteem-thieves"** in our journal—the topics that circle around in our heads, weigh us down, and trouble us emotionally.

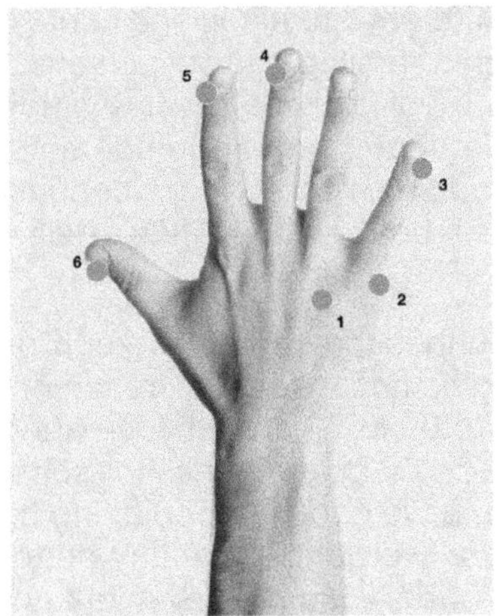

Adobe Stock Prostock-Studio

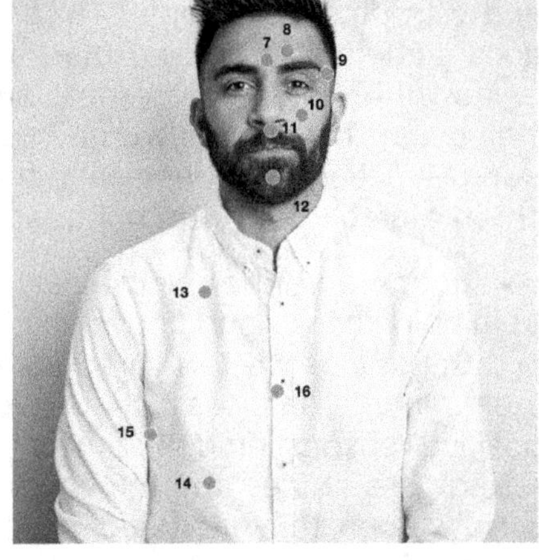

Adobe Stock Krakenimages.com

2. When we stumble on a topic that awakens strong fear or other overburdening emotions, we can look squarely at the topic while simultaneously resorting to **tapping the acupuncture points** on our fingers, head, and chest (in the order seen in the diagram) while concentrating on the tapping. We will notice immediate relief because our brain only has a certain capacity for processing information and by concentrating intensely on tapping the acupuncture points, we reduce the space our fear can occupy. We crowd our fear out. Furthermore, since the acupuncture points have big representational areas in our brain, the stimulation is more intense than in other places on the body. The physical stimulation overrides our overactive limbic system more easily, and our prefrontal cortex regains control faster. Physical tapping usually helps calm oneself down quickly and offers quick relief for emotional topics. With the experience of self-calming comes the experience of self-effectiveness, memory tracks in our brain are overwritten with the new experience of this memory (the memory with the tapping experience), making it more bearable and manageable. We can use this technique purposefully for working on basic emotional topics or emotional situations that we experience every day. For more complex ones, it is important to work on the big five developmental blockages, and if one is traumatic, it is important to get professional help.

3. When we have written down our "self-esteem-thieves," we go through these false stories one by one, searching for their **false benefits** and touching ourselves in the area between our heart and shoulder (see picture) in a circling motion like a caress while we say aloud: "Although I believe ... (the false belief), **I love and accept myself just the way I am, and I stay in my strength and security**!" We go through the whole list, one by one, saying this phrase for each. For example: "Although I believe I can't handle difficult situations and I panic, I love and accept myself as I am, and I stay in my strength and security!"

4. We then create strong, passionate **self-esteem affirmations** or power phrases that can substitute our old **cognococci** (thought infections/false beliefs). "I am a strong, intelligent person and can manage difficult situations, as I have done so many times in the past." Nossrat Peseschkian called these healing affirmations **psycho-serums** and employed them for healing.

5. We **repeat our new affirmations** in the morning and the evening during the day, over and over, until they become the empowering truth of our inside world.

Example of addressing the energy-robbing thoughts of a school-teacher with a fear of teaching:

1. Brainstorm or journal freely about "**self-esteem thieves.**"

2. Look fear in the eyes and **tap it away** when we stumble on sensitive topics.

3. Look through our stories and truths; **look at the benefits** we receive from them and **give ourselves love, strength, and autonomy**. For example...

    a. Looking through our **stories and truths**:

"I am really worthless as a teacher." (=> "But somehow my colleagues do ask me for advice") (*Blaming myself*)

"I'm such a fraud." (=> "But somehow, I passed all my exams at school and college and am a teacher now.") (*Blaming myself*)

"If the parents would take better care of their children, teaching would be easier, and I wouldn't worry about how I am relating to all my students." (=> "Sometimes I expect too much.") (*Blaming others*)

"The parents should respect my efforts! They shouldn't take out their frustrations with their children on me." (=> "I always expect it, but it never happens.") (*Expectations*)

"I am afraid standing in front of the class, and sometimes I shrink and feel incompetent" (=> "But I keep managing it every day and then I'm happy.") (*Regression*)

"Nobody likes me; the kids hate me." (=> "Although the kids give me gifts for Christmas.") (*Blaming myself*)

"I'm so afraid of failing my students." (=> "Although I prepare well and more conscientiously than my colleagues.") (*Blaming myself*)

"Someday I will fail." (=> "Somehow, I made it through the last fifteen years.") (*Blaming myself*)

"I never have time for myself. I follow in the steps of my father, who was a workaholic." (=> "Actually, I really dedicate a lot of time to the children.") (*Dysfunctional loyalty*)

b.   We look for the **benefit we get out of it**:

"I am afraid of admitting I am good. People could have expectations of me. And I want to be better than others. Maybe this is narcissism I want to conceal. I don't want to be envied."

c.   And **giving ourselves love, strength, and security** for each one of the false beliefs:

"Although I believe I am really worthless as a teacher, I love and accept myself just the way I am and stay in my strength and security!"

"Although I believe I am such a fraud, I love and accept myself just the way I am and stay in my strength and security!"

And so forth for each of her false beliefs...

4.   **Creating new affirmations**:

"I am a dedicated, well-educated, and lovable teacher who really cares for her current and former students and deserves to be seen as such!"

"I am proud of what I have achieved in life, and a little pride and admiration will make me feel good. As for my students, they will be even happier to learn from a happy, fearless teacher."

"I also have the right to leisure time, relaxation, and fun, so I follow my own path. My father can be proud of me anyway!"

"Whenever I feel incapable and immature, I have the tools to return to my actual capability and maturity readily."

"I am a happy, lovable teacher, and my family and friends support me."

An excellent book for working more intensely with Process and Embodiment Psychology is *Bitte Klopfen* (*Please Tap*) by Dr. Michael Bohne.

How to systematically search for and find our false beliefs

We can systematically search for false beliefs by going through our four dimensions:

- Who do we believe we are? What do we believe is life?
- What are our beliefs about our bodies, health, and sexuality?
- What are our beliefs about our profession, money, work-life balance, and teamwork?
- What are our beliefs about our friendships, family, and love?
- What are our beliefs about our spirituality, hobbies, and plans?

We then work through Michael Bohne's technique for creating self-esteem.

Creating self-esteem with a thankfulness diary

One way of strengthening our self-esteem, our appreciation of ourselves, and what we experience in life is through writing ten things we are thankful, happy, and proud about every evening. By focusing on gratitude, we are not omitting our difficulties and disappointments but transforming or reframing them. Instead of asking, "Why did this happen to me?" we ask, "How can I learn from this?" When we have high self-esteem, feel self-efficacy, and act like a proactive optimist, we see positive experiences as consequences of our own actions, which in turn heightens our self-esteem.

Negative experiences don't need to have such a big impact on us; they can be ascribed to external circumstances. Pessimists with low self-esteem and a low sense of self-efficacy experience the exact opposite. They ascribe the good things that happen to them to the action of others and the bad things to their own account, and therefore they tend to get sucked into a downward spiral of negative thinking about themselves. "Reality is merely an illusion, albeit a very persistent one," Albert Einstein wrote. Self-esteem is a product of our own healthy thoughts and feelings about ourselves; there is no objective sense of self-worth but only a subjective experience of how we have experienced ourselves reflected by others. Self-concepts aren't stable; they are context-dependent and can change with time.

There are situations and contexts within the four dimensions of life where we feel at home and have strong self-worth, and in others, we feel less confident. Our self-esteem also varies depending on the people we are around.

The use of anchors in everyday life for consciously getting back to resourceful states

When we get up in the morning and feel down, we can envision how moving our bodies will help us wake up and energize us. We visualize this experience mentally before getting up and then moving about much easier. Our mental state is fundamentally dependent on what we are expressing with our thoughts, emotions, and body in each moment we are living. During the day, our mental states are in constant flux. Just recall the common situation when a parent sees her daughter coming home. The teen is feeling down and doesn't want to do anything but lie down in bed. Suddenly, a text message from her heartthrob brings about an instantaneous change of mood. She jumps up and starts dancing. Our mood fluctuates and changes at various times during the day, even from moment to moment. In the morning, we may be in an exuberant mental state, and in the evening, fall into a depressive one. We might be sad, and then, when our best friend calls, our spirits lift. Our minds may be full of terrible ideas in one moment, and then, after a meaningful conversation, all these depressive fantasies evaporate and disappear.

A nice tune that we recognize on the radio or the scent of a delicious cake in a restaurant may carry us back in time to a wonderful experience. It lets us relive the memories and emotions from that period within ourselves. A song and a wonderful scent are examples of **anchors.** The same thing can happen with other sensory triggers that are also unconscious anchors. Most importantly, we can create conscious triggers to alter our state of mind when we are down. Our personal conscious anchors bring us into a desired state of mind whether it is happiness, power, peace, or security that we need. For example, we can use conscious anchors as we prepare for a sports competition or a presentation to release our greatest power and potential.

Creating an anchor

We must know what state of mind we want to achieve and where we have already experienced it. Then we can go into meditation and recreate this state. We must internally connect to it with all our five senses by remembering everything we experienced initially.

We recall the immediate surroundings and landscape, all the colors, scents, and sounds. Once we make a sensory reconnection (for example, tranquility), we make a subtle, inconspicuous gesture with our hand or foot (touch our ear, cross our legs, or so on). We imagine a word and a color that fit the sensation and continue focusing on our internal imagery for a few minutes, uniting our elevated emotion with the word, color, and physical gesture. When we finish our meditation, we smile, move, look about, and maybe even dance or sing. Then, after a few minutes, we meditate again. We repeat the process a few times so it becomes rooted and can easily be reproduced.

There are manifold anchors we can create to help ourselves in difficult, challenging situations or to relax quickly. We can create as many anchors as we want and need to remind us of tranquility, love, power, or security. In the beginning, let's create only one anchor and practice bringing it to mind at least once a day.

We can then create as many as we need according to the situation where we need support. We write down the times when we could use anchors and start the process of creating them, think of where we could use them right away, write them down, and practice.

Staying strong with composure instead of regressing under stress

Self-esteem and composure are closely related. When our self-esteem is strong, we deflect verbal attacks as with a shield, and we don't take them personally. We are in our balance, remaining self- and not other-related. The often-used playground rebuttal applies: "Sticks and stones can break my bones, but words can never hurt me."

When someone pushes our buttons, we feel we are under attack; inner wounds are triggered, and we tend to identify with the attacks. Then our self-esteem falls apart, and we regress to a younger age. One of the best defenses is to heal our emotional wounds so people can't hurt us. We heal by finding consolation and understanding and by changing our faulty credos by creating and repeating affirmations. These steps strengthen our self-esteem, so we become less sensitive.

We can also use a **rapid self-defense method** to protect ourselves from emotional harm. First, we must learn how to quickly become aware of the emotional vortex that has triggered our descent before. Secondly, we must practice a rapid self-defense technique so we can get out of our paralysis immediately. The moment we notice that we are regressing to a younger age, when we start to feel vulnerable and small, we can say "Stop!" and, in our imagination, take a step forward toward our true age, strength, and maturity. We raise one hand as a shield, or we bring our whole body into the fighting position of a **Tai Chi master,** ready to deflect whatever aggression is coming. This way, we can stop identifying with the defamations and being pulled into a rabbit hole of fear. We need to practice this technique regularly so it becomes a reflexive anchor. We do so by repeatedly embodying the pose we want as a mental attitude in our mind through physically acting it out, role-playing our internal measures, and experiencing them with our whole physical body. We stand erect and take a step forward to a position of strength and maturity. If necessary, we can go as far as assuming the position of a Tai Chi master, ready to react and dodge while still staying receptive and objective, reading the incoming messages of the underlying feelings and needs of our counterpart.

Embodying what we want to create as inner pictures and future visualizations helps us activate our resilience and maintain assurance and sovereignty.

Another useful picture is to imagine ourselves in an **impenetrable bubble** or in a combat suit that protects us from harm. We learn to become aware of downward spirals and get out of them by catching ourselves before we fall, sidestepping them, or simply stepping out to avoid the painful drama. We refocus on the things we want. We must patiently persevere and trust in the process.

We shouldn't let ourselves be driven by the fear that others will laugh at or berate us; we should not give a damn about what others think of us. The only things we should care about are if what we are doing or wanting will take us in the direction we want to go. And here we are, not talking about that if someone will feel offended. Since everyone interprets things differently, **we can't be responsible for everyone's feelings** about our actions. But we do need to consider if our actions could really hurt someone. We want to be independent, stick up for ourselves, and not base our self-worth on others' opinions. We can ask ourselves why we are doing what we are doing. If our reasons are to be liked, get rid of insecurity, or take revenge, we should reconsider our actions. If, however, we are acting based on our personal motivation to follow and develop our talents, inspirations, and inner calling, we should continue. We can let our intuition guide us by connecting to ourselves in a quiet moment. We can always feel good and be proud of ourselves if we do something with integrity, based on our values, and in the best way we can. Although we learn to be more and more independent of others, we can at the same time benefit from the external input we get by **taking criticism constructively** and evaluating the sincerity of compliments by asking, "Can these comments help me or others develop?" If so, if others can help us dedicate ourselves to making a change in our lives to become a happier and fuller version of ourselves, it is worth listening to them.

Having an inner mentor, a role model, always by our side

When we want to **develop a characteristic**, it is helpful to look for people who already have the excellence we are seeking and to observe their behavior closely so we can understand their ideas, beliefs, speech, and behavior regarding our objective. It's up to us if we want to work on ourselves to acquire the excellence another has already mastered. People who have the attributes we are hoping to incorporate into our lives become **role models** for us. They can also be a mentor or coach whom we can ask for advice when we can't solve an issue. Role models can be a person from real life or fiction or even an avatar that we invent to support and advise us as needed. If we want to become an entrepreneur like Richard Branson, we can be attentive to his unique behavior patterns. If we want to be courageous, we can consider what a brave person like Reinhold Messner would do in our situation. If we want a spiritual guide, we could read Thích Nhất Hạnh. Through our alter ego, we acquire his strengths and feel that we handle the situation by enthusiastically looking through a different lens. We observe the way he thinks, talks, and acts, and we try to do the same.

- **Establishing our inner mentor:** For establishing our inner mentor, we get into our usual meditative state by sitting upright and relaxed; we inhale and exhale a couple of times and then imagine our mentor with his physique, dress, manners, facial expressions, movements, core values, and emotions. We envision as complete an image as possible so we can have him present in the future when we need him. When we head into challenges, we can open ourselves up, and instead of focusing only on the difficulties, we see all the opportunities around us. We can even invent a whole council of advisers based on the people we admire, each one to use in a different situation.

The four phases of learning

Learning all these coaching techniques will take time, but learning is an inherent and natural process. Because life is in constant flux, learning and unlearning are continuous and necessary processes.

From birth onward, we adapt to our environment and must learn useful skills and then unlearn them again to replace them with new skills as we tread new paths and open ourselves to new possibilities. Our unconscious contains and **elaborates** much more information than our conscious. Of what we perceive, **12%** is elaborated **consciously**, some **88% unconsciously**. Most of what we process from moment to moment are contents arising from within ourselves. Our subconscious continuously keeps us alive by managing all the vital processes (heartbeat, breathing, digestion). When learning or reading a book, we are assimilating the information consciously and unconsciously simultaneously. Past experiences are stored in our subconscious without our conscious recall. Remembering everything consciously would be a burden and not leave room and openness in our mind for the important. Whatever we gather in our subconscious can be either a motivation or an obstacle for us. The enormously expansive world is too complex for consciousness to grasp it in its totality.

We humans tend to believe that the only things that exist are in our conscious mind, but consciousness is only the tip of the iceberg. Noel Burch describes **four phases of competence,** which include the unconscious. The path we take when learning is from **unconscious incompetence** (we are ignorant that we have something new to learn) to **conscious incompetence** (we are aware and recognize that there is no way around it, maybe rebelling against it or opening ourselves with curious joyfulness to the new). Then we move into a mode of **conscious competence** where we are learning, but every action is still a conscious process. Finally, we achieve **unconscious competence** or mastery, when the skill has become a habitual, unconscious process. Remember when we learned to drive a car? As a child, we were ignorant of it, but as we matured, we realized that it was a necessary skill. We became conscious of our incompetence, so we signed up for driving lessons. At first, driving required all our focus and conscious attention. We were aware of turning the wheel, adjusting the stick shift, and pumping the brake. But with time, everything became so routine that we were able to talk to someone while driving. With patience and perseverance, our emotional health can follow this pattern as well.

"It's not bad to fall down as long as you get up again."
- Nossrat Peseschkian

Working with defeat

Instead of looking at what and how we have "failed" at something, we can see it as a temporary hurdle, as a point of reevaluation and considering how to do things differently, where we can ask ourselves what we have learned in the last months. Our consideration directs our focus onto the process and away from the result. Michael Jordan, for example, missed the basket 9000 times, lost 300 games, and missed the deciding point 26 times. Failure, he concluded, probably made him a winner. Years later, our "failures" appear in a different light. We often say, "I'm lucky this happened to me years ago." If only we could apply that future perspective to a current crisis, we might see a crisis for what it is: a watershed or turning point.

Many of us are stuck and languishing in life. Too often, we don't dare to go beyond our comfort zones and risk failure. We feel secure within our comfort zones. However, if we don't see new horizons and face new challenges, there will be no personal development. If we really want to get out of our comfort zone, we must pose the question of what is important and worthwhile to us. We must be conscious of and give the necessary priority to what we value. **Important** things are related to our essential meaning in life but often need longer time periods to be realized. Therefore, we often postpone them and do what seems more **urgent** and pressing to us. Things usually become urgent issues if we don't do anything about them, but we get less credit for doing things right away. It is the silent runners who usually make things work and are the foundation of society and every business, although the emergency rescuers are usually the ones to be remembered. But this shouldn't keep us from doing the things important to us because, in the long run, they are the most gratifying. Walt Disney said that **when our priorities—the things that are important to us—are clear, it is easy to make decisions**. In getting what is important to us, we want to be **effective** because this gets us closer to our goal and **efficient** at the same time, because we are making good use of our resources. We aren't effective if we don't get closer to our goal. And we aren't efficient if what we do isn't useful in advancing us toward our goal. Most of us intend to do what we believe is right, but we aren't conscious of what we are doing. We try to be effective, but often we don't look up to see where the ladder is leading; we may be efficient but going in a direction we don't really intend to go. Therefore, the **quality of our life depends on finding our direction and using our energy wisely**. We will still encounter plenty of unexpected detours along the way.

We can remember the following principles:

- Things get **urgent and pressing** if we don't do anything about them, which then becomes stressful.

- The **earlier we complete our tasks** and solve our problems, the better. If we get active before it gets urgent, it takes less effort, and we achieve better results. This is a sort of double-lever effect. Just think of buying presents the day before Christmas with all the hassle of long lines. We are faster and less stressed if we buy presents beforehand or when we see something nice and fitting for our loved ones.

At the same time, **often it is only pressure that gets us going** since urgent things trigger an alarm in our limbic system. So, if we want to accelerate things that aren't urgent, since there is no external pressure, we must make them urgent for ourselves, **motivate ourselves**. And remember, as Harry S. Truman said, "If you don't have your own goals, you will be doomed to work toward someone else's." Mark Twain aptly remarked, "When we lose our goal from sight, we redouble our efforts." One of the purposes of setting goals is establishing motivation and getting away from immediate gratification. The ability to set objectives and follow them through is a sign of maturity.

"If I had six hours to chop down a tree, I'd spend the first four sharpening the axe."
- Abraham Lincoln

Personal mastery and resilience

In his book *Flourish*, Martin Seligman notes that having a so-called **positive character,** as Lincoln called it in the nineteenth century, is a helpful trait for leading a healthy, prosperous, and happy life. In Lincoln's day, politics, morality, and psychology were all attributed to the character. His inaugural speech addressed the "better angels of our nature" and made each individual responsible for his own destiny. After the events on Haymarket Square in 1886 in Chicago, when labor unions sought to bring more justice to the working class with bloody protests as a result, a turning point came for this perspective. It wasn't the **character** anymore that made for the difficult destiny of an individual; instead, the **environment** was the key to producing prosperity or crime. It was a great change in paradigm, and individuals were not held responsible for their actions. The environment, which had a positive or negative influence on them, was the cause of all difficulties. Therefore, Seligman describes the **psychology of victims** and psychopathology caused by the environment as a result of Haymarket Square. But as true as this new perspective— making **society accountable** for the well-being of man— was at the time, we also must see how failure and success do stem in due part from the character of the individual, not only from the system. **We have both influences and need strong individuals in a just and prosperous society**. As Seligman demonstrates, in a family with abusive parents, usually one child fails in life, one makes it through with complications, and one has the resilience to get out of the mess his parents created and lead a successful and happy life.

Learned helplessness: In the laboratory, Seligman has shown that dogs, rats, mice, and even cockroaches **become passive and give up in the face of adversity** once they have first experienced **noxious events that they cannot control**. Humans react similarly in experiments. People who believe the causes of their setbacks in life are temporary and changeable do not readily become helpless. People who believe a situation is going to last forever will undermine everything; they believe there's nothing they can do about it and become helpless. Research indicates that pessimists are far more prone to depression than optimists.

However, **mastery strengthens a person**, as the following experiments have shown. In an experiment, rats that had been implanted with a tumor with a 50% mortality rate were submitted to painful electrical shocks. One group had escapable painful shocks, a second inescapable painful shocks, and a third, the control group, received no shocks. In the first group with the escapable shocks, only 25% died. In the second with inescapable ones, 75% died, and in the control group, 50% died. An investigation of those suffering from cardiovascular diseases had similar results; it showed that **optimism is the greatest factor for surviving** longer. No other risk factor, such as blood sugar or high cholesterol, predicted health or death as strongly. Of the 16 most pessimistic men, 15 died. Of the 16 most optimistic men, only 5 died.

It has also been proven that positivity helps in improving flu symptoms. Even faking positive emotions helps. So, in essence, we recognize that **what we think and feel influences our future. Optimism might be a distortion of reality, but since it makes positive outcomes more probable, it's advisable to embrace optimism.**

"I am all for realism when there is a knowable reality out there that is not influenced by your expectations. When your

expectations influence reality, realism sucks!"
- Martin Seligman

The key to reaching our goals

If we are to be **motivated and not dependent on immediate grat-ification,** the goal must be attractive to us. *Why do I want to get there?* If we have set an **attractive goal**, we can then **visualize** it so we can gain energy by seeing it before our internal eyes whenever we need to. We can establish some **rewards** for achieving different **milestones**, which provide intermittent satisfaction. We have to be aware of and calculate **the cost** of reaching our goal and ask our-selves beforehand if it is worth all the effort we must put into it. And if it doesn't work out, was it worthwhile? Once we have done this, we write out our **plan** by defining our milestones with dates and possible rewards. That way, we will make a real **commitment**. If we hesitate because of fear, we must remember that we miss 100% of the shots we never take. And remember that continuous success isn't possible either. We will always have moments of doubt and moments in which we believe we failed. But if we get up, reevalu-ate, and start going again, we really will make our way. We should work with **high self-motivation paired with an excellent mood**. If we maintain our motivation and mood, we will notice our success grow-ing like the frost flowers on a windowpane. Success follows success, and it grows faster and faster.

But we must take care! Danger lurks when we become **dependent on our successes,** and we work ourselves into **burnout**. We must keep in balance with life, using all our four dimensions as resources for health, success, and happiness. That way, we will always be full of energy and high-spirited, and when we have difficulties, we will always have someone or some resource to turn to. We always seek to work, efficiently, effectively, smart—and not hard.

On average, our mood determines more than 70% of how much life satisfaction we report. How well we judge our present life deter-mines less than 30%. So, life satisfaction is disproportionately tied to mood. Nonetheless, some people living under very dire circum-stances can pull out more life satisfaction through their judgment of how they are leading their life than the mood their circumstances bring them.

"Who doesn't have harmony within himself has enemies everywhere."
- Nossrat Peseschkian

Depression and getting out of its downward spiral

Most emotions come and go; some linger for a while, but with time, our bodies and minds usually heal themselves. When we experience a loss, we feel sadness and grieve. The process goes on for a time, but then our soul has the inner capability to heal its wound, to let go and continue. But when our current sadness is consciously or subconsciously connected to past episodes in which we have experienced shame, blame, guilt, inadequacy, worthless, helplessness, or hopelessness—especially if these feelings were a major part of our childhood—then these thinking patterns can be reactivated and pull us into a downward spiral of depression. Sadness and frustration in the face of a seemingly unsolvable situation (cognitively arrested alternatives), caused by a macro-trauma or a sequence of micro-traumas, allow negative thoughts and feelings to arise about us and our capability to manage the situation, and we turn inward. We try to repress our feelings, think our way out. We get lost in comparisons and self-critical thoughts of self-blame and lost self-esteem. We try to "soldier on" or "just get over it" by working harder, but we become more alienated from life and depressed until we are completely exhausted and emotionally numb.

There is a difference between those who have never had a bout of depression and those who have. Depression forges a connection in the brain between sad mood and negative thoughts so that normal sadness reawakens major negative thoughts. When depression occurs, we usually attempt to repress our negative feelings and think our way out. But this only results in rumination and dredges up regrets or conjures future worries. In our head, we experiment, play, and replay different solutions but soon feel bad for not being able to find a way of resolving our problems and alleviating our painful emotions. We get lost in comparisons of where we are and where we want to be, and soon we live almost entirely in our heads. Feelings of low self-esteem and self-blame—accompanied by powerful self-critical thoughts in which we berate ourselves as failures or as useless, unlovable losers—surge up within us. We become preoccupied and lose contact with the world, with those we love and who love us the most. We deny ourselves the tasty, rich input of living a full life. As we sink into a depressive state, we become exhausted because we try to deal with our problems by working harder. Research shows it is better to stop trying to solve the problem and rather let go of regrets and future worries so that we can get back in touch with the full range of our inner and outer resources through which we can learn, grow, and heal.

The four dimensions of **feelings, thoughts, body sensations,** and **behavior** are essential to the understanding of depression and overcoming it.

Feelings: Normally, emotions come and go, but depressive feelings linger and appear connected to anxiety, fear, irritability, anger, hopelessness, and despair. Irritability may be the most marked and strongly experienced symptoms of depression, even more than sadness, especially in the young. Depressed people may be prone to outbursts of anger. In major depression, we feel sad, agitated, lost, down, fatigued, and listless most of the day. We have difficulties concentrating, thinking, or deciding. We lose interest in most things and cannot find pleasure in anything, in all the things we used to enjoy. Feelings of worthlessness or extreme and inappropriate guilt dominate our thinking. We can suffer a significant decrease in appetite with weight loss or, inversely, weight gain with an increase in appetite. We may have difficulties sleeping at night and feel tired during the day. We have recurring thoughts of death or suicide, with or without specific plans to end our lives. As we funnel down into depression, we may attempt suicide as the final expression of our despair.

Thoughts: Our emotional reactions depend on the stories we tell ourselves. Our minds interpret the data we receive through our senses. This interpretation and reaction can be described using Albert Ellis' ABC model.

- A (Activating event) is the facts of the situation or how a video camera would capture the situation.

- B (Beliefs) is the interpretation of our mind as the running subtitles to the video.

- C (Consequences) is the reaction of our body, our response to the sensations, and emotions that result from the interpretation of the video we have seen.

Often, we see the situation A and the reaction C but are completely ignorant of our interpretation B. We think it was the situation that caused our reaction, while it was actually our interpretation. For example, when we walk down a street and a person we know doesn't respond to our greetings, we may start thinking, *What a bad-mannered person he is!* We don't know anything, though, about the difficulties he has experienced throughout the day, which have caused his reaction. When we feel down, we are likely to focus and elaborate on the most negative interpretations. Themes of worthlessness, blame, inadequacy, and isolation arise. We take these toxic and distorted thoughts about ourselves as unassailable truths, and they drain our energy. Unhappiness is not the problem but rather the harshly negative views that can be triggered by an unhappy mood. When we adopt this negative and destructive concept of ourselves, transient unhappiness devolves into persistent unhappiness.

Body: 80% of people with depression have physical pain. Our thoughts have a profound effect on our feelings and on our bodies. It is also true that our bodies influence our emotions and thoughts. A scientific experiment demonstrates this interconnectedness. It seems we experience a cartoon as funnier when we watch it with a pencil clenched between our teeth, smiling, than we do with pursed lips. Another study shows that we perceive information to be more positive when we nod our head affirmatively than when we shake our head negatively.

Behavior: Since we are too shameful or weak to show our emotions, and we were taught to simply "soldier on" or "just get over it," we try to do just that. Our thinking revolves around the core themes of self-blame, inadequacy, and unworthiness, perpetuating the belief that depression is our fault, and we have to sort it all out on our own. We give up our nonessential and unimportant activities, ones that might improve our mood rather than deplete our energy. This leads us to spiral down even more. When we then try to work harder without fruitful results or breakthroughs, we descend lower into depression and blame ourselves for our failure. This cycle can result in burnout and exhaustion.

Aversion towards ourselves: Our emotions are sophisticated and vital messengers that have evolved as signals to meet our basic needs for self-preservation. Their inner and outer expressions and messages are eloquent and complex. The most prominent, as we've seen, are happiness, disgust, sadness, fear, and anger. Happiness shows us when our goals are met, disgust that we are confronting something highly unpleasant, anger that an important goal is blocked, fear that we are confronting a dangerous situation, and sadness that something precious has been lost. But emotional reactions evolved to be temporary, and our initial emotional reactions usually last only as long as the subject of our alarm persists, often only for seconds or minutes. If they lasted longer, we would become insensitive to further changes in our environment. A gazelle bolts in fear when it senses a lion nearby and then minutes later starts grazing again.

However, some situations in our lives endure, and so do many of our reactions to them. For example, the loss or death of a person can bring enduring sadness or sadness that comes in unexpected waves. But even with this kind of loss, our mind has the capability to heal with time. Depression and sadness outlast the situations that triggered them because we have emotional and cognitive reactions to our own emotions, and our thoughts perpetuate them. This is the problem with our reaction to our emotions. When our emotions are signaling that something isn't as it should be, we feel intensely uncomfortable, and this is the appropriate and healthy response. Our feelings are precisely designed to make us act, to clarify and rectify the situation. When we are facing a charging bull or a roaring funnel cloud, we experience fear and must act. Our brain mobilizes a whole chain of mostly automatic reactions that help us deal with whatever threatens our survival. We call this reaction **aversion**. Our aversion reaction is for coping with the external world but counterproductive and dangerous when it is directed toward our internal world, our thoughts, feelings, and our sense of self. There is no way and no place we can run to escape ourselves. Once our aversion mechanism is switched on, our body tenses up as if we were getting ready to run or bracing ourselves for an assault. When we are preoccupied with how to eliminate our sad and self-berating thoughts, we are disconnecting from the outside world, and our whole existence becomes one of contraction. Our mind drives us to focus on the compelling but futile task of getting rid of these feelings, and we close in on ourselves. As we eliminate external input, we feel cramped and boxed in, and the choices available to us seem to dwindle. We feel increasingly cut off from the wider space of possibilities that we long to connect with. None of us can run away from, fight, or eliminate our inner experience. As we try to control our thoughts, we experience more anxiety, sadness, and frustration as all these feelings are imbedded in our DNA.

Doing and being mode: When we walk down a street, memories and emotions from past experiences arise. Deep-sea divers remember things they learned underwater when they are diving and those they experienced on land when they are on land. Mood can function as an internal context, bringing back memories and patterns of thinking associated with times when we were in that mood. Mood swings happen automatically without our consent. If the main thing that made us sad in the past was a loss, we would feel passing sadness when the memories of that loss come to mind. We will feel sad again but usually have no problem acknowledging our loss and then shifting our focus to other things while the echo of grief fades in its own good time. But if our previous moods of sadness were evoked by situations leading us to a thinking and feeling of worthlessness, if they were a significant part of our childhood, the thinking patterns that made us depressed are likely to be reactivated. These feelings endure and do not fade easily. This is why we can react so negatively to unhappiness. Our experience is not one simply of sadness; it is sadness accompanied by feelings of inadequacy. Feelings reactivated by our moods force their way into our consciousness. They increase our unhappiness and bring up the urgent priority to occupy ourselves with our "deficiencies" and focus primarily on them. When these feelings dominate our consciousness, it is difficult to switch our attention to anything else. Instead, we try to get to the bottom of what is wrong with us or with the way we live our lives. We try to think our way out of our depressed moods by working out what's wrong and trying to fix it.

Critical analytical thinking is a high achievement of humanity in solving many problems. It is aimed at closing the gap between the way things are and the way they should be. But critical analytical thinking is the wrong faculty to apply to our inner lives; the logical approach fails as well. *I should be feeling happy because it is a sunny day* makes us only feel worse.

Comparing how we feel to the way we want to feel only increases our unhappiness and takes us further away from where we want to be. We think of who we want to be and who we fear we could become if our sadness persists. The resulting defeating self-talk persists, and what it tells us seems real. The more we have experienced it in the past, the more familiar it is to us, and the more we believe it to be true. We begin to ruminate.

Ruminating is a vortex of thinking, thinking, and thinking. When thinking in a depressed mood, we conclude that we are the problem. That discovery is so painful that we want to get rid of it right away. We ruminate when we feel low because we believe it will reveal a way to solve our problems. But research shows it does just the opposite. When we are depressed, our ability to solve problems deteriorates markedly. Rumination is part of the problem, not part of the solution.

Awareness, on the other hand, is. Through awareness and creating space for the experience, we can get out of our heads and see and feel the world directly without the relentless commentary of our thoughts. We can open ourselves up to limitless possibilities for happiness. We can see our thoughts as mental events that come and go like clouds and start living in the present moment. We disengage from our autopilot and become more aware of ourselves, our senses, our emotions, and how our mind works. We sidestep the whole cascade of mental events that lead to depression, and we stop forcing life to be a certain way just because we are uncomfortable right now. We can create awareness through mindfulness. Jon Kabat-Zinn defines **mindfulness** as "the awareness that emerges through paying attention on purpose, in the present moment and non-judgmentally to things as they are." It is completely intentional, purely experiential, and relentlessly non-judgmental.

So, we learn how to bring consciousness into our lives. When we feel depressed or anxious, we can enter a state of mindfulness. In this state, we can feel and experience our anxiety and or depression from a meta-level, distance ourselves from it, and see it with more objectivity. Mindfulness lowers our emotional load so we can see beyond our difficulties and rediscover life and our resources. It helps us discover new solutions to our crises.

In 1904, researcher Richard Semon defined **engramming** as the physical process of creating memory. We have **engrammed** our negative experiences from the past or physically locked them into our brains. So now we take a path of reverse engramming. This process entails letting go of the identification we had with our experiences and emotions; we check and experience reality, then progressively widen our perspective and take action to make new positive experiences. With time and repetition, our new feelings, our new ways of thinking, and our positive behavior are progressively engrained into our brains.

In PPT, we use the whole toolbox we have described above as well. We work on our needs by finding new strategies for fulfilling them; we work on our actual, basic, key, and inner conflict using the five steps of treatment, four dimensions of life, stories, proverbs, positive interpretation, and changes of habits and beliefs. Along with this whole suite of strategies, mindfulness is an additional and welcome tool that helps us re-perceive our world.

Simple mindfulness practices can be:

- Eating a raisin slowly and mindfully

- Bringing mindfulness to routine activity

- Breathing or meditating mindfully while lying down or sitting

- Walking mindfully

- Body scanning

- Mindful yoga practice
- Sitting meditation (mindfulness of breath and body)
- Mindfulness of hearing
- Mindfulness of thoughts and emotions
- Choice-less awareness—opening ourselves mindfully to what is.

"Crisis as an opportunity"

A handsome young man once fell in love with his beautiful young neighbor. He saw her every day and yearned for her every night until, without notice, she moved to another part of the city with her parents. When the young man couldn't see her anymore, his longing grew ever more intense until it became heartbreaking lovesickness. He didn't know what to do, and so one night he wandered the streets of Bagdad. At that time, there was a curfew, and nobody was allowed to go out after sundown. When the night guards noticed him, they chased him down the streets. He ran as fast as he could, running down one alley and up another, dodging his pursuers through the parks and around shops, but the night guards stayed close on his heels. Then he turned around a corner and found himself in front of a wall. Not knowing what more to do, he called on the name of the Almighty, and just before his pursuers caught up, he jumped over the wall. Falling to the ground, he lay on the grass, and looking up, he found himself looking into the bewildered but enamored eyes of his beloved one.

– Retold after Nossrat Peseschkian (*Oriental Stories*, p. 56)

Basics in the art of creating psychological fitness through positive emotions

The key to psychological fitness, according to Martin Seligman, is resilience and positive emotions, which are our resource builders.

Positive emotions work for us in two ways: drawing attention and coordinating a response.

- Admiration alerts us to the chance to rapidly learn a culturally valued skill.
- Joy alerts us to opportunities for new experiences.
- Pride, in an appropriate dose, alerts us of our own skills and talents, and allows us to take credit for them, and sets us up for future success.

- Gratitude marks opportunities to solidify relationships with people who seem to care.

We can find out what inspires us, makes us laugh, and gives us hope and learn to cultivate these emotions.

For building mental toughness, Seligman also recommends we cultivate the **five factors for positive mental health, PERMA,** which are **Positive emotion**, **Engagement**, **good Relationships, Meaning**, and **Accomplishment**. As already mentioned above, these are present in Nossrat Peseschkian's **Four Dimensions of Life**: body, work, social life, and future/spirituality. Cultivating our four dimensions is the equivalent of cultivating the five factors. Either path will improve your outlook and mental health.

CHAPTER 6

MINDFULNESS, MEDITATION, AND YOGA FOR ENJOYING THE PRESENT AND BRINGING MORE CONSCIOUSNESS AND BALANCE INTO OUR LIFE

"Yesterday is history, tomorrow is a mystery, and today is a gift of God; that's why it's called the present."
- Bill Keane

A path to experiencing life

We tend to think we need something more or must be somewhere else to be happy, but we have already arrived, and happiness is here with us at this moment. If we recognize, *Life is great right now! I've arrived,* and we live our life here in this moment, this moment is truly where we can be happy. This moment is perfect, so let's live it in peace and grow naturally from moment to moment without trying to force our will on life. Instead of continuously seeking more and running around in our life and our head, we can live in the consciousness that we already have it all. Plenty consciousness is understanding that all we need to be happy and thrilled is already here in this very moment. We must give some consideration to what will happen in the future, but life is lived and can only be savored today.

"I arrived, I am already at home, my destiny is in every step with peace and freedom."
- Thích Nhất Hạnh

We can practice experiencing the feeling that we have already arrived at our destination and savor it with every step and movement. Whatever happens, right now, we have the chance to live our life fully. So, let's stop living in an imagined future in our heads and missing our real life in the present. Carpe diem. We can enter the moment and love ourselves and life while we still have a chance to do so, while we are so fully alive. Deep down, next to the everyday pleasures and happiness we seek in the outside world, every one of us is looking for peace within. Being at peace with ourselves and experiencing the silent happiness deep within us is very satisfying. When we find that internal joy, it will illuminate our lives. It can carry us through difficult situations and bring us more gratification than our continual search for happiness in the next experience. We tend to jump ahead mentally and desire the next experience without even realizing the wonder of our current experience. Then in the next moment, when we have finally achieved that desire, we are already thinking of what will follow. If we find happiness and peace, we can continue experiencing and enjoying life, but from a relaxed, fulfilled interior stance. The process of creating ourselves must be consciously connected to the process of finding ourselves. If we have everything but still aren't satisfied, it is time to get out of our automatic mode of grappling from one pseudo-satisfaction to the next. The pleasures we experience through craving to have something, getting it, and then quickly losing interest in it are transitory and unfulfilling. It's as if we tear open a candy bar, take one bite, and then throw it away. Craving becomes a trap that makes us look for satisfaction continually. Whatever we have, we will still be looking for more. We will never feel really fulfilled or happy.

Instead, we must learn to savor our lives, experience eudaemonia—lasting gratitude— and nurture our souls. Owning and achieving remain empty pursuits if they are devoid of mindful savoring, gratitude, and spiritual connectedness to everything. If we want to live happily, it's fundamental to live in peace with ourselves, our fellow people, and with the eternal. To wake up, become conscious living beings, and live with our mind and senses calm and clear while residing in our internal happiness and peace is fundamental. When our mind is calm, it is able to grasp the deep sense of life. It is capable of consciously choosing its destination and the path leading there. In calmness, we are open to the various challenges of each day; our energies are at our full disposition. We think and act in flow and can follow our path willfully. If we let ourselves be carried away by our negative thoughts and emotions, we become enmeshed in the past and fearful of the future. If our source energy resides in the present, we live in joy and peace. While each of us works on ourselves, our action spreads to others. By working on ourselves, we begin the process of transforming this world into one of love, compassion, happiness, and harmony.

"The art of living is neither careless drifting on the one hand nor fearful clinging to the past on the other. It consists in being sensitive to each moment, in regarding it as utterly new and unique, in having the mind open and wholly receptive."
- Alan Watts

Vedic mythology envisions the charioteer with a passenger in his chariot as a metaphor for our human existence. "Know that the Self is the rider, and the body the chariot; that the intellect is the charioteer, and the mind the reins" (Katha Upanishad 1:3:3). The chariot is our body, the horses our emotions, the charioteer our thoughts, and the passenger our essential being. The chariot follows the path of our life, and it is up to us to decide and navigate our way. To do so, we have to keep body, mind, soul, and spirit healthy and in balance, so we can consciously walk the path and be the masters of our life, being in control of our thoughts and feelings.

The chariot: Keeping our bodies healthy is essential for living a happy and fulfilled life. Our physical condition affects our mental state and vice versa. If we are healthy, we feel good, full of energy, and can concentrate and think powerful positive thoughts. If we don't take care of our body—lack good nutrition, sleep, cardiovascular and muscular strength, and maybe even abuse our energy reserves, do drugs, and work excessively—our soul and mind will suffer.

"The body is your temple. Keep it pure and clean for the soul to reside in it."
- B.K.S Iyengar

Therefore, it is important to be aware of our physical condition and take the best care of it. In the morning, we can begin by drinking a glass of water with a squirt of pure lemon juice for good hydration. Throughout the day, we eat two or three wholesome appetizing meals and drink 1.5 to 2.5 liters of water. We do yoga or other exercises three to five times a week and sleep at best eight hours a night. For healthy mental hygiene, let's not forget to limit our online time and turn off our gadgets for at least an hour before we go to bed. We need breaks to clear our heads during the day and time for calming down before going to sleep. Doing meditation, a body scan, and reading some spiritual or self-help books before going to bed can help us clear our minds and prepare for sleep as well. If we are fit, we are happier and more productive in life.

"Between stimulus and response, there is a space. In that space is our power to choose our response. In our response lies our growth and our freedom."
- Victor Frankl

The horses: If we want to be the protagonist of our life, we have to lead our emotions and not let them control us. There are different ways of reacting to our emotions. One is to *ignore and repress* them. But ignoring them isn't getting rid of them, as we may strongly wish to do. In reality, the contrary happens. We simply push repressed emotions such as anger, fear, and sadness down into a deeper layer within ourselves, where they may not seem to dominate but are nonetheless active. They will show up in the form of psychosomatic reactions since they are expressions of our unfulfilled needs that must be attended to. In the analogy, this corresponds to not looking after the needs of our horses. On the other hand, if we *identify too fully with our emotions,* and we let them drive us through life, a simple sadness can carry us off to ever-stronger emotions that leave us living in perpetual drama. This corresponds to allowing our horses to control our direction. We should never make a decision when we are very sad or mad or happy or fearful. We should wait a moment to clear our mind. The third way of acting is to recognize the emotions as they are, *become conscious of them,* and allow ourselves to feel them. When we feel sadness, we don't become sadness itself, but we recognize sadness as a transitory feeling. Recognizing the emotion is honoring it in its just measure. Observing its origin, what has caused it, and how we can respond is respecting the emotion. We then consciously choose the path we want to take without judging and reproaching ourselves. When we use this distancing technique, we discover we aren't the emotion but the observer of the emotion, and we can look for what we need according to our intuitive and cognitive evaluation.

When we experience strong emotions, we take a step back and evaluate what they are telling us. Behind every emotion, we find needs such as security, autonomy, and connectedness that have to be fulfilled, emotions that are interpreted by our thoughts. By becoming conscious of them, we can trace them to their source and look for a way to satisfy these needs. If we ignore our emotions, they will remain with us; if we focus on them entirely, we'll be dominated by them. To live in peace and freedom we have to recognize our emotions, discover their basis, and freely decide how to address our imbalance so we can be happy again.

The charioteer: "Tell me what you're thinking, and I'll tell you what you're feeling." The interpretation of our outer and inner worlds, the needs we are facing, and our thoughts dictate many of our emotions. It is fundamental that our charioteer is in balance with himself and that he benefits from the energy and strength of his bridled horses. If we become conscious of how our thoughts interpret a given situation and what our needs are, we realize that these two create our emotions. With that knowledge, we can decide how to change our thoughts and find a satisfactory way to meet our needs.

The passenger: When we identify with our mind and not with our higher self—consciousness observing from a meta-plane—we are living in autopilot mode, living all the beliefs we have accumulated in the past about this world, including all the false beliefs, fears, and excuses we have created around them without questioning. Whenever we become aware that we are in autopilot mode, we can come back to consciousness and remind ourselves that we are not our thoughts. Our thoughts are not reality but our instruments for understanding reality. We become aware of the present and can acknowledge that we can change our thoughts and bring them into alignment with reality. Mindful living, meditation, and yoga can open our way to a conscious, self-determined life and recognizing things as they are, as Zen master Shunryu Suzuki counsels. Our emotions will then change along with them. To take a fulfilling, happy, and adventurous ride through life, our mind, body, and soul must be aligned with one another. We also have to make the choice to let the fear go as we learn to live with more love and connectedness.

"It's great to be here; it's great to be anywhere."
- Keith Richards

Mindful attention shows us a simple but powerful way to get out of our automatic mode and take control of life. We can learn how to align gratefulness with attention, how to live in the present and reinvigorate our contact with life, our vitality, and wisdom so we get out of our heads. We learn how to take back into our hands the direction and quality of our life, our relationship with ourselves, our family, and our work.

Mindfulness diary

We take a notebook and write down our observations about topics, what we feel about them, and what we need that moves us throughout the day. Then at the end of the day, write what we discovered and learned and what it was good for. Every night, we write down whom we would especially like to thank and why. At the end of the week, we write down the same topics concerning the week: What we discovered, what conclusions we drew, and what it served us for our everyday life.

Meditation and mindfulness

"Your challenge is to discover your world and devote yourself to it with all your heart."
– the Buddha

Man has always sought fulfillment. Many of us are busy and occupied but are unfulfilled because we have lost our connection to life. We find that we are preoccupied with matters that have no emotional connection. We have lost our connectedness to others as well. When we lose these connections, the world becomes meaningless, we become resentful, and we don't perceive our everyday struggles as struggles of growth and learning but useless agony looming over a nothingness inside. Loneliness appears even more threatening; wishing to be relieved from this suffering can lead us to the border of our existence.

Meditation and mindfulness in **gratitude and love** for existence give us an intimate connection to ourselves and the world around us. It's as reassuring as the tender gesture of a friend putting his hand on our shoulder. Through meditation and mindfulness, we tenderly lay consciousness on our breath as it goes in and out of our nose and into our lungs. As we concentrate on our breath, our muscles relax, and our mind opens. Meditation and mindfulness can be used to slowly clear our minds of thoughts and emotions. With practice, we achieve states of deeper relaxation and become aware of the realms of consciousness. This ultimately leads us to a lighthearted and high-spirited state. Through meditation, feelings of power, happiness, and bliss, which are at the root of our being, well up. This connectedness to ourselves, the world, nature, and God gives us a foundation, a center, and a home in the midst of the events and activities of our lives. We feel that our lives are fulfilled and meaningful when we create beauty, truth, and love wherever we are. Meditation and mindfulness lower our stress level, promote more restful sleep, develop our creativity, improve our concentration and memory, and develop our emotional intelligence. With all these benefits, we can become more productive and happier people.

And all these benefits occur because meditation fosters our inner process of maturing. By practicing introspection, we become able to "see" our thoughts, emotions, and motivations with increasing clarity. We learn that we have the innate ability to transcend them instead of reacting to them. This is not a process of suppressing our emotions, as some may think, but rather the process of becoming more conscious of our inner world and learning to take clear, insightful, and purposeful action. Meditation truly yokes body and mind consciously (the definition of yoga), so we become free, willing individuals. Meditation can strengthen our self-esteem or our will by using mantras and affirmations. Meditation and mindfulness also center us in the moment, bringing us to a clear perception of the present. We let go of the frustrations of the past and the worries of the future. When we relax our whole body, we find the ability to focus on the present and rely on our intuition and inspiration to make manifest what we desire. Meditation can also strengthen our understanding and empathic capabilities. We welcome all these benefits of meditation.

"The whole universe surrenders to the mind that is quiet."
- Lao Tzu

Meditation and mindfulness techniques

"Do you have the patience to wait till the mud settles and the water becomes clear? Are you able to wait without moving till the right action arises by itself?"
- Lao Tzu

- **Body scan:** A recommended position to meditate is lying comfortably on our backs, maybe with cushions beneath our heads and our knees, so our whole body is more relaxed. We take three deep breaths to settle down physically and emotionally and follow our breath for a minute or so. We then direct our attention progressively, first to our feet and then slowly but continuously moving upward through our whole body, perceiving what we find wherever we are observing. We experience without judgment whatever we find, be it warmth, cold, tension, relaxation, pleasure, or pain. We realize how our pure attention to any discomfort can soothe it, help us dis-identify with it, and that it lessens our tension and suffering. To heighten the benefit, we can imagine bringing warmth and relaxation to the parts of the body we find in need of them. We can also imagine that light is entering our body and relaxing every muscle or that our breath travels through our muscles. Once we have gone through all major parts of our body systematically, we can bring our attention back to our breath and how its movement goes through us all the way to our fingers, toes, and head; we experience how it enlivens us with gratitude. We can stop here, stretch, and move our limbs before getting up, but if we have time and feel the pleasure in it, we can continue to go deeper into our experience and observe our heartbeat and its vibrations pulsing through us. We thank our heart, our blood vessels, and our blood cells for bringing life and energy into our whole body. We can then direct our attention to our stomach and feel its activity, thanking it for always being there, silently, unobserved but carrying on with its work of preparing our nutritional intake to become our life elixir. We can feel grateful for how our body, with all its collaborating organs, gives us the possibility to live our lives creatively. We can then go even a step further and imagine how in nature, everything is masterfully working together to sustain life. How the farmer sows his grain, how the seeds grow with the nourishment of soil, rain, and sun. We imagine how the grain is harvested, brought to the mill, and ground into flour, which a baker uses to make bread. We begin to see more expansively how collaboration is everywhere. We rest in thankfulness, vowing to be part of life's collaboration, creativity, and growth, finding solutions to our challenges. We return our mind to our body once more to discover what changes may have occurred. When we have thoroughly experienced our being, we return to our daily lives full of energy, relaxed but ready to appreciate and find pleasure in whatever awaits us. We stretch, move our bodies and limbs, and we are happy to be.

- **Meditation on breath**: Regular meditation is beneficial since it feeds the spirit, calms the mind, and adds to our well-being. We sit upright or lie down comfortably, inhale and exhale three times through our nose, do a short body scan, and if we find any tension, we relax it. By relaxing our bodies, we also relax our minds since they are intrinsically connected. We practice with open or closed eyes, whatever we prefer. When we begin to feel at home and well in our bodies, we put on a smile. We continue to follow our inhalation and exhalation, our breath going in and out through our nose, letting go of thoughts and feelings as they arise. With time and practice, we learn how to go further into clarity and perhaps experience pure consciousness and the light and happiness that emanates from it through us. Our breath is our guide for concentration, but we can also use the voice of an audio, a mantra, counting, ocean waves, or the flame of a candle to help us concentrate. We meditate for ten minutes in the morning or whenever it is right for us. Our consistent practice will guide us to inner peace.

- **Mindfulness meditation**: We begin as in the meditation on breath, but in this practice, our initial focus on breath shifts to our interior and exterior world simultaneously, welding them together as one with time. As we go deeper and deeper into our interior world, we find endless space within us where we experience peace and a profound sense of happiness and inner light emanating from it. In the outside world, we experience our body and the presence of the environment that surrounds us, with all its sounds, smells, and images. We judge nothing but accept everything as it comes.

- **Loving kindness meditation for others and ourselves**: Contrary to what some would think, doing the Buddhist "loving kindness" meditation for family, friends, and "enemies" often brings us more peace and works better for our own self-worth than when we meditate for ourselves. Instead of looking through our habitual glasses of fear and projecting all the potential dangers and threats we may have experienced, or instead of projecting the caution we exercise to protect ourselves, we try to envision our fellow human beings smiling in the natural, authentic, peaceful, and defenseless state we all have deep down inside. We wish them: "May you be filled with loving kindness, may you be well, may you be peaceful and at ease, and may you be happy." We can do so while meditating or in our everyday life when we see or meet people. When we see others through these new lenses, we learn to see them in a new light, accept them, and even come to love them in their humanity. And by doing so, we learn to accept and love ourselves more as well. With growing self-esteem our sense of self-efficacy is strengthened, and we learn to stand up for our values and rights, take others' opinions and needs into consideration, and do what we believe is right, even in critical situations. We can of course, also use it directly for ourselves: "May I be filled with loving kindness, may I be well, may I be peaceful and at ease, and may I be happy."

- **Mindfulness in everyday life**: We practice mindfulness by giving our attention to whomever we are with. The person who is with us is, at that moment, the most important person in our life. We also practice mindfulness when we focus completely on whatever we are doing. To make it easier, in the beginning, we can say whatever we are doing with a loud voice and to do everything a bit slower. We can start with conscious eating. Hippocrates: "May your medicine be your food and your food your medicine." It's important not only to eat well but to have a good relationship with food by bringing consciousness to eating. For example, once a week, by eating alone, consciously, and silently, we can develop better eating habits. We should always ask, what am I eating? Is it healthy for me? How do I eat this? Slowly and consciously while enjoying every bit. Why am I eating? Am I tired, sad, anxious, or alone? We don't want to address our emotional needs by eating. We want to find the unfulfilled needs behind them and fulfill them suitably. By improving our emotional state, we can also change our diet. We may have many unhealthy beliefs about eating; perhaps our parents said, "Clear your plate or I will punish you." Every time we eat, we should sit down and concentrate on enjoying our meal with all our senses. How does the food look, smell, feel, sound, and ultimately taste? We eat as if it were the first time by becoming a beginner. We practice gratitude for our food, asking ourselves how the food got to our table, how it was prepared, and who grew it. We close our eyes and practice a moment of gratefulness before eating. Between bites, let's put our forks down. We can try eating with our non-dominant hands. We learn to start distinguishing between hunger and thirst.

- **Mindfulness with practice of silence**: We practice a week of silence, being as silent and awake in mindfulness as possible. We reduce the input by turning off our television and radio, reducing time on our phones. We enjoy doing other things and listening to the silence. As Buddhism tells us, we don't wash dishes just to clean them, but also with the knowledge that every act is important and precious in itself and should be honored. Buddhists also believe that the present is the best, most beautiful, and most important moment of our life. When we make a ritual out of every moment of our life and give full attention to every moment, we find happiness. Mindfulness is the practice of staying in the present and living it fully. We abandon thoughts about the past and future since they don't have anything to do with this very moment. Since our thoughts are repetitive 80% of the time, we will not overlook anything. Instead, we will experience a full life in the present.

- **Light meditation**: We begin as in the breath-focused mindfulness meditation and then imagine a light beam coming from the sky. It shines through our head and penetrates our body with light, energy, and well-being.

- **Mantra or affirmation meditation**: This form of meditation brings calmness and strength at the same time. We choose a mantra fitting our purpose. Then we begin with some breath-focused mindfulness meditation. We bring our mantra into an open space within our mind and repeat and visualize it with all its imagined attributes, so these qualities grow roots in the calmness of our mind and personality. An example of a broadly affirming meditation:

  - "I trust in you, my powerful, creative, loving cosmic nature; you live through me, you live through everyone, you are everything."

- **Meditation with an intention/prayer**: We begin with our breath-focused mindfulness meditation, get quiet within ourselves, and release a question into the void, our subconscious, our source within, or the collective subconscious. Then we open ourselves to whatever inspirations comes to us.

- We can also use **CDs, YouTube videos, yoga studios,** and **teachers** for guided meditations and chanting to arrive at a meditative state.

Meditative intermezzos

"A small fire that gives you warmth is better than a big fire that burns you."
- Carlo Goldoni

Meditative breaks bring more clarity, consciousness, and peace to our day. They force us to stop our automatic robot-mode of activity. We can become more aware of ourselves and our environment, see more clearly and take off our glasses of projection when we take a meditative break.

"One cannot add days to one's life but life to one's days."
- Anonymous

Saying *Stop!* and coming to our senses: Whenever we need to get clear about something, or we are under pressure and our mind is in disarray, we can become more conscious and cease rushing. We can use any of the following meditative breaks:

1. **Stopping to breathe:** We step away from our activity and take three deep, conscious breaths deep into our abdomen, where our sense of autonomy resides. Then, when we feel a bit calmer, we observe what is really happening around us before we give an answer or proceed with our activity.

2. **Tongue to the palate:** When we bring our tongue to our palate (the roof of our mouth), we notice how our inner dialogue stops. It's as if, without subvocalization, the words stop.

3. **Instant body scan:** When we feel physical tension, it is always accompanied by mental tension. Because body and mind are intrinsically connected, when we relax one, we relax the other. Throughout the day, we can check in on ourselves to see how we are doing. When we feel tension, anxiety, insecurity, or stress, we can relax and bring ourselves to an upright position so our breath can flow freely again. We locate the areas in our body where there's tension and imagine bringing warmth and relaxation to that area. To bring even more relaxation, we can use post-isometric relaxation by contracting all our muscles for five seconds and then releasing them again. Mental and physical relaxation will appear simultaneously. Our body is always in the present moment while our mind is always moving from past to present to future and back. So, if we are in our body, we are in the present, where there is more safety and happiness than in any unresolved thoughts of the past or fearful thoughts of the future. When we reconnect with our body, in a sense, we come home to ourselves. We notice that when we listen attentively to our bodies, the noise in our minds stop automatically. When we are very stressed, we can ask our body where we are. It will always answer. To live in the present, we focus our attention on our bodies. When we sit, we bring our attention to our posture. When we walk, we bring our consciousness to our steps, how we walk, and the sound we create walking. When we are lying

down, we bring awareness to the position in which we are lying. When we are talking, we observe our voice and gestures and become present in them. We continually adjust our body, relax our feet, shoulders, face... These little observations bring us into the present moment and liberate us from confounding and challenging thoughts. This concentration on our body gives us clarity and peace.

4. **Change of posture:** When we walk, stand, and sit like a burdened or depressed person, we feel depressed. When we feel triumph and exhilaration, our body will reflect that too. We think of the state of mind we want and bring our body into a representative posture.

5. **Respiration:** Breathing is an essential function of life. With conscious breathing, we can manage our feelings and find mental calmness. While watching a movie or giving a speech, we might hold our breath out of suspense. We breathe deeply when we are sad, and often we sigh. Our breath accelerates when we are mad and will become more subtle when we embrace a close one softly or when we give a tender kiss. Let's breathe with mindfulness during the day, feeling how our breath is fresh when we inhale and a bit warmer when we exhale. When we notice that it is altered, let's stop for a moment and take three profound breaths consciously through our nose before we resume our activity. If in certain tense situations, we feel that we want to breathe deeper, then let's do so with exaggeration.

6. **Mindful walking:** Take a moment off and go outside to walk mindfully until we regain our senses.

7. **Tapping our thymus gland:** Whenever we feel exhausted but know we must continue, we focus on our thymus gland by tapping on the sensitive tissue above it on our breastbone for a minute or two. This tapping brings back concentration and energy.

Living at peace with our past, present, and future

"When I didn't have anything to lose, I had everything. When I stopped being who I am, I found myself."
- Paulo Coelho

The way to live in peace with our past is to ask ourselves, why did this happen to me? Everything we've done, we've done with a positive intention, and we did it with the tools we had at that very moment. Everything that has happened in our lives happened so we can learn something important. Maybe we'll suffer until we get the answer. We must trust in life. We will always learn from it, and nothing happens by chance.

We tend to get sucked into a whirlpool of thoughts continuously shifting between worries about the future and frustration about the past, going from one extreme to the next, creating an ever-greater inner movie-drama. When we are obsessed about our future, we are spinning wild theories and torturing ourselves about what mayhem may be awaiting us. Yet we never find an answer about what is to come. When we get caught up in frustration about the past, we continuously ask ourselves why this happened to us and why we didn't react differently, thinking up numerous different versions about how we could have reacted. Yet we cannot change what happened. Thinking about our future and past are, of course, legitimate, sane forms of reflection. They only become maladaptive when they take over our present and begin a life of their own. But when we live with our automatic pilot turned on all the time, doing things automatically, our thoughts constantly racing back and forth from past to future and back, we have no control over them nor over our mind. This mode of reflecting is immensely tiring and takes away our ability to concentrate on anything in the present.

Obsessive ruminating, as has been shown, although seemingly an alluring way of reacting and trying to solve one's problems, is counterproductive. It is healthier to create some space in our mind by re-focusing on another topic and not letting ourselves be controlled emotionally as we are pulled into a depressing vortex, an approach that brings more insecurity and instability without offering a way out.

We can find more security through mindfulness, which grounds us in the present. We may think it is tiring to concentrate on the present moment. But it isn't. It's more tiring to carry the past and the future, with all their concomitant anxiety. Moreover, when we are looking at the dangers ahead, we usually magnify their size and quantity. Most of our anticipated fears never happen, and when they do happen, we suddenly find ourselves calm and steady as we face them. So why worry that we aren't prepared for imaginary disasters? We can have a more resourceful state of energy by concentrating on the here and now. Sometimes we ask ourselves how much time we still have before we die, but we can't know that either, so the only option is to say carpe diem and live in the moment with gratitude. If we live every day as a unique one, as if it were our last, we will be at peace with ourselves when our day comes.

In summary, then, we live in **peace with ourselves** when we learn to calm our mind and live in the present, **practicing mindfulness and gratitude** in our everyday lives, overcoming our anxiety for the future and our sorrow about the past. **Meditation and yoga** can further help us live consciously every moment of our life, knowing that each one is unique, not repeatable, necessary, perfect, and truly magical. We were born with pure enthusiasm for life, and if we can return to this joyful state, we will find enduring happiness. We recognize this happiness within ourselves when we feel complete, confident, compassionate, and serene, even when we are facing an adverse reality.

Preventing anxiety and hyperventilation through grounding with mindfulness

Mindfulness can be very helpful for anxiety and panic attacks:

Inhale, counting slowly to three, and exhale slowly, counting to six. Look around and look for:

- Five things that you can see
- Four things that you can touch
- Three things that you can listen to
- Two things that you can smell (smells that you like)
- One emotion that you can feel.

How to stop hyperventilation with mindful breath-work

When we are in a panic and start hyperventilating, we feel dizzy, lightheaded, or spaced out. We experience tingling in the arms and legs or maybe even cramps; we can do some conscious breathwork that will get us out of the difficult situation within minutes.

- We inhale, counting to three.
- Exhale, counting to four.
- And hold our breath, counting to five.

During this time, we focus on our counting and our breath and notice how our anxiety and physical sensations rapidly diminish.

Basic life attitudes for mindfulness, meditation, and yoga

The following basic life attitudes deepen the effects of our meditative and mindfulness practice:

1. **Being open and dropping judgements with a beginner's mind**

"The real voyage of discovery consists not in seeking new landscapes, but in having new eyes."
- Marcel Proust

Judging is an automatic reaction we have learned. It helps us orient ourselves by distinguishing between like and dislike, helpful and not helpful, good and bad. Although it usually is a necessary tool for survival, it also puts everything into predefined categories and establishes stereotypes and shortcuts in our thinking so that we lose our openness to life. The expert in our mind always has a prepared opinion on everything. But we can let go of our omniscient or know-it-all thinking and our prejudices by becoming aware of our judgments, holding them a second in our mind, and then letting them go. We can then see with a clear mind, a beginner's mind, and find new qualities in individuals and groups that we had not seen before. When we begin to see everything with new eyes and meet every instant with a fresh mind, we get carried away by new discoveries, observe them with great interest and see our world and how it develops in its ever-new magic. Beginner's mind is a way to live non-judgmentally, open, aware, and concentrated.

"In the mind of the beginner, you have many possibilities; in the mind of an expert, few."
- Shunryu Suzuki

We can when let go of our prejudices and become more conscious human beings instead of sleepwalking through our life. When we observe everything with an open mind and curiosity, it becomes colorful and amazing.

"Observing the world with new eyes and an open mind, the beginner will see things that escape the expert."
- Salvador Méndez Piñón

When we live with open-mindedness, we also let go of believing we have intuitive knowledge of the intimate realms of another's mind and that we have "divine divination." We recognize that, by observing their behavior, we believe we know exactly what our counterpart thinks: "He's watching the soccer match on weekends, so it's obvious he doesn't care for me." It's far better to ask someone what you want to know rather than make assumptions based on limited data. Guessing what someone is thinking is very risky. Open and understanding communication is essential for a well-functioning friendship and relationship.

2. Accepting and letting go

"Life is a series of natural and spontaneous changes. Don't resist them; that only creates sorrow. Let reality be reality. Let things flow naturally forward in whatever way they like."
- Lao Tzu

Complaining doesn't feel good, and people get bored listening to us when we are wasting our time and theirs, lamenting while we could be searching for a solution to our problems. So to be happy and successful in life and as social human beings, it is best to substitute our penchant for complaining with a solution-oriented approach. We can focus on going over, under, through, or around a problem to reach our goal instead of moaning continuously about our bad luck and the obstacles others are putting in our way. Sometimes we need some empathy for our situation, and we might need help in finding a way out of it. We can search for the consolation and considerate advice we need, but then stop our repetitious complaining about the same problems and get to work solving them. When we change our mindset, we realize that our difficulties are like fertilizer, which can be a stimulant to our growth.

"They say that the lotus flower, one of the most beautiful flowers, grows in the mud. The flower and the mud are equally necessary. The difficulties we confront, the errors we commit, and the suffering we take on ourselves aren't anything else than fertilizer. Instead of thinking of it as something bad and stupid, we can transform it into an excellent organic fertilizer."
- Brenda Shoshanna

We can change the vision of our past, present, and future instead of continuously complaining. Non-stop rumination and grumbling about one's dissatisfaction are manifest proof that we don't recognize and accept reality. We don't acknowledge that things are the way they are and that everything carries a message for us to learn and evolve. When we hear ourselves complain, we should ask ourselves questions like the following:

- What is this situation telling me?
- Is it really a failure?
- Is it an obstacle or a challenge?
- Should I be frustrated about it?
- Can I view it as an apprenticeship?

We can then replace our complaint with gratitude: "I'm tired of my work, I'm really fed up" => "Thanks to my work, I know many interesting people." If a complaint keeps arising, then we should look for a deeper reason for its persistence. Am I seeking a change? Let's not waste our energy and time by complaining. Accepting what is and getting into flow with life gives us the energy to be the masters of our lives. Things are the way they are— instead of lamenting or resigning ourselves to them, we act intentionally so we can learn and grow from them. When we stop clinging to things, we become free. Nothing lasts forever, not our belongings, health, friendships, or circumstances. They all change with time; we enjoy, take care of, and value them, but when the time comes, we must let them go. To address things we don't like in the present or things that we severely reject from the past, we ask ourselves, *What was it for?* We look at the situations that made us feel bad and try to discover what we can learn from them, find a new path, and continue. As a second step, before going to bed, we can go through our day and accept and let go of everything we have experienced, emptying our minds of all the dislikes or regrets we have.

We see that next to changing our present and future (although it is generally believed that we cannot change the past), we can also change our *perceived* past that is fixed in our memory with this change of perspective. We don't change the real events but rather the experience and the flavor that linger by changing the meaning and context, accepting it, and letting it go.

3. **Use trust and patience to relax**

"Patience brings roses; impatience neurosis."
- Nossrat Peseschkian

We run from experience to experience every day. Often, we go so fast that we don't even notice what is happening around us anymore. We must turn off our automatic pilot and reduce our speed with this reminder: "Don't hurry; go slowly" and repeat it whenever necessary. We can learn to go slowly, and when we are in a hurry and hastening unconsciously, we can use mindfulness to slow our pace. Patience is good for our health; impatience harms us. Patience means respecting the moment as it is. "Patience can be an essential quality that we invoke when the mind is agitated and can help us accept how erratic it is, reminding us that we don't have to let us be carried away on its trips," says Jon Kabat-Zinn. We trust whatever we meet; we give everything a chance. We practice trusting ourselves and live moment by moment, day by day. We trust in our own developmental process and our path in life. When we start trusting in our path, we become patient. We learn to experience the moment as it is and not rush everything just to get to the end, forfeiting our happiness on the way. When we are patient, we stop forcing things, so they come naturally, and we can relax into them. We can leave things as they are and approach them naturally without force, fighting, or sacrifice but with intrinsic power. We call this *doing without doing.*

4. **"Mature envy"**

"Be careful about what you want; you might get it."
- Nossrat Peseschkian

Making comparisons is a necessary habit in a competitive environment. Like any other habit, we don't even notice when we are comparing. This faculty of discriminating or discerning is essential to our life, and at the same time, it creates the illusion of complete separation. We experience ourselves as separate, yet we are completely interconnected parts of the all; we are an ocean of matter and energy in movement and with memory. Therefore, believing in our own superiority and complete autonomy is an illusion. We cohabitate in one world, so it is essential that we get along with one another, get in sync, and harmonize so that all can flourish. When we compare ourselves to someone and think we're superior, our pride, the driver of our ego to maintain a strong self-image, dominates us. When we feel inferior, again, it is our pride and our ego talking. In reality, others compare themselves to us and would like to be like us in many respects.

We need a more mature and respectful form of pride and envy. Not one that says I am superior or inferior, but one that shows us both the beauty in ourselves and in others. It is a pride in ourselves and an envy that has let go of fear. Comparing without feeling fear enables us to be aware and share our capabilities. At the same time, it lets us be grateful for the capabilities of others and see them as developmental potentials for ourselves. It gives us the possibility to appreciate others' gifts and talents, their contribution to all of us, since we all complement one another in this world of diversity and possibility. We can cease comparing ourselves to others in terms of scarcity, and instead admire ourselves and others and feel the love and abundance around us and the possibilities and potential in everyone. We can live authentically and be grateful for the uniqueness of each individual with his or her inherent capabilities. We are perfectly lovable human beings just the way we are, yet we have the possibility to continue growing. When our comparing is dominant, and we create an energy of scarcity, we first have to become aware of it and then let it go. Then we consider how to appreciate the other person, become aware of her beauty as different from our own, and say thanks that the cosmos has created such an abundance of potential.

5. Forgiving and finding inner freedom

"We build too many walls and not enough bridges."
- Sir Isaac Newton

Forgiveness is powerful. It can transform feelings of anger and bitterness into equanimity or even better, into positive emotions. When we are consumed by anger, hate, self-pity, and resentment, we see only the damage of the past and how we can get revenge. When we are thinking negatively, we don't analyze how we can learn from this experience for the future. We can choose to either brood about our most painful and sorrowful moments or let them go and forgive those who caused the pain. We can pick the scabs of our emotional wounds, preventing them from healing and perhaps causing infection, or we can heal through forgiveness. We have an erroneous belief that dwelling on them will create justice for our suffering in time or that we can exact revenge for what was done to us. But the only person we are hurting by wallowing in these painful memories is ourselves. It may be that our perpetrator isn't even aware of our torment and the expectations we have of him. We can't expect the other person to make amends for something they may not even recall. By keeping these experiences alive in our minds and reliving the emotions, we are dragging the heavy loads of hate and resentment around with us, weighed down and in pain—"I'll make sure you pay for what you've done. Even if I have to carry this around for a lifetime." But this fixation on past injuries is like taking poison and waiting for the perpetrator to die. Once a war veteran asked another veteran if he had already forgiven his enemy. He said no, why should he?! The questioner replied that he had done so because he didn't want to spend any more time in the same prison in which he had already spent much of his life. Weighing ourselves down with shame, guilt, resentment, and self-loathing is self-destructive and a waste of time. We will not change what has happened by continuously ruminating on it. So, let's throw it out. If we have a problem with someone, we go and tell them about it, express ourselves, and forgive them, regardless of what becomes of it. If they understand, great; if not, there is no other solution than we let it go anyway. Otherwise, we will continue obsessing about it, and it will continue eating at us. If we have shared our feelings, we can at least say that we have given it our best and can then eliminate that person from our lives with a good conscience. We lay down the weight of pain and resentment and become free once more. Forgiving someone is not only about being nice to the other person but just as much about being nice to ourselves.

What can we do to be able to forgive?

Be happy rather than right: We are the ones who can choose to be happy and free or right and tormented. What is it worth to us? What are we holding on to that is worth our happiness?

Understand and find empathy: Forgiving someone is dressing an inner wound. First, we take the poisonous arrow out of our soul, then we clean and dress the emotional wound until it can heal completely. It is painful in the beginning, but after enduring suffering for so long, we are taking the steps we need to heal. To facilitate this process, we can imagine the person we fault as the innocent child he once was and, deep down, still is. We acknowledge that he is someone who acted out of fear and ignorance. Usually, people are in pain and fear when they try to protect themselves by hurting another.

Take our part in "response-ability": Do we want to continue dragging around the weight of pain and resentment, or do we want to leave this experience behind, solve the problem, and move forward toward our goals? Everyone has a viewpoint on an issue in a confrontation. We have to be inquisitive and not reproachful. We ask, *How did I contribute to the problem?* People see the same movie and have different reactions and responses. What they see is very much about themselves; their perspective is determined by the feelings and ideas they project onto the cinematic experience. If people have vastly different responses to a movie, it follows that they will have a variety of responses to real events. It's wise to reflect on our actions before we condemn the other person. We ask:

- Why did this happen to me?
- How did I contribute to the issue?
- Did I provoke this in any way?
- How can I make the best of the situation?
- How can I understand and empathize with all those involved?
- How can we evolve together?

We can use a personal conflict for growth and not for wallowing in our pain and angry emotions. When we apply these kinds of questions to a personal conflict, we transform our pain and anger to personal growth. We can use our awareness of our own negative emotions to understand ourselves and others better and achieve a positive outcome. Since we all project our ideas and concepts on the world, and we always suppose our beliefs are the right ones, this is our chance to revise and question them instead of being slaves to them. We can look at the experience from new angles, let go of our rigidity, and when relaxed, see how our anger dissipates. We can develop a clearer vision of our genuine personalities and somewhat less-than-admirable character traits instead of thinking of ourselves as saints. We can examine why we are reacting so strongly to what others are doing and where our shadow self is acting out. Do we really know what's going on, or are we simply assuming or guessing? Evidence of how we can jump to conclusions occurs when we misinterpret a text message. How often do we project our inner life onto those kinds of cryptic messages? What are our projections, and how accurate are they really? We have to continuously take responsibility for examining our part in conflict.

Use the energy stored inside

When we are really angry, we are full of energy that has to be released. We can let it go with some clay, a pillow, a punching bag, or the keys of a piano. At best, we can use it for tough physical training and fortify ourselves. That way, we can clear our heads and return to finding solutions.

A forgiveness letter

When we've gotten to the point of letting go, writing a forgiveness letter with all the topics and related emotions will provide an emotional cleansing. If the situation dictates, we can deliver the letter; if not, the writing will bring us personal freedom.

Remember, whatever it is, will soon belong to a forgotten past

When we look back and search for the many anger-provoking situations we've lived through, usually only vague memories of them still come to mind. There are countless other events that we don't remember at all. Some events, which we now look back on more objectively, used to be highly emotional. Most of them became meaningless with time and disappeared soon afterward. Remembering how short-lived other tension-filled incidents were helps us to release our tension over current situations more quickly.

Forgive and leave it behind

When we forgive, we should do so not only in words but really liberate ourselves and open ourselves again towards the world with a beginner's mind, expecting the best. We will see many new positive aspects in everything when our tunnel vision broadens, and the dark haze of anger dissipates.

6. Gratitude

"Man looks back in time and sees that his bad luck turned out to be his good luck."
- Eugen Roth
"When you are grateful, fear disappears,
and abundance appears."
- Anthony Robbins

People usually do what we want if we ask them to do so in a nice and friendly manner. If we are rude, they probably won't comply. There is no reason to be unfriendly in the first place. When we warmheartedly enter into dialogue, we feel connectedness and gratitude with the other person, and since they are more likely to respond when we initiate a conversation politely, we have a chance to participate in the natural flow of positive give-and-take. Good manners are not enough because they can emanate from mechanical or soulless politeness. But manners combined with gratitude is a force that is difficult to resist. Gratitude is an enduring feeling of thankfulness.

Feeling grateful means being aware of and appreciating the true miracles of life happening to us each day. With gratitude, we experience an inner fullness, become high-spirited, feel that we can authentically be ourselves, and sense our connection to the divine. This fullness radiates and sends out positive emotions and energy, which in turn reflect on us. Since every action has an equal opposite reaction, we reap what we sow.

When we approach others in gratitude, we are filled with positive energy, which contributes to our physical well-being and our mental health. With gratitude, we experience the power of our existence. We sense our self-efficacy and are alert to the pleasure in our actions. We know that appreciating the many little wonders we encounter every day makes our lives full. And when life bestows on us the great gifts it has in store for us, we know their value and sense there are many more gifts to come. When we don't live in gratefulness, we feel empty and soulless. Gratitude also gives us the power to work with others; we know that cooperation is the best form of potentializing one's effectiveness. Mutual gratitude is an effective social glue. When we actively send gratefulness out, we receive it back, and in doing so, sense an even stronger connectedness to all humans and nature. Deep down, we realize that with each exchange, an intuitive understanding arises that we are not only connected to everything but one with everything. Inspired by this universal truth, we have the inner security and power to realize our dreams and make a difference in this world. Moreover, with this understanding of our intrinsic connection to the world, we know instinctively that we are the world, and by being grateful to the world, we are grateful to ourselves. The more grateful we are, the more connected we become, and the more our faith in ourselves and others grows. The more we give, the more we receive, and the easier and sooner we realize what we want to create.

Bring gratitude into any moment of our day: Showering, eating, meeting someone, commuting, working, or exercising. When we become aware of our thoughts, reminded that we aren't our thoughts, and we focus on the things we are grateful for, happiness arises. Our mind is our tool; we can use it wisely and learn to master it. Once we start practicing gratitude, we become more joyful, and we see how contagious our gratitude and happiness are when they spread to others.

Increase our satisfaction and savoring: We increase our satisfaction and savoring by experiencing them intensely by using mindfulness on every small wonder of life. We learn to "reduce to the max!"

Practice everyday gratitude: Whenever something wonderful happens to us, we actively appreciate and give gratitude to whoever bestows it on us. Whenever anything not quite so wonderful, mediocre, or bad happens to us, we still search for some ways to be grateful. Sometimes this is difficult, but it is how we make the best of the challenging situations in life. When we learn from a situation we have experienced, we are able to get over it more easily. We look for what we can learn so we can move forward in life. Let's not think, *Why did this happen to me?* but rather, *What can I learn from this experience?*

Listen actively: To understand and connect better with whomever we meet, we can listen actively to our family and friends.

Recognize and celebrate individual character strengths of others: We respond actively and constructively to what an individual, using his personal capabilities, has brought us. On occasions, we celebrate them.

Thank someone every day: We can thank someone every day for something, whether it is their existence, an action, or a word. By repeatedly extending gratitude, we create more connections with others.

Write a letter of gratitude: We write a letter of gratitude to somebody we have never thanked and send it to her.

Be mindful of our success: For more self-esteem, we can add mindful moments of gratitude for recognizing and appreciating our success every day and congratulating ourselves.

Keep an evening-blessings journal and visualize: Before going to bed, we review the importance of cultivating positive emotions and write down at least ten things we are grateful for. If we write only our gratitude for the nice things, we will be happier, but if we are thankful for the difficult ones, we will also grow. We can also include the success we have had using our personal character strengths in our gratitude list. Just before going to sleep, we visualize and experience with gratefulness the wonderful things that happened to us. We can fall asleep with positive reinforcement.

"I never feel so given to than when you take from me. When you understand the joy, I feel giving to you, and you know my giving isn't done to put you in my debt, but because I want to live the love, I feel for you. To receive with grace, my gift may be the greatest giving. There's no way I can separate

the two. When you give to me, I give you, my receiving. When you take from me, I feel so given to."
- Ruth Bebermeyer

7. Faith

"Faith is having the audacity to believe in the not yet seen."
- Jen Sincero

When we have faith, we realize we can release the abundant reservoir of energy, intelligence, and intuitive creativity that is dormant within us. When we live in fear, all this positive energy is blocked and inaccessible. Faith helps us get out of our comfort zone and is the anchor we rely on when we are scared. When we have unwavering faith and passionate gratitude at the same time, we get into the flow of creating and realizing our dreams. We can cultivate the intensity and duration of positive emotions by savoring and relentlessly practicing gratitude. So, let's practice being grateful not only for what we have but also for what we want to receive. And remember, it is a fact that "satisfiers" (people inclined to say, "This is good enough") achieve greater well-being than "maximizers" ("This is not good enough") in the long run—especially if we experience gratitude towards them.

8. Positive start of the day

"You cannot exercise much power without gratitude; for it is gratitude that keeps you connected with power."
- Wallace Wattles

When we wake in the morning, a thought appears. It can be positive or negative and is usually related to whatever issues we have at that moment. The next thoughts or worries are influenced by this initial, directive thought. If our first thought is, *Another day of boring work*, day after day, it will infuse our whole day and life with its limiting negative contents and accompanying emotions. If we can change the initial thought, our whole day will have a different flavor. If our initial thought makes us happy and content, then we are on the right track. If it makes us unhappy and anxious, we can change it through gratitude. When we are thankful that we are alive, that we breathe, have new opportunities and another day to do good work, we feel gratefulness in in our heart and our whole body. The energy of thankfulness can change everything.

9. Detachment from objects

"They should tell you when you're born: have a suitcase heart, be ready to travel."
- Gabrielle Zevin

To create more space for joyful things in our lives, we can practice detachment. Let's get rid of five things every day that don't make us happy. Ask the question of each object, "Does it make me happy?" If not, then let's give it to someone who would love it, and if none comes to mind, then just throw it out.

10. Generosity

"It is one of the beautiful compensations in this life that no one can sincerely try to help another without helping himself."
- Ralph Waldo Emerson

Gratitude, love, compassion, and generosity go hand in hand, creating fulfillment. By practicing gratitude for being alive, breathing, for all we encounter and love, we learn to appreciate ourselves and the world, strengthen our own personality and happiness, and become fulfilled. We start looking at the world with love and compassion and learn to accept and love what is, while fear and hate dissolve. We become more compassionate by profoundly understanding others and wanting to help them out of generosity, not out of our own self-interest. Having compassion for ourselves means understanding and wanting to help ourselves without judging and denigrating ourselves with negative names. Day by day, we fall more and more in love with ourselves, others, and all. We become more generous beings, letting our wealth flow to others and watching how it flows back. We recognize ourselves in the minds and hearts of others and come to peace with ourselves and the world. Generosity and giving are a great joy and a demonstration of fearlessness and power. They are based on our trust that life has plenty to give and that when we give, we also receive. Generosity increases our freedom and raises our level of happiness as we become radiantly inspired human beings.

We can create a flow of giving and receiving with all our connections. When we get greedy and fearful of losing money, we cut off the natural flow of reciprocity between ourselves and others. Money means responsibility. We are not meant to waste our resources but to invest them in what we believe, in the values we cherish. Generosity that comes from the heart will always bring back surplus amounts of valuable gifts in return.

- Let's smile, compliment, and increase people's joy every day.
- Let's make a habit out of doing good deeds every day.
- Let's give someone our time, one of our most precious resources.
- If someone is being unfriendly, let's give them "the love"; let's not retaliate and bring ourselves down to their level.
- Let's give something we really love to someone who will really appreciate it.
- Let's donate regularly to a cause that is important to us.
- Let's make a habit of leaving a bigger tip than we have before.
- Let's say yes to invitations we would normally not accept because we think we might be inconvenienced.

"Love lives on loving trivialities."
- Nossrat Peseschkian

We practice these ten basic actions each for a week in rotation throughout the year.

CHAPTER 7

RISING THROUGH THE DEVELOPMENTAL STRAITS OF LIFE: OUR NATURAL ART OF SELF-DEVELOPMENT

"The sum of all man's days is just a beginning."
- Lewis Mumford

Spiral dynamics

One day a cube met a triangle and told him he would take him to a new dimension. The triangle became a pyramid, and from then on could never go back to seeing himself as only a triangle.
- Source unknown

What follows is an interpretation of Nietzsche's metaphor from *Thus Spake Zarathustra*, which provides insight into human evolution. From our beginnings as spirit, we undergo three metamorphoses, transforming from one level of consciousness to the next. Nietzsche describes how this evolution of the spirit of one individual parallels the history of humanity. Growth toward freedom of a single human being has three equivalent stages in the history of mankind.

Each stage is identified with an animal. The first stage, called the era of the camel, occurs in the first four millennia of human history. A camel is an apprentice who absorbs the rules of society and endures the difficulties of life. The camel is the preserver of tradition who bears the burdens of others. This laden, long-suffering animal is the weight-bearing spirit. The second stage, Nietzsche calls the epoch of the lion. Instead of preserving tradition, the lion rises up in defiance. This beast throws off traditional restraints or the "shalt nots" of the previous era, and wills change. The lion says *no*—no to poverty, no to tyranny, no to plague, and no to ignorance. Beginning with the declaration of the Magna Carta in 1215, the Western world has been on an trajectory of saying no to the severe conditions of life. What will become possible when the lion becomes successful? What if humanity becomes successful in eliminating all the disabling conditions of life? Nietzsche says that then our spirits will transform into the third stage of development, represented by the innocent child, the "child reborn." The child asks, "To what can we say yes?" The child is the best version of ourselves.

"The world is an interesting book, but it is useless for those who cannot read it."
- Carlo Goldoni

In the 1960s and '70s, Clare W. Graves researched human development; he described his model in a presentation at Union College in Schenectady, New York: the Emergent Cyclical Double Helix Model of Adult Personality and Cultural Institutions. Don E. Beck and Christopher Cowan then further elaborated on Graves' model and renamed it Spiral Dynamics. These researchers developed the model into a coaching method for enterprises and personal growth, which the philosopher Ken Wilber then further refined and used in his Integral Theory. As a psychology professor, Graves had the task of teaching his students personality-psychology and found himself confused by the number of different theories on personal growth and maturity, theories that often contradicted one another. The three predominant teachings at the time were the psychoanalytical theories of Sigmund Freud, C. G. Jung, and Karen Horney; the behavioral concepts based on the empirical research of B.F. Skinner and Ivan Pavlov; and the humanistic theories of A. Maslow, C. Rogers, and F. Pearls. The humanistic theories neither describe the human being as a drive-based being nor as a trained biological learning-machine, but as a consciousness-endowed being in search of meaning, self-realization, and transcendence.

So Clare W. Graves set out to research the topic of personal growth and maturity by studying his students. He spent nine years exploring what a healthy, mature personality is, and he found that a human being goes through a whole scale of development. In general, one can say that every person develops from rigidity to dogmatism towards openness or from autistic to absolutistic to relativistic thinking. Freedom and originality in thinking develop progressively and lead to quantity and quality in problem-solving. His research had similar results as well as some differences compared to Maslow's theory. Maslow's model demonstrated five levels of personal growth, while Graves discovered more than eight on an open upwards scale. He also found that personality development isn't linear as in Maslow's model, but cyclical, with a pendular movement between self-control and control by outside forces. We develop as an interaction between ourselves and our environment. Each developmental stage correlates to external factors, and conditions of existence prompt conditions for existence. The scale for human growth opens upwards and is theoretically endless. It is a continuous incrementation or augmentation of the complexity of our cognitive structure and cultural information. These units of cultural transmission are called *memes* (Dawkins). These memes don't describe typologies of human beings but instead refer to biopsychological forms of organization of personality and human societies since every human being goes through all the developmental phases humanity has gone through, just as an embryo goes through all the developmental stages of evolution that animals go through.

Each stage transcends and includes its predecessor, which simply means that each new stage of development includes its previous stage but then adds something new and emergent (bigger, higher, wider). This is an evolutionary or developmental sequence. Arthur Koestler called these developmental entities **holarchies**. Each senior stage transcends and includes its junior stage. In development, we have evolved from atoms to molecules, to cells, to organisms, to animals, to human beings. If something goes wrong with the "transcend" part—if, that is, the higher stage fails to cleanly and clearly move beyond the previous stage—that part of the new stage remains fixated or "addicted," as Ken Wilber calls it, to the previous stage. On the other hand, if something goes wrong with the "include" part—if the new stage doesn't include or integrate the previous stage but dissociates, rejects, and splits off parts of it instead—then it will develop an "allergy" to those disowned and unwanted aspects of itself. These addictions and allergies are the two universal problems built into each stage of evolution because of their inherent transcend-and-include nature. When we start out at a stage, we are identified with it. For example, at the survival and instinct stage, we didn't have the desire to eat; we were ourselves that desire to eat, the world was all food, and we were all mouth. Therefore, Freud called this stage the "oral stage." Depending on how strongly we are still identified with this stage, we have a food "addiction."

Normally we should eventually dis-identify with each stage, letting go of our identification exclusively with its needs and drives while maintaining awareness of the stage. We no longer *are* it; we only hold it in our awareness and "transcend and include" it. But if our dis-identifying goes too far or is too extreme, we won't just dis-identify from it but disown and dissociate or repress it. If this happens, we will have a food "allergy" such as bulimia or anorexia.

"Growing up": The stages of human and personal development

In the following summary of the human and personal developmental stages, I have assigned the individual stages colors Ken Wilber has given them instead of names since any single characteristic would be too reductive and not encompass the whole scope of its attributes. Nonetheless I have chosen as subtitles some of the more typical names and traits that have been attributed to them over time, in an attempt to describe them in a more succinct way. I have also added the corresponding yoga chakras (psychophysical energy centers of the body) since yogic wisdom has obviously anticipated our modern knowledge in this field by many centuries, not to say millennia.

Spiral dynamics has given me a profound understanding of my personal development as well as the development of mankind. It furthermore inspires hope in me for the future of mankind and the world during an age in which our human development sometimes seems to have become stagnant and simultaneously ever more in danger. I hope the following pages can convey this understanding and let us gain faith in ourselves and become more responsible individuals.

Infrared stage: Instinctive, archaic self

"Instinct is a marvelous thing. It can neither be explained nor ignored."
- Agatha Christie

Physiological, survival-oriented, instinctive

Muladhara Chakra (base of spine, earth element)

Starting *250,000 years ago* in human history and developed at the age of *0–18 months*, this is our *symbiotic stage* when, at approximately four months of age, the "hatching" or the *"physiological birth"* of our self—the ability to distinguish between our body and our physical environment—occurs. This is also when our primal sense of trust is developed, and the limbic system of our brain, with its sensory-motor and physiological instinctive capabilities accumulated during evolution, has fully matured. The limbic system works unconsciously and non-deliberately with the immune system, digestive system, and respiration. It also coordinates our instinctive understanding and reactions to nature, our search for food, water, and shelter, based on the experience of our ancestors. As infants, we begin to discover our world orally and later, in the course of time, with our hands and the rest of our bodies. We still perceive ourselves as a "dual unity," largely fused with our mothers, and we can't tell the difference between our emotional self and that of others. Our emotions are those of a primitive and basic libidinal self, indicating hunger, thirst, pleasure, pain, fear, disgust, and rage, seeking satisfaction and avoiding pain. We are libido itself and haven't developed a real mind, language, or individual self. We haven't learned to look at ourselves from the outside as an object and, therefore, still completely identify with ourselves.

In the development of humanity at this stage, we lived together with others in survival bands. Our main *quests* were survival and procreation as individuals, thereby maintaining our physiological stability by living instinctively and self-centeredly with our undifferentiated autistic narcissism. Our *methods* were instinctive survival mechanisms such as scavenging whatever we needed, reacting reflexively to outer stimuli, and communicating through emotional contagion and rudimentary signals and sounds. Our *gifts* at this stage were our survival instincts; we intuitively sensed what we needed and how to get it. We also sensed imminent trouble. Our *spirituality* consisted of pure symbiosis with nature, while our main *fears* related to how to stay alive, so we prioritized water, food, and shelter. At this stage, the *typical drugs* we consumed were natural plants.

A *developmental crisis* was presented to us by a sudden, unprecedented lack of resources, which made cooperation necessary and let us discover the benefits of working together.

An example of this stage is a population discovered in Uganda around 1980. This population was organized in bands; if there wasn't enough food for all, the grandparents were left to die so that the rest could subsist.

Today there are only very few adults at this stage, usually suffering from brain damage such as Alzheimer's disease or extreme war trauma. It is possible, however, to have some aspects of awareness become attached or fixated to this stage—oral fixation or oral dissociation, which leads to oral addictions or oral allergies. *Afflictions that have their roots at this stage are autism, bulimia, and anorexia (not differentiating the second-person perspective, staying fixated, or becoming dissociated from this oral level).*

Mindfulness practice for the infrared stage

To become aware of and discover this stage and its quality, we can do a body movement scan, move our body mindfully and experience it, and discover our senses by eating mindfully.

Magenta stage: Animistic, emotional, sexual self

"Indubitably, magic is one of the subtlest and most difficult of the sciences and arts. There is more opportunity for errors of comprehension, judgment, and practice than in any other branch of physics."
- Aleister Crowley

Shared identity, magic

Svadhishthana Chakra (lower abdomen, water element)

Starting around *200,000 years ago* in human history, during our migration from Africa, and developed at the age of *1–3 years* of an individual: At around 18 months of age, we experience our *psychological birth* by discovering the fundamental difference between our emotional libidinal self and our physical self. We begin to experience that we not only have a physical body but are full of emotions. Along with the distinction of our emotional self, our instinctual drives begin to flower and differentiate, with early bodily feelings becoming more distinguished. Early emotions such as happiness, disgust, fear, sorrow, and anger develop beyond the rudimentary sensations that primarily seek pleasure and avoid pain. At this stage, our psychological and somatic intelligence are impulsive, situated in the present, seeking immediate gratification. The emerging, more sophisticated sensations and early feelings are still not seen through introspection but are unreflectively felt. In our encounter with nature, our awaking brain is confronted with immense amounts of information; many forces and experiences of seemingly unknown origin within and outside of ourselves affect us constantly. We try to make sense of them, to predict and control them so we can find security and protection. But since our emotional self is adapting to its differentiation from the outside world, and we still can't experience the origins and boundaries of our emotions and thinking, we develop an anthropomorphic —or animistic—worldview. To us, the flower, the rock, the mountain, and the sea have souls and take on human-like qualities. In our animistic perception, we can believe that a volcano erupts and thunder strikes because they want to kill us and that flowers bloom when we fall in love. Since our emotional selves have no limits, we believe that we can influence the outside world through our thinking and emotions. In our effort to understand and defend ourselves in this incomprehensible world around us, we seek to magically control the world. We resort to superstitious and magical thinking such as Santeria, believing in the evil eye and bad omens such as that black cats bring bad luck or that a person is ill because she is possessed by evil spirits. We try to influence the weather through a rain dance or hurt and punish others with voodoo dolls and curses. We believe in our voodoo-doll trick because, on the one side, our brain has already learned to create images (picture "Lassie" the dog) and symbols (word "Lassie") during this pre-operational stage (described by Piaget), but on the other hand, we still tend to confuse them with what they represent. We can see magical thinking when a three-year-old hides his head under a pillow and believes that everything around him has disappeared. The Christian Bible has many instances of magical thinking, such as Moses parting the Red Sea and Jesus turning water to wine, walking on water, making the blind see, and raising the dead. As adults, we often still have tendencies towards magical thinking and are attracted to the magic in religions. But we must recognize that although there is consciousness and life full of purpose all around us in nature, we still must learn to differentiate our emotional self from our surroundings so we don't attribute our individual human characteristics to them.

At this stage, our ancestors lived in tribes of 30 to 40 individuals whose relationship was determined by blood lineage and defended by aggression towards outsiders. Encounters with other tribes often led to war. Infanticide was practiced when there was a lack of food, and the survival of the tribe was at risk. We performed magic rituals to tame nature. Our *quest* at this stage was safety and security, keeping our tribe's home safe and the spirits of nature and our ancestors happy. Our *methods* for this were customs and traditions, including rituals for the gods, which never failed our ancestors when they venerated them in the right way. In this stage, *gifts* are rituals, awe, wonder, fun, and play. Bonding and the primary capabilities are learned at this stage since they also help secure survival. Our *fears* lie in the loss of shelter and territory and are, therefore, the origin of our social fears. When someone trespasses on our territory, we are aggressive so we can protect our taboos and possessions. The *afflictions* of this stage are emotional instability within the border-line, the non-development of further perspectives with continued self-centeredness such as in early narcissism, the inability to connect to others such as sociopathy and omnipotence fantasies, and spontaneous and instinct-driven animistic hallucination. A fixation at this early stage often results in difficulties developing proper willpower. Impulses and the desire for immediate gratification are strong and make sustained, willed action for future goals hard to realize. *Spirituality* is practiced through shamanism with rituals. Typical *drugs* of this stage are mushrooms, peyote, natural herbs, and opium in ritual. The *developmental crisis* arises through decreasing fear of survival, bonding within the tribe, and making the individual's obligations to the community seem less important. These changes, as well as our own experiences that don't correlate with handed-down customs and doctrines, promote the awakening of the ego. An example of a culture living at this stage has been found in Papua New Guinea.

Mindfulness practice for the magenta stage

Through mindfulness training, we can discover this stage and become aware of, transcend, and include any magical, superstitious thoughts we might have. Through our attention and direct objective awareness, we can either transcend and break any fixations at this level, or touch the object, break any dis-owning of it, and "include" it back into our personality. A "magical" fixation occurs when a magical or superstitious thought arises in our mind, and we don't dis-identify with it ("I have this thought, but I am not this thought"). When we dis-own our magical thoughts, we dissociate and deny them completely ("This thought isn't mine"). With this dissociation, we repress them into the depths of our unconscious. From there, we usually project them onto other people, so that "out there," many people believe in silly superstitions.

Red stage: Pre-conventional, I-emergent, early mythic self

"Power will intoxicate the best hearts, as wine the strongest heads. No man is wise enough, nor good enough to be

trusted with unlimited power."
- Colton

Impulsivity, power, safety

Manipura Chakra (solar plexus, fire element)

Starting 10,000 years ago, during the feudal and explorative empires in humanity, and developed at the age of 3–6 years: During this early age, we discover our I-identity; our ego develops and manifests itself with the pure enthusiasm and pleasure of being. We experience our body and express ourselves through it with unrestrained vitality, spontaneously and impulsively with the brute elemental force of our power drives. Through this self-assertion, we develop our capacity for honesty, autonomy, and initiative, as well as early secondary capabilities. This was the age of empires, characterized by heroes fighting for honor and glory, individuals asserting themselves against others, and God against all. Shame and humiliation provoke blood-vengeance, an eye for an eye and a tooth for a tooth. The self-assertion of the strong against the weak results in the muscular survival of the fittest and the exploitation of the frail. The ego comes into being and erupts defiantly, throwing off the tethers of group morals and norms. The ego asserts, "Here I am; I am alive!" "I will do as I please!" "I can take what I want!" and "After me, come what may!" In maturation, our early impulsivity can transcend into vitality, passion, spontaneity, and creativity. Our power-drives are our solid foundation for self-protection and self-assertion. This stage is also called the "opportunistic," "naive hedonistic," or "power gods" stage because it is narcissistic, self-centered, and immensely charged with power. At this stage, the descriptor of narcissism does not mean being occupied and self-consciously absorbed with oneself and one's self-image but rather ruthlessly doing whatever one pleases without any reflexive self-awareness. Self-awareness simply isn't possible yet, since we as humans at this stage cannot stand back and look at ourselves from a distance, criticize ourselves, or reflect on ourselves from a different perspective. We are unreflectively identified and stuck with ourselves in the first person "me/mine" perspective. We cannot yet introspect and see our interior as something that can be investigated or seen phenomenologically as an object. We remain on the simple subject of doing the seeing.

We act like four-year-olds in this stage. When we ask a four-year-old with a red and green ball in his hand to tell us what color he sees when the red side is facing him, he will say red. Although he is aware that the ball has two differently colored sides, he cannot understand that we see green on the opposite side, since he cannot yet put himself into our shoes. The four-year-old has a hidden map, his basic grammar rules; he still doesn't have the capacity to recognize the real existence of another person and see the other's perspective. At the red stage of development, morals consist of the naive, hedonistic, pre-conventional egocentrism where might makes right, the stronger person dominates, seeks pleasure, ensures their own safety and security, and uses pure brute power to achieve these ends. At this stage, there is no sense of guilt, remorse, or self-blame. The ego-driven person demands respect, allegiance, and unconditional obedience. Always seeking security and power, our power drives are the hidden map of unconscious grammar rules controlling our behavior. In adulthood, fixations to this stage can be excessive cultivation of muscular power, easily resorting to physical violence in conflicts or to get what one wants, criminal behavior, corruption, or leading a gang—all awash in the pleasure of power.

The difference between an animistic and mythic worldview depends basically on where we locate the "miracle." When we see the world during the animistic stage, we still believe that we are the ones capable of making miracles happen. We think we can make it rain by performing a rain dance or kill someone by wishing him dead. In this stage, we cannot clearly differentiate the thoughts and images in our heads from the phenomena we perceive in the external world. When we enter the mythic stage, we begin to understand that we can't really perform magic, but power-gods, spirits, yogis, and other supernatural beings, as well as godlike emperors, and of course, "Mommy" can. So, we locate the magical powers in mythical beings, and we try to influence them or please them through rituals and prayer. The first great military empires were usually headed by godlike emperors such as Caesar, Ramses, and Alexander the Great.

According to Piaget, this is the concrete operational stage when the capability of forming concepts and schema first appears. Now concepts such as "dog" representing all dogs, not only Lassie, are becoming possible. The emergence of symbols in the magenta stage makes the expansion of our emotions possible. For example, rage can expand to anger. When we understand concepts in the red stage, anger can expand towards hatred. Our positive emotions are also continuously differentiating and expanding. Basic rudimentary pleasure extends to pleasure and then the beginnings of joy, yet all these emotions are still self-centered. With the emergence of power, concepts, and intentionality, a basic form of willpower becomes possible, enabling a child to build Lego structures and arrange furniture in a dollhouse. This basic willpower is still largely limited to the present moment.

Our *quest* at this stage is to be a hero-warrior with power and glory through passion and self-expression. Our *method* is impulsive and egocentric. We seek immediate gratification and have low frustration tolerance, conforming to the pecking order and aligning with power, taking whatever we need whenever we can work through force and power. Our *gifts* are individuation, power, passion, courage, risk-taking, creativity, and learning to set boundaries. We find our *spirituality* in polytheism and myths. Our *fears* are of physical aggression from others, humiliation, and the loss of our personal power. *Afflictions* are a "power addiction," which is a strong fixation and hidden identification with this stage; it lets us glorify power in the extreme forms of martial arts, militarism, body cultivation, and ultimate business success. Afflictions also appear as failed anger and emotional management and the inability to build stable relations. A "power allergy," where we repress and project our power drives, means we act as spineless, dependent children who give way to anybody else's will. We act as if the whole world is controlling us and has power over us. This allergy results in anxiety, depression, phobias, and excessive shame. Typical *drugs* used on this level are crack, heroin, and tobacco. A *developmental crisis* appears when the dominance of the powerful and rich is no longer accepted, and the poor and oppressed band together to defend themselves and fight for their rights. To succeed in this collaborative rebellion, the need and the desire for structure and discipline grow. The newly emerging understanding that one must die (no matter how strong) initiates a search for meaning, transcendental order, and authority. We see this occur when young people throw off the restraints of family rules during puberty. Some cinematic examples are *Gomorrah* by Matteo Garrone, depicting the gangs in Naples. The movie *Sin Nombre* (2009) shows the similar social order of Mexican gang life. Perhaps best known is *Lord of the Flies*, based on a novel by the English writer William Golding about schoolboys stranded on an island who regress to this stage.

Mindfulness practice for the red stage

For this stage, we can use our mindfulness technique for our repressed power drive. It often makes itself heard as an inner critic or inner controller, watching and chiding us with a negative, critical, and controlling voice. This inner critic always puts us down and makes us feel like inferior losers. We can work on this inner voice, our sub-personality, with mindfulness by asking it to dialogue with us. We take the roles of our cognitive self and our controller self and let them converse. We begin when the normal self asks the controller self, "What do you want? Why are you critical of me? Why do you always try to control me?" We then take the role of the controller and try to answer these questions. Through this process, we make our inner critic turn from a hidden subject into an aware object. We become capable of looking at it instead of through it. We act like a videographer.

We all have an inner critic within us. We initially created it by introjecting other people's ideas, judgments, and criticisms into our psyche. We were so successful with this process that we made them seem like a part of ourselves. Those critical ideas became like an infection that we have difficulty curing, one that continues to impact our mental health. These negative, internalized "infections" usually come from our parents, family, and teachers and can be called "parento-cocci." We can often still hear them in their original speaking voices. To slowly become masters of our inner critic, we can use the dis-identification technique, which consists of a number of steps.

- "Unearthing" or searching for it
- Noting or becoming aware of it
- "Videotaping" or holding it in awareness as an object
- Letting go or disidentifying from it.

Amber stage: Mythic, conventional, authoritarian, conformist, premodern self

*"Learn the rules like a pro, so you can
break them like an artist."*
- Pablo Picasso

Rule-role mind, meaning, order, belonging, belief in an absolute truth

Anahata Chakra (heart, air element)

Starting *5,000 years ago,* during the age of monarchies, nation states, and authoritarian religion in humanity and developed at the age of *7–8 years*: At this stage, we discover the *second-person perspective* and become able to take the role of the other. Now we can attune ourselves not only to our own emotions but also to those of others. We experience empathy, extended love, and belongingness and adhere to peer groups, which give us a true "we" identity or a "mythic membership." When we understand the role of another person, our identity expands from egocentric to ethnocentric as we extend our sense of belongingness from our self to belonging to various groups—our family, clan, tribe, political party, nations, and religions. We develop a drive and desire to interrelate and connect with others and study their behavior for clues of feeling so we can conform and fit in. At this stage, we also discover our mortality, which makes us seek and adhere even more to the absolute truth that is represented by the authorities of the group we belong to. This adherence promotes concrete, "absolutistic" or "mythic literal" thinking. Examples in our contemporary world are fundamentalist Christians, Muslims, Marxists, Taoists... Christian fundamentalists read the Bible literally, believing that God killed all firstborn Egyptian sons, and Elijah drove straight to heaven in his chariot. Our group's absolute truth grants us security, and by attuning ourselves to it, we gain meaning and identity. The absolute truth of our group is expressed in its dogmatic books—the Bible, Koran, Bhagavad Gita, Pure Land Sutra, Marxist writings, or the text of whatever group we identify with. To be sure of our membership, we avoid conflict, seek harmony, and conform to peer pressure.

Learning the second-person perspective also means that we begin to gain distance from ourselves and develop intra-personal awareness, a rudimentary proto-awareness of ourselves and our interior spaces. We begin to become introspective, to look within. During this developmental period, we discover the advantages of discipline and courtesy, and we ripen our secondary capabilities. A clear vision of a good, virtuous life comes into view, as does the demarcation between sinners and saints. Our desires become controlled and channeled into the construction of a holy order based on our group's absolute beliefs. It is the birth of our mortality based on the group's rules and a god who rewards the faithful and punishes the negligent. We adapt our morals to the ethics of the group, whether they conform to any notion of absolute morality or not; what's more important is that we believe what our group believes. We do what our group does. The group upholds the standards of absolute truth and absolute goodness. We abide by law and order, behave nicely, and believe in "my country, my group, my religion, right or wrong," which is why this level's moral stage is referred to as conventional or conformist. We know that disagreeing with our group or breaking its laws has grave consequences. Law and order are the glue for our societal coherence. The Ten Commandments are a typical example of the governing laws for this stage.

In this stage, our belief in rules enables us to find meaning, direction, and purpose in life, and therefore it enables us to get predetermined outcomes. We develop total and unquestioning subordination to the system, take laws literally, and obey them strictly without challenging authority. Historically at this stage, social institutions are established, so punishment isn't executed by the individual, but the accused are tried and condemned according to the laws of the group. Fundamentalists quote verbatim from their holy scriptures, and with the ardor of belief, they enforce some of the rules barbarically. An adulteress is stoned to death, while a thief has his hands cut off. Willpower becomes dominant at this stage, making a significant sacrifice of present pleasure for future gains possible, hoping to achieve religious goals by fasting, practicing celibacy, or engaging in self-flagellation. This strong willpower can also be seen in child gymnasts, ballerinas, pianists, and chess prodigies. This willpower and the other attributes don't have to manifest in exaggerated versions but usually occur more often in healthy ones that are crucial for our flourishing in life. Our somatic intelligence continues developing as well, and our body has learned how to operate concretely in the world. It can learn to play different songs on the piano, coordinate its movements with others, and play individual and team sports.

Most of the great empires of the past—Mesopotamia, Greece, Rome, India, China, and the Ottoman Empire—were driven by this mythic belongingness stage. It began some 6,000–7,000 years ago and dominated up to the rise of modernity only 400 years ago.

Our *quest* at this stage is to find belonging, meaning, and order, thus defining good and evil, and allowing us to follow a safe pathway way to the good. Our *method* is to have faith by following the given rules and filling them in or completing them when needed. The *gifts* we develop are empathy, discipline, impulse control, and gratification deferral. We find our *spirituality* in monotheism with rituals. We *fear* the loss of control, chaos, straying off the path of the good, loss of faith, and retribution from a punishing god. The *afflictions* we encounter at this stage are archetypical role identification, script pathology, fundamentalism, fascism, and compulsiveness. Criminal networks also have strict laws and codes of behavior, such as the Cosa Nostra, imperialistic and colonialist empires, and governments with ethnocentric identities. Especially if infested with any lingering power drives, they tend to be authoritarian, corrupt, and villainous. Those who belong to fundamentalist religious or to the political far right prioritize law and order and traditional family values (or "God's values"). They appear nationalistic, anti-immigration, fear the ruin of family values and work ethic, and oppose gun control. The typical drugs adhered to at this stage are alcohol, tobacco, and medications. A *developmental crisis* arises when we begin to think, *Why should I wait for the gratification of my needs and desires in the afterlife? Why can't I satisfy them now?* In the Middle Ages, the plagues prompted just doubts about God's holy order, since everyone—pagans and saintly priests—all died alike. God didn't offer safe harbor to those who followed his rules.

Mindfulness practice for the amber stage

For this stage, we can use our four-step mindfulness technique of unearthing, noting, videotaping, and letting go. We can apply this technique, for example, to our feelings of righteousness or to the opposite feeling, when we repress our need to stand up for what we believe is right. How often do we want to I say "I told you so!" and how important does it feel to us? How often do we believe we are right and compulsively impose our opinion? When do I simply let others impose their opinion without standing up for myself? We learn to dis-identify, transcend, and include, so we can express our-selves freely, not compulsively or with inhibition. We can also use our mindfulness practice on our need to belong to a group.

Orange stage: Rational, achieving, modernist, post-conformist self

"The beginning of wisdom is the definition of terms."
- Socrates

Reason, freedom, achievement

Vishuddha Chakra (throat, ether element)

Starting earliest from *6,000–7,000 years ago*, it began dominating 300 years ago with the rise of modernity and is developed at the age of *9–14 years*: This is the stage at which we discover the *third-person perspective* or our objective, scientific, universal perspective. It is the formal operational mode, according to Piaget, and is the moment we become aware of our thoughts. This awareness allows us to stand back and use our logic and personal experience to criticize and substitute outer authority with our own rational opinion. Once we start thinking with autonomy, we start living with self-determination instead of with fatalistic heteronomy. This liberation enables us to address self-esteem needs and unleash our drive to achieve and accomplish. In this stage, we can develop our intelligence quotient, win merit, excel in a number of arenas, and contribute to the progress of mankind.

This also means that emotions surrounding purpose, goals, and aims come to the surface, and we become particularly attuned to the emotions and feelings of others that reflect on our own success and advancement. Instead of viewing others as either sinners or saints, we now see them as winners or losers. At the same time, formal operational thought, metarule, lets us advance from ethnocentric conformism to the third-person world-centric view, and a world-centric consciousness and tolerance that considers all of us begins to emerge. On the other hand, we learn to act out of our own self-interest again and strive for our own personal pleasure. We value success and merit in competition with others, which fortifies our willpower and develops frustration-tolerance and self-discipline for reaching long-term and more complex goals. We can now make decisions relying on our rational, pragmatic, individualistic thinking, independent of any moralistic dogmas or group conventions, which gives birth to our first true individual personality. As individuals, we now strive for success within the boundaries of regulations and legislation but also come to question them and bend them according to our individual necessity by affirming that "the end justifies the means." We now feel that our former belief of being at nature's mercy and having to appease this force or find favor through rituals is ineffective and outdated. Instead, we try to understand nature and use it to our benefit. This approach brings about an incredible development of technologies. Since we now actually become aware of our thoughts, we learn introspection, become self-reflective, and truly conscientious and develop a universal identity with a growing cosmopolitan awareness, accompanied by a post-conventional sense of morals. This enables humanity's what-if thinking. The government can now be understood not as a monarchy created by divine rights where everyone is the ruler's property but as a governing body that is erected on a social contract or agreement between the governors and the governed. Out of the idea of the individual rights of citizens, the idea of universal rights of all humankind arises. This expansive paradigm leads the way for alternative realities, such as the abolition of the monarchy, slavery, fundamentalist religion, and patriarchy. Universal rights became the foundation of the moral understanding of the French, American, and Russian revolutions and the development of the modern world. This moral view is still the basis of representative democracies in the world. The US Declaration of Independence, the Constitution, and the Bill of Rights are all representatives of post-conventional universal morals. Some 300 years ago, Western Enlightenment or the Age of Reason fostered a belief captured in this statement: "I am a human being, nothing human is alien to me." In the Renaissance, which preceded the Enlightenment, democracy, science, and a capitalistic, market-driven meritocracy slowly evolved and became the state order. The development of the third-person perspective enabled humanity to stand outside the present moment for the first time, to become aware of historical time, compare the present with the past, and conceptualize a new future. This cultural shift and a new view of time enable us to imagine improvement, which becomes the origin of our newly developed drive for accomplishment, achievement, excellence, merit, and progress. Mythic time circled back to nature's seasonal rhythm, whereas historical time continuously unfolds before us.

In their teens, most young people go through the inner chaos of puberty, the "reason and revolution" stage, at which their self-esteem needs begin to emerge, and they reject conformity and follow their individualist impulse to stand out and be different.

With the development of the third-person perspective and intrapersonal intelligence, comes the discovery of the three-dimensional space within, with length, height, depth, and perspective that can be visualized in introspection. The two-dimensional artworks of the Middle Ages give way to the three-dimensional paintings of the Renaissance like Raphael, Michelangelo, Rembrandt... and our developing introspection allows us to monitor our inner status. We ask ourselves if we are happy, anxious, sad, elated, guilty, depressed, or regretful. This personal monitoring helps us evaluate if we are fulfilling our basic needs and complying with social norms but also whether we are meeting our needs for self-esteem and life fulfillment. Our willpower now takes a significant step from its concrete expression of controlling matter and body (such as diet, sex, and behavior) to controlling our thoughts and ideas. Philosopher Ken Wilber writes, "Just as formal operational cognition operates on concrete operational cognition, which operates on the concrete material world, so the formal will operates on the concrete will, which operates on the concrete material world. In each case, the field of phenomena operated on expands from matter to bodily emotions to mental thoughts." We learn to hold inner phenomena such as images, symbols, concepts, thoughts, ideas, rules, roles, values, goals, and aims in our consciousness, making them objects of our will, analyzing and transforming them. Many of our cherished skills and capacities require our minds to keep a steady and constant focus and not wander wildly and randomly. We now consciously and willingly become able to work on our personality, consciousness, and thoughts to mentally transform ourselves through coaching, psychotherapy, meditation, and so forth. We also become increasingly able to mentalize and understand what our counterparts are thinking so we can anticipate their next moves. In our somatic intelligence, we learn to train our body to accomplish activities and performances with multiple skill sets such as how to play the same tune on different instruments or as athletes to perform the multiple skillsets of different sports. This ability allows us to excel as athletes, dancers, painters, pianists, and surgeons.

Our materialistic *quest* is to create a better life using our logic, reason, strategic thinking, and internal drive to enjoy life and gain materially. We are individually the architects of our future. Man is his own god. Our *method* is using thought, introspection, and science to learn how to set goals, and then compete, achieve, and excel in meeting our measurable goals. Our *gifts* are discovering and creating our critical thinking, our IQ, and an early global perspective showing the way to individual rights, democracy, modern science, medicine, and industrialization. We live our *spirituality* in the form of atheism, science, or a more transcendent, liberal form of religion. We *fear* the loss of status and position, money, or honor. We fear losing control of life and not having the reins of our destiny in our hands. The *afflictions* of this stage lie in an identity crisis (industry/inferiority), role confusion, consumerism, ecological crisis, workaholism, goal-fixation, burnout, and over-attachment to successful methods. Typical *drugs* are cocaine, crystal meth, speed, and other amphetamines. A *developmental crisis* arises when we start experiencing senselessness and loneliness despite having material success. The awakening of a need for a greater sense in life lets us transcend our limited goals of personal pleasure and well-being and start thinking in wider human terms and engage in projects of public welfare. Historical examples include Martin Luther's reformation of the Catholic Church and the contributions of empirical scientists Kepler, Galileo, and Newton.

Mindfulness practice for the orange stage

For this stage, we can use our mindfulness technique for our need to stand out or our rational achiever mentality. We can further use it for the differentiation of our orange, green, or other levels: Do we like conforming or deciding for ourselves? Do we want to belong to a group or be an individual? Are we intensely patriotic, or do we feel we are more a part of a global village? National or cosmopolitan? Do we think mythically or with reason?

Seeking the truth about ourselves is essential to personal development: When we become able to tell ourselves the truth, we become able to stand up and tell others the truth. Although it is sometimes more diplomatic to keep some truths to ourselves, it is never wise to close our eyes to them or keep them from ourselves. When we can see and accept the truth, we can internally improve. In the evening, we can take some time to reflect on our interactions with other people during the day and become honest about our feelings about them. We take a few moments of awareness of these judgments, let them sink in, and then continue. After this exercise, we can maintain our composure out of integrity instead of falsehood. We must clean up all the little white lies, the diplomatic falsehoods we use when we talk about ourselves. Over time, we believe them and develop habits that cripple our emotional intelligence to function authentically. We can tell ourselves the truth about our job or our relationship and, through truthfulness, assume responsibility for our choices. Our emotions are not just feelings but necessary information. As adults, our emotionality has to have matured to be trusted; we recall our previous phases of fantasies, magic, and narcissism, and we have outgrown them. A good practice is to report on our feelings and each time affirm our belief about what these emotions are telling us. Because our feelings are an important dimension of our reality, we learn to follow our path toward truthfulness and to trust our feelings; they are an important dimension of our reality.

Green stage: Pluralistic, sensitive, postmodern, egalitarian, collectivist self

"When awareness is brought to an emotion, power is brought to your life."
- Tara Meyer Robson

Community and quality

Vishuddha Chakra (throat, ether element)

Starting around *150 years ago* with the social democracies, this movement included student revolts in the 1960s and focused on human rights. The development of our *fourth-person perspective, which is acquired at the age of 15–21,* is the awakening of compassion and conscience, where social orientation becomes more important to us than success, cooperation more important than competition, and we begin to consider people as our equals with same rights (egalitarian, pluralistic). We can say this is the discovery of our EQ, our Emotional Quotient. At this stage, we take an even deeper plunge into our interior world while simultaneously emphasizing the caring dimensions of community and solidarity. We become aware of the division and merciless competition in our world that has led us to differentiate the strong from the weak, the good from the bad, sinners from saints, rich from poor, and superior from inferior. We become compassionately opposed to these differentiations and want to eradicate them. Our perspective has broadened to include rational facts as well as emotions, human needs, and values. After discovering ourselves, the fourth-person perspective allows us to focus on discovering our fellow human beings. We discover their multiple viewpoints and come to believe that all these differences deserve to be respected. The development of our fourth-person perspective means that our intra-personal intelligence can now become aware of and criticize our third-person rationality and its conclusions. Our expanded vision of morals lets us believe that all morals are relative. "What's right for you is right for you; what's right for me is right for me. I do my thing; you do your thing." Neither can nor should be ranked, judged, or challenged. Universal judgments and guidelines become suspect to us. We want all people to be allowed the maximum amount of freedom to pursue their own individual truths, values, and preferences. Our multicultural, pluralistic view increases the capacity of our willpower even further. We adopt a critical stance about the third-person rational mind, investigating it for its deficits in the area of feelings and intuition.

This stage of thinking enables the development of social democracies, recognizes the value of a pluralistic society, and encourages human rights activism. It is the natural outgrowth of the Enlightenment and has empowered the civil rights and environmental movements worldwide. Other characteristics of this postmodern era are the growth in feminism and multiculturalism and a sensitivity for the marginalized. It is postmodern, relativistic, sensitive, and multicultural. The dominant point of view is pluralism, where multiple approaches coexist. Gone are universal truths or guiding principles that are true for everybody. In their place are local, culturally constructed beliefs. Universal claims of knowing the truth are recognized as attempts to impose one's own view and values on others. They represent the menace of subjugation, oppression, and domination. So, postmodernism critiques all "isms" or "big pictures," including capitalism, Marxism, and fundamentalism. The new paradigm is not based on abstract rationality or logic but on the "heart", on feelings and intuition. The old paradigm is now equated with all the "isms," which are Newtonian-Cartesian, rational, analytic, and divisive. The new paradigm operates by the rules of the new quantum physics; it is holistic and organic, caring and loving and not fragmented or mechanistic.

With this shift in paradigms, all rankings and hierarchies become taboo, even excellence and achievement. Being better and more successful than others becomes another form of oppression. The success of a meeting is defined by everyone having a chance to exchange their feelings about a subject and not by the decisions made or conclusions drawn. Through our further development, the capacity for multiple skill sets across all five sensorimotor areas continues to increase. A master card dealer can, for example, not only shuffle a card deck thoroughly with one hand but is able to end up with a pre-decided card on top.

Our *quest* at this stage is for dialogue and consensus because we care for friends, family, and the people in our groups. Care for others becomes more important than for us, and our care now expands to the whole planet. Our *method* is to listen and appreciate diverse views, emphasize group needs, and marginalize no one. Our *gifts* are empathy and social skills (EQ), tolerance, social justice, pluralism, spirituality with inter-religious faiths, the worship of nature, and concern for the planet. Our *fears* arise from not being tolerant enough, not belonging and contributing sufficiently to our group and not getting enough social confirmation from its members, not being sensitive enough and not contributing to the health of our earth. The *afflictions* are lack of discernment, excessive relativism, over-indulgence, self-complacency, inauthenticity, and deadening. If we take our pluralistic thinking to extremes, this can lead to aperspectival madness with a sense of paralysis arising since we experience all elements as contextual constructions, and so they all seem equally untrue. Typical *drugs* of this stage are LSD and marijuana. A *developmental* crisis emerges for us when our continuous struggles for consensus, harmony, and well-being for our community deplete our energy, and our own feelings and needs begin to impose themselves urgently on us again. The stronger this dissonance becomes, the more we feel the need to walk our own path again. Culturally this paradigm is reflected in songs such as "All You Need Is Love" by the Beatles. A more formal declaration of the values of this paradigm can be seen in the passage of The International Bill of Human Rights by the United Nation in 1966.

Mindfulness practice for the green stage

For this stage, we can use our mindfulness technique to observe ourselves when we judge others for judging or how we reproach others for ranking. We recognize that we condemn others for our own character defects of judging and ranking. We like to say that we do not force our views on our counterparts. "Believe what you want to believe. I would never want to force my belief on you." But deep within, we feel the impulse to make others comply with our belief of tolerance, and we deeply detest all people on the **orange** level. But by becoming aware of this judgmental process, we are able once again to unearth, note, videotape, and let it go. We can shift our perspective from judging and recognize that our behavior is ubiquitous, unavoidable, and natural. Then we can accept it and let it go, so we can use it resourcefully.

The **red** power drive sees the world in schemata of predators and prey and thinks only of itself and treats only itself morally. **Amber** is fundamentalist and sees only sinners and saints, with only true believers belonging to its group, which it treats morally. **Orange** recognizes that all human beings have human rights since it demands them for itself, but it competes in a world of winners and losers and despises all the equality jargon. **Green**-level thinking, for the first time, recognizes equality as a value and embraces pluralism. So, by looking at this development, we can recognize and acknowledge that there is a natural growth hierarchy as opposed to a dominating or unhealthy hierarchy. Natural growth is a vertical development ascending from archaic to magic to power to mythic to rational to pluralistic. This development rises upwards to a wider, deeper, more embracing, holistic, and loving worldview. As Hegel put it: "Each stage is adequate, each higher stage is more adequate." We must include our judgmental thinking in our transcendence. By transcending, we let go of judgment itself, and by including it, we simply rest in the awareness of it without identifying with it or condemning or negating it.

Whenever we let go of identification and allow a subject to be the object of our awareness, we grow and open ourselves to new realms of development. These new realms are waiting to emerge, and once we identify with them, naturally, we initiate the entire process of growth all over again.

The distribution of the population in the developmental stages in the United States around the year 2000 was approximately:

40% Amber traditional, mythic

50% Orange modern, rational, scientific

25% Green pluralistic, postmodern

These are the three stages involved in culture wars. This distribution adds up to more than 100% because these stages are overlapping. These stages are often at the heart of political disagreements where one set of values confronts the others. In the rhetoric of these disagreements, we hear ambers espousing traditional religious values, oranges advocating modern scientific values, and greens championing postmodern multicultural values. Unless people from one stage reach the next higher level of development, the **yellow** stage, they will not gain the fundamental insight that all stages have value and are irreplaceable and necessary. Religious fundamentalists accept God's truth without looking for scientific proof. Orange, rational thinking doesn't accept religion and despises the green pluralists for their lack of scientific approach. And postmodernists don't accept science or religion because they consider both to be social constructions.

The second tier

Beginning at the following yellow stage, a "momentous leap" happens—or, as Clare Graves puts it, "a chasm of unbelievable depth of meaning is crossed." All stages up to and including the green postmodern pluralism stage believe that their truth and values are absolute; they are the only truths and values in the world, and all others are misguided, confused, or simply wrong. But yellow and the subsequent stages believe that there is some significant truth in every single earlier stage, viewing all of them as phases of growth and development. Just as we can't go from atoms to molecules to cells to organisms by skipping molecules, every stage of development is essential and important. The first six stages are therefore called first-tier and the new levels second-tier. We can distinguish **deficiency needs** (first tier) and **being needs** (second tier). While the first-tier levels are "partial, narrow, excluding, superlative and driven by deficiencies," second-tier levels are "inclusive, embracing, comprehensive, integral and driven by abundance" (Ken Wilber).

Yellow stage: Cognitive, systemic, integral self

"It is very important to understand that emotional intelligence is not the opposite of intelligence; it is not the triumph of heart over head—it is the unique intersection of both."
- David Caruso

Self-realization, but not at the cost of others

Ajna Chakra (forehead)

The cognitive-systemic self is a world-centric meshwork of flex and flow and an interlocking dynamic system. It is the repeating of infrared at higher levels of self-sense, integrating the whole spiral and the search for the survival of the human species through growing healthy hierarchies. This stage started around *50 years ago,* and there is *no specific age* for the beginning of this new *systemic thinking* that combines head with heart, emotions, intuition, and thought. This system of thought requires us to live responsibly and fully as an individual while still being conscious of our past and our potential future. It's not about surviving, being part of a group, or proving anything anymore. Our physiological and psychological existence as an individual and self aren't existentially in question. We now have the freedom to dedicate ourselves to the topics that interest us. We have lost patience with trying to find consensus in our group and want to live our individual freedom and creativity. But we also recognize that we now have to widen our perspective, and that isn't about safeguarding ourselves as individuals, because much more is at stake. It is now the survival of humanity and our endangered world. The modifications of our environment are not egocentrically—or ethnocentrically—based. Now we must operate from a global or universal point of view. We follow the maxim to bring our self-expression into harmony with the needs of others and the environment. We do so more freely and with more authentic individual creativity, since we are not so dependent on others' consent and approval.

All this is possible because of vision-logic. The fifth-person perspective emerges, and we see beyond differences and recognize communalities and universal principles. Vision-logic gives us the ability to question our fourth-person perspective. Postmodernism, described in Ken Wilber's words, understood that "truths are culturally constructed" and "that there are no universal truths" or that "all knowledge is context-bound, and contexts are boundless and thus depend on interpretation." Our fifth-person perspective realizes that postmodern claims that there are no universal truths are, by their very nature, universal claims supposedly true for everyone, everywhere, and through all times. To make such a universal claim is self-contradictory. We now understand that although knowledge is context-bound and that there are universal contexts and universal principles, more truths can be discovered and further developed and deepened as our understanding grows. All the previous levels up to now believed that their truths and values were the only truths in the world. Their either/or mentality assured them that all other values are wrong, confused, misguided, or infantile.

But at vision-logic, we now understand and see that without exception, every previous level has touched a part of the truth and has significance, and all levels are steps in our growth and development. We understand just as physical existence must go from atoms to molecules to cells to organisms, so too must we progress from level to level. Skipping any of the steps is fatal because all the stages of our psychological development are essential and must develop integrally without dissociation or fixation. Clare Graves called this level of human consciousness a "momentous leap," where "a chasm of an unbelievable depth of meaning is crossed."

Graves identified the first six stages leading up to this pinnacle of human consciousness as the first tier. In the first tier, we are driven by deficiency needs. The second tier is significantly more inclusive, embracing, comprehensive, integral, and driven by abundance. All this expansion happens from the first to the second tier. Here at the integral level, our multiple intelligences developed throughout our life and as humans begin to influence and form each other. Through introspection, we gain insight that our cognitive, emotional, somatic, spiritual, and moral intelligence all influence each other; the end-product is wisdom. From here on, evolution even more intensely begins to remake and refashion all aspects of our identity. Genuine outreach, inclusiveness, and true wholeness show up in whatever we do worldwide. We become capable of advancing science, art, and the humanities. This results in further development of spiritual maturity, improved government, and more egalitarian economics. Our *quest* at this stage lies in integral synthesis, procedural thinking, and networking. We understand that although everything is in flux and transformation, there are still foundational commonalities. The only constant is transformation. We, as humans, also understand that we are all enmeshed in a social system of reciprocity. Our *method* is leading the self—first to interior clarity and then acting elegantly with a maximum of possible evolved intelligence, integrating diversity with discernment. We help others develop themselves in harmony with all. Our *gifts* lie in a decrease of fear, flexible and multiple perspective-taking, and a continuous increase in our cognitive complexity (polarity/ambiguity management) with the integration of cognitive, emotional, somatic, spiritual, and moral intelligence. We become continuously more capable of deeper creative solutions to all problems facing us. *Fear* and aggression aren't the defining elements for action anymore. We are still afraid and can feel aggressive at times, but these feelings become subordinated to the needs of humanity and the world. Impulsivity and fear slowly dissolve. The *afflictions* we face are aborted self-actualization, existential angst, or bad faith.

We face another *developmental crisis* when we begin to acknowledge that we will never be able to know everything and never gain control over everything. Even if all natural forces were scientifically understood, humanity and the world would always be, to a certain extent, at their mercy. Examples: Creative, self-sufficient, independent people who place their capabilities at the disposal of everyone, such as Albert Schweitzer, Mother Teresa, Paul Farmer, and Nelson Mandela and the film *Tomorrow: The world is full of solutions.*

Mindfulness practice for the yellow stage

So, with mindfulness, let's focus our awareness on the feeling or notion of wholeness. Where and when do we experience this wholeness? In ourselves, our culture, the world, and the universe? How do we feel and experience it whenever it appears in our life? Let's focus on it whenever it is there and take a step back and unearth, note, videotape, and let go, turning this subject into an object and opening ourselves to whatever emerges. At this stage, we will also want to focus on our drive to understand and manage the world and help others develop. What understanding will lie beyond this belief?

Turquoise stage: Holistic self

"Knowing others is intelligence; knowing yourself is true wisdom. Mastering others is strength; mastering yourself is true power."
- Lao Tzu

Humility and acceptance of the limits of our mind and understanding

Ajna Chakra (forehead)

This stage started some *30 years ago* as collective individualism in humanity and begins at *no special age* of the individual. We have arrived at an *intuitive level* of being, experiencing and living with humility, reverence, and acceptance. We know that our understanding is limited and that there is way more out there in the world than we will ever be able to apprehend and manage. Therefore, we become devoted to what is and actively open our consciousness beyond rational thought, and we experience what can't be captured by our intellect. We live in an ecology of perspectives, with a deep experience of oneness and the wholeness of existence through our conscious mind and spirit. Our *quest* at this stage is to bring harmony, joy, and thriving to the whole of humanity throughout the spiral and to bring peace to our world. Our *method* is to do deep interior work on ourselves so we can let go of false belief in our control of external forces. We accept life as it is—unmanageable, in flux, and full of paradoxes. This acceptance allows us to use our accumulated knowledge and intelligence to work intuitively or to "dance with what arises" and live our power through our presence and radiance. We help warmheartedly by accompanying people through their developmental levels. Our *gifts* lie in our abundant experience, our multiple intelligences, and our newly acquired intuitive intelligence.

It is the return of **magenta** at a higher level through ritual, joy, awe, and a profound stable connection to all that is. *Afflictions* that confront us are pathologies of the soul and developmental crises. With vision-logic, we see everything interconnected and harmoniously working together. This interrelatedness can lead to difficulties in recognizing which element is more significant to us than another, often leaving us paralyzed because everything seems equally true and important. This stalemate can continue until we learn to discriminate between greater and lesser wholes. This discrimination is always possible since all wholes come in **holarchies** or nested holarchies with more and less inclusive **holons;** thus, the will can connect with some element. When we do so, we become powerful and effective. Examples are Taoist sage Lao Tzu and people who connect spiritually with the non-visible universe and who open their consciousness to these realms.

Mindfulness practice for the turquoise stage

Through mindfulness and meditation, the continuous work of unearthing, noting, videotaping, and letting go of whatever arises in our mind, over time, we find internal rest. As Lao Tzu said, "Do you have the patience to wait till your mud settles and the water is clear? Can you remain unmoving till the right action arises by itself?" We rest and settle until I-am-ness, our original face, true nature, Christ, arises, and we can stay here bathing in its bliss.

Coral stage: Unitive, trans-rational, transpersonal, super-mind self

"Be content with what you have; rejoice in the way things are. When you realize there is nothing lacking, the entire world belongs to you."
- Lao Tzu

Sahasrara Chakra (crown)

When we reach the coral or clear light stage, the super-mind looking within becomes seeing without. We become able to transcend subject-object dualism, and instead of experiencing the subject in here and the object out there as separate, we enter non-dual suchness, and the knower becomes the known. Our observing self, our interpersonal intelligence becomes transpersonal intelligence and doesn't identify with any object or event anymore, but we become able to identify with all, with everything, with the entire universe. At this stage, our willpower joins our multiple intelligences to operate as a truly spontaneous unity in the best interest of humanity, the world, the universe, all. Our *quest* becomes to realize ourselves as integrated, free, functioning human beings.

Continued evolution

"The way to do is to be."
- Lao Tzu

Since evolution never stops, there are further levels opening before us and humanity. Some that are postulated are indigo para-mind, violet meta-mind, ultraviolet over-mind, and white super-mind. Readers who wish to know more can read works by the philosopher Ken Wilber.

The universe, as we know it, inherently has the capacity to develop continuously, bringing forth new elements that then transcend and include their predecessors. It is an intimate process of coming into being, apprehending (touching), and becoming aware of the previous subject and then making it its object. When we touch an object, this, of course, affects and influences us, so this is also the continuous process of the previous moment influencing the present moment. The causal influence of the past determines the present. But the evolution of the universe isn't predetermined since there is always novelty and creativity built into each act of evolution, making every new step of growth and transcendence an individual, creative one. This process of evolution is what Neoplatonist philosopher Plotinus called *efflux.* It is the universe's process of developing itself materially and unfolding consciousness back to the divine from which it originated through *influx* at the beginning of eternity. It thereby gets the chance to recognize itself.

Leibniz said, "We live in the best of all possible worlds." He meant that although we have many difficulties and much suffering in our world, we, as humankind and the universe, also have this extraordinary opportunity for development and experience.

Memetics

According to the theory of memetics, *memes*, the basis of individual and collective development, are conceptualized units of information such as ideas and thoughts. They reflect the individual emotional and intellectual capabilities that are then communicated in the culture. The brain is a breeding ground in which thoughts incubate. Those thoughts then spread much like a rumor from host to host, continuously mutating like genes from generation to generation. As our intestines are populated by bacteria that help us digest food, our brains are inhabited by memes, through which they develop ever greater comprehension. When distinct memes build coherent complexes, they become WMemes, which form our opinions and cultural characteristics and define the way we clothe ourselves, communicate, and build relationships. These WMemes can be harmonious or in competition with each other, always trying to integrate and elaborate a greater order to themselves. Each developmental stage consists of a characteristic complex of WMemes, each stage of WMemes thus transcending and including its predecessor.

When memes work together on a harmonious developmental scale, they can express themselves as a successful, integrated person who works their way up (orange) through the hierarchy of an organization (amber), understanding and using its rules to their benefit. They will also be able to play competitively (orange) on a team (amber) and work for a charity for the homeless in their spare time (green).

"Man, you will turn into what you love; if you love God, you will be a God; if you love the earth, you will be the earth."
- Angelus Silesius

According to Clare Graves, the development from one stage to another becomes possible when:

- Problems of the current stage are solved.

- The potential for further development is given.

- A disturbance in the inner or outer environment appears and makes change necessary.

- Insight is developed.

The process leads to the removal of hindrances and the consolidation of new pathways.

Phases of transformation

Graves describes five phases of transformation from one developmental stage to another. These phases follow a pattern of relative stability alternating with phases of destabilization and uncertainty:

1. Alpha: Stable and balanced
2. Beta: Time of insecurity and questioning
3. Gamma: Time of confusion, fear, and anger
4. Delta: Understanding and inspired enthusiasm
5. Alpha New: Stability within the new value system, on the next level of development.

The whole developmental spiral is traditionally also referred to as the great chain of being or great nest of being, with complexes of ever more integrated holons contributing to ever greater holons.

"No master falls from the sky"

Once in the far east, a sultan hosted a magician at his court. The sultan was so awed by the magician's presentation that he stammered repeatedly, "What a wonder, what a genius!" His wise adviser, the grand vizier, was less impressed and commented, "Just a question of practice." This comment enraged the sultan, prompting him to respond: "My dear Grand Vizier, obviously you have lost your wisdom and are of no use to our court anymore. Off you go to prison in a tower! So you may have company of your own kind, a young calf may accompany you." The imprisoned grand vizier regularly carried the animal, his only companion, up and down the stairs of the tower on his shoulders. As the calf gained weight, the prisoner grew stronger by the day. In time, the sultan noticed that the affairs in his empire weren't going so well and wondered what had become of his former advisor, so he summoned him from the prison. When he saw the man enter the palace room with a full-grown cow on his shoulders, he again stammered, "What a wonder, what a genius!" but the grand vizier repeated the wisdom that had initially led to his imprisonment: "Just a question of practice."

– Retold after Nossrat Peseschkian (*Oriental Stories*, p. 131)

Within the described spiral, we find the development of multiple intelligences. They are the answers, the solutions we have found to the questions and problems we encounter. Each of these has been intensely investigated by authoritative scientists. Ken Wilber has based his advanced description of human and individual development on all these discoveries.

"What am I aware of?"	Cognitive line – J. Piaget/ K. Fisher
"Who am I?"	Self/ego line – J. Loevinger

"What is significant to me?"	Values line – C. Graves
"What should I do?"	Morals line – L. Kohlberg/ C. Gilligan
"How should we interact?"	Interpersonal line – R. Sellman
"What is of ultimate concern?"	Spiritual intelligence line – J. Fowler
"What do I need?"	Needs line – A. Maslow
"How shall I physically do this?"	Kinesthetic line – H. Gardner
"How do I feel about this?"	Emotional line – D. Goleman

We are all faced with these questions in life, but most of us draw upon only one or two lines because we aren't aware of the others. We have the chance to open ourselves and develop ourselves in even more of them by questioning ourselves in the sense of Positum, the given, and our potential. Depending on what we want to do and our individual contexts, we also may need to discover and develop our own individual questions.

"Waking up" within the states of consciousness.

"Consciousness is a singular of which the plural is unknown."
- Irvin Schrödinger

In yoga, *Saguna Brahman* means spirit or consciousness taking on qualities and form, and *Nirguna Brahman* means spirit or consciousness without qualities.

As there are **stages (waves/levels) of personal growth** for "growing up" towards fullness, gaining more and more perspectives, there are states of consciousness to which we can "wake up" towards ever-growing freedom. **"Growing up"** and **"waking up"** are achieved through the continuous widening of our awareness and consciousness. While "growing up" is a natural process that can be facilitated through *mindfulness practice* and *meditation, "waking up"* is primarily attained through the continuous practice of these. We use the process of *unearthing, noting, videotaping,* and *letting go* that we mentioned beforehand. It enables us to transcend and include ever-new levels of consciousness and thereby lets us grow as individuals and as a collective in an endlessly unfolding universe and consciousness.

"Waking up" is the gradual and sometimes abrupt attainment of stages of consciousness on a path to expanding freedom—experience of ultimate reality, enlightenment, awakening, metanoia, great liberation, realizing one's greatest identity, transcending the sense of self as separate, uncoiling of the self-contraption, felt oneness with everything that is arising. This brings with it diminished fear and anxiety, grasping and addiction. Through conscious surrender and a process of continuous dis-identification, one goes from grasping and identifying to intentionally letting go and transcending.

In both Buddhism and Christianity as well as most other religions, we have contemplative practice. In Buddhism, it is typically accompanied by the practice of compassion and in Christianity by the practice of love. The practice of compassion and love are essential for creating a continuously growing connection to life and our fellow human beings while we are seeking freedom through meditative practice at the same time.

The states of consciousness

According to Wilber, each state of consciousness builds on the previous ones. Each state consists of an expanded consciousness of a physically existing mind-state and becomes accessible to clear awareness through the mindfulness and meditation process.

- The **waking state** is attributed to the gross body-mind or gross reflecting self (ego), which is sensory-motor. It operates on the body, the physically real, and thus material objects. Its peak experience is called nature-mysticism (unity-experience with nature) and is also experienced as flow-states (dissolution of subject and object, timelessness, and sense of oneness are experienced). Examples are when jogging or becoming one with what one is doing.

- The **dreaming state** is attributed to the subtle body-mind or subtle reflecting self (soul), which operates on emotions and thoughts, thus emotional-mental states. Its peak experience is called deity mysticism and comprises the experience of higher "luminous forms" or "deity forms," (which are Jungian archetypes interpreted according to the culture of the experiencer). This state gives a sense of oneness and identity with the divine.

- The **deep, dreamless sleep** state is attributed to the causal body-mind or causal reflecting self (true self/spirit), which operates on primordial archetypes (not Jungian but first forms of manifestation out of emptiness), divine spiritual realities. Its peak experience is formless mysticism.

- The **witnessing state** peaks as the experience of the true self, of I-am-ness and "siddhis." (True paranormal powers such as ESP, precognition, telekinesis, remote viewing, spontaneous healing, synchronicity can be experienced at the highest levels.)

- The **non-dual state** (spirit/suchness/supreme identity) has as its peak experience the union of emptiness and form.

Brainwaves correlating to individual states

An interesting and, at the same time, logical fact is that each of the states of consciousness corresponds to different brainwaves and can be measured with an encephalogram:

- Beta: Gross waking state 13–30 Hz

- Alpha: Gross relaxed waking state 8–13 Hz

- Theta: Subtle dream state 4–8 Hz

- Delta: Causal deep, dreamless state (meditation) 0.1–4 Hz

- Delta plus slight alpha: Awake at sleep

Developmental drives

We can differentiate two different directions and drives for development that are the basis of "growing up" and "waking up." They can be described as two different axes, each one having opposite poles:

Agency and communion

- **Agency:**

- The drive toward autonomy and self-containment

- In extremis leading to alienation, separation, fragmentation.

- **Communion:**

- The drive to be part of something, an aspect of a larger network, a relationship

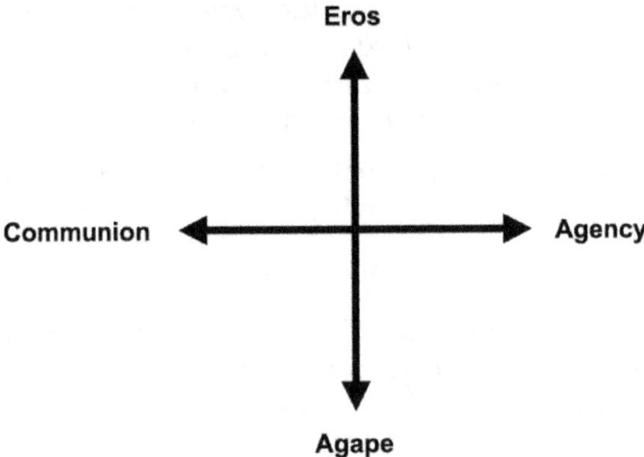

- In extremis, it leads to dependency and symbiosis.

Eros and agape

- **Eros:**
- The drive to ever greater wholeness, transcending, moving up to higher levels.
- In extremis, it leads to **phobos**, the escape from the lower into the higher, which is repression- and fear-driven instead of transcending.

- **Agape:**
- The drive of the whole to embrace the parts, reaching down to embrace all the lesser elements.
- In extremis, it becomes **thanatos**, the death-instinct, regressing, moving down toward lower levels.

In personal development, it is important to find one's balance within these and maintain one's patience at the same time.

Differences between men and women

As the saying goes, "Girls have roots and boys have wings." Men and women have different tendencies within the drives for personal development.

- **Men:** agency-eros
- **Women:** communion-agape

As Ken Wilber describes in his books and lectures, science is continuously providing more evidence that the more men and women develop, the more they **integrate** their **contra-sexual drive** and become balanced and integrated.

CONCLUSION

"The real question isn't if life exists after death but if you are alive before death."
- Osho

The "Tree of the Mensch"

The Jewish traditional "Tree of the Mensch," as described by Bruna Martinuzzi, is a wonderful metaphor for the human being and is precisely what Nossrat Peseschkian saw in men and women.

- The **roots** of the "Tree of the Mensch" consist of humility, authenticity, and empathy.

Humility helps us nourish ourselves by seeing things openly, with big minds or the eyes of a novice, opening ourselves to development and possibilities and being able to listen and learn humbly. Authenticity means being ourselves, living our values—the ones that give us roots in life—even through hardship. Empathy is being present for and considering others at all times.

- The **trunk** of the "Tree of the Mensch" consists of optimism, responsibility, and mastery.

Optimism, a positive attitude, nurtures our ability to inspire and convince. We need the willingness to be responsible for things that need to be done and fix the ones that went wrong. It gives reliability. We must live a life of mastery, always staying calm, no matter what we face, and being honest and clear in our communication. We should listen more than we speak. Listen to what the other person has to say, and talk only when he has finished, not dominate the conversation.

- The **branches and leaves** of the "Tree of the Mensch" consist of enthusiasm, generosity, appreciation, and confidence.

If we exhibit a good mood, are enthusiastic, generous, and appreciative, a creative atmosphere will surround us. Generosity is giving abundantly to others, including giving second chances and convincing others that they are important. Confidence in ourselves and the sense of self-efficacy, according to psychologist Alfred Bandura, give us the ability to perform efficiently. It gives us the power to face challenges and failure confidently and courageously. Our performance in challenging times gives us mental strength and health.

"Everyone is his own luck blacksmith as long as he is not afraid of touching a hot iron."
- German proverb

Everyday practice for growing and living a fulfilled life

Of the following, we must use what is useful to us and select those for which we have time. We add as we find and create more time. The ones with the * are essential; the others are highly beneficial.

"Small acts change the world."

- Begin the day with a glass of water with a squirt of lemon juice.
- *Meditate or pray and visualize our day.
- Write the morning pages.
- *Eat healthily and consciously two or three times a day and always ask ourselves: What am I eating, how do I eat it, why do I eat it?
- *Engage in sports activities at least three to five times per week and always stretch afterward.
- *Listen mindfully and talk attentively, always with the best attention.
- Use anchors when they are necessary.
- *Bring consciousness to the body and breath with mindfulness to come back to the present and ourselves whenever we are under stress.
- Make decisions with the "triad" connecting to heart, body, and mind.

- *Keep the seven basic attitudes present (beginners' mind, acceptance, trust and patience, mature envy, forgiving, gratitude, and generosity) for living in peace and in the present.

- *Connect to people who inspire.

- *Keep a good routine, break bad habits, and get out of your comfort zone regularly.

- *Never take our age into account.

- *Achieve calm and quiet for the last hour of the day without messaging and news. Instead, read some spiritual or inspiring literature that will bring us healthy sleep and further inner development during the night.

- *Do a short reflection on the day, with meditation and bringing our life goals to mind as visualizations.

- Diary

- To finish the day, do a body scan and breathe with the abdomen for preparing to sleep.

- *Sleep at least six to eight hours.

- *Allow time every couple of weeks to reflect on what we want for the future, set new goals, and give thanks for what we have lived during the last weeks.

- Repeat exercises from this book and from other inspirational books as well.

"Epiphany is a visceral understanding of something you already know."
- Jen Sincero

Thanks

Dear Reader, we are coming to the end of the book. It originated from my personal questions about life and outlines the answers that I have discovered up to this point. It reflects my continuous struggle to understand myself and the world. I am always trying to make sense of the world and find my reasons to live in it.

I am so grateful to all my teachers, five of whom I venerate as well as so many more who played key roles in my development. First among the five is Nossrat Peseschkian with Positive Psychotherapy, who helped me find fulfillment and gave me all the tools and the model I needed to heal so that I could thrive personally and professionally. Second is Marshall Rosenberg with Nonviolent Communication, who showed me the way on my quest towards peace and connectedness with others. Third, Ken Wilber's teachings on integral Spiral Dynamics gave me a deep understanding of the psyche and human development with its multiple perspectives and intelligence, along with an abiding hope for further human development and prosperity. Fourth, Shunryu Suzuki gave me a foundation in spirituality through which I could find a common basis in the wisdom traditions of other religions so I could circle back to find my own spiritual self. And last, Michael Bohne added to my toolbox with Process and Embodiment Psychology and gave me techniques for working with fear, trauma, and low self-esteem.

My search for knowledge and understanding started as a youth when I was looking for a religion that would quench my desire to know where we are coming from, where we are going, and why we are here. I read countless books and frequented churches, temples, mosques, and seminars, but I eventually felt I had to throw religion out of my life. I simply couldn't find the universal key that would let them fit together, let me find a universal truth within them, and let them grow together as one great spiritual background. There were too many myths and stories, too many incoherent descriptions about the afterlife, and too many overly idealistic paths to God that my reason couldn't accept. But my constant inner desire to understand myself and the world and find my personal connection to the universe was unquenchable and pushed me on. Although I felt miserable and lonesome in this field sometimes, my trip was worthwhile in the end. My way back to religion, or better said, forward to finding myself and the common ground of spirituality, was inevitable. I continued my search by studying physics and biology at school and later medicine and psychology, interesting myself in music and art, all of them filling me with pleasure and enthusiasm, as did life itself. But the fundamental question was only solved when Shunryu Suzuki's teachings let me learn to let go of all teachings and go into the experience; Ken Wilber's books explained the evolution of religion and everyone's path away from dogmatism towards openness and pure spirituality, the path traditions of wisdom.

Looking back, I can now recognize all the steps of psychological development I experienced within the spiral dynamics of developmental psychology. I lived intensely through them and am happy and mostly at peace with myself now. I am glad for all the religions I have studied; I found deep spirituality in each wisdom tradition I came to understand. Knowing that all are based on spirituality and love despite their differing cultures gives me inner peace. In the end, the essence of my trip through psychotherapy was a spiritual one, the search for understanding myself and the world. It was the strongest inner drive I have felt in my life.

So, as you can see, this book is the essence of what I have discovered, understood, and continuously tried to practice. Of course, I didn't practice all that I have recommended at the same time but rather at a steady pace, whatever was helpful to me at a given time. Psychotherapy and coaching are a path in life I have opened for myself; they have become immense sources of happiness and self-development.

I hope some of my discoveries will be of help to you as you search for your personal path to health, happiness, success, and prosperity. Continue looking into how you can flourish. Be proud of your past, do spiritual practices as you need them, and don't stop looking enthusiastically into the future. And make your present a wonderful adventure as it has been for me and continues to be.

I still want to thank many more of my friends and teachers. I learned a great deal from my friend Carmen Kauffmann, a wonderful communication coach with whom I have had the deepest spiritual and professional conversations and fun. I also feel very strongly connected to John Okoro, an intimate soulmate. I want to thank all my

Ethiopian friends from whom I have learned so much working in their beautiful country during the last decades. I am incredibly grateful for the guidance and friendship of my teachers, Dr. Nawid Peseschkian, Dr. Hamid Pesseschkian, Arno Remmers, Dr. Gunther Hübner, Birgit Werner, Sheyda Rafat, and all my colleagues of PPT.

I also want to thank all those from whom I learned enormously by devouring their books and who are all represented in this book: Martin Seligman, Mihály Csíkszentmihályi, Daniel Goleman, the classical psychologists as Rogers, Freud, C.G. Jung, Abraham Maslow, and Aaron Beck. I am grateful for spiritual masters Yongey Mingyur Rinpoche, the Dalai Lama, Bahá'u'lláh, Abdu'l-Bahá, Jack Kornfield, Lao Tzu, Patanjali, the Bhagavad Gita, Hazrat Inayat Khan, Thích Nhất Hạnh, and great coaches such as Paz Calap, Jen Sincero, and Sandra González. Consider my inclusion of their names on this list as a recommendation to read their works.

And thus, the wondrous cooperation of many individuals orchestrated this book's full spectrum and radiance. May it help you prosper, find life fulfillment, and shine into many hearts.

I will see you again with Positive Psychotherapy and, of course, with its friends. Make it your daily practice! Thank you for staying with me. I wish you the prosperous life you deserve and can create for yourself. Get enthusiastic about your life!

References

Antonovsky, Aaron: Salutogenese. © DGVT Tübingen 1997

Beck, Aaron: Cognitive therapy and the emotional disorders © Penguin 1991

Beck, D., Cowan, C.: Spiral Dynamics. © John Wiley and Sons Ltd 2005

Beck, Judith S.: Praxis der Kognitiven Therapy © Beltz 1999

Bohne, Michael: Bitte klopfen. © Carl-Auer-Systeme Verlag Heidelberg 2010

Bohne, Michael: Klopfen mit PEP. © Carl-Auer-System Verlag Heidelber 2010

Calap, Paz: Quiero Paz. © Editorial Planeta. S.A. 2019

Cameron, Julia: The artist's way. © Profile Books 2020

Csíkszentmihályi, Mihály: Creativity. © Gildan Media Corporation 2015

Csíkszentmihályi, Mihály: Flow. © Harper Perennial 1991

Dawkins, Richard: The Selfish Gene © Oxford University Press1976

Ellis, Albert: The essential Ellis Albert: Seminal writings on psychotherapy © Springer 1990

Freud, Sigmund: An outline of Psycho-Analysis. © W. W. Norton & Company 1989

Goncharov, Maksim: Conflict operationalization. Khabarovsk

Kabat-Zinn, Jon: Wherever You Go, There You Are © Piatkus 2004

Kauffmann, Carmen: Diplomatie im Alltag. © Haufe-Lexware, 2015

Kauffmann, Carmen: Sich durchsetzen. © Haufe-Lexware, 2008

Martinuzzi, Bruna: The Leader as a Mensch © Six Seconds 2009

Peseschian, H., Remmers, A.: Positive Psychotherapy. © Ernst Reinhardt Gmbh & co. München 2013

Peseschkian, H., Messias, E.: Positive Psychiatry, Psychotherapy and Psychology. © Springer 2020

Peseschkian, Nossrat: Positive Psychotherapie. © S. Fischer Verlag GmbH, Frankfurt am Main 1977

Peseschkian, Nossrat: Psychotherapie des Alltagslebens. © S. Fischer Verlage, Frankfurt am Main 1977

Peseschkian, Nossrat: Der Kaufmann und der Papagei. © Fischer Taschenbuch Verlag GmbH. Frankfurt am Main 1979

Peseschkian, Nossrat: Positive Familientherapie. © S. Fischer Verlage, Frankfurt am Main 1982

Peseschkian, Nossrat: Auf der Suche nach Sinn. © S. Fischer Verlage, Frankfurt am Main 1983

Peseschkian, Nossrat: 33 und eine Form der Partnerschaft. © S. Fischer Verlage, Frankfurt am Main1988

Peseschkian, Nossrat: Psychosomatik und Positive Psychotherapie. © S. Fischer Verlage, Frankfurt am Main 1993

Peseschkian, Nossrat: Das Geheimnis des Samenkorns. © S. Fischer Verlage, Frankfurt am Main 1996

Peseschkian, Nossrat: Der nackte Kaiser. © 1997 Pattloch Verlag GmbH & Co. KG, München

Peseschkian, Nossrat: Es ist leicht, das Leben schwer zu nehmen, aber schwer, das Leben leicht zu nehmen. © Herder Verlag, Freiburg 2006

Peseschkian, Nossrat: Wenn du etwas haben willst, was du noch nie gehabt hast, dann musst du etwas tun, was du noch nie getan hast. © Herder Verlag, Freiburg 2007

Peseschkian, Nossrat: Glaube an Gott und binde dein Kamel fest. © Kreuz Verlag, Stuttgart 2008

Peseschkian, N., Aziz, A.: Lexikon der Positiven Psychotherapie. © S. Fischer Verlage, Frankfurt am Main 2009

Peseschkian, N., Battegay, R.: Die Treppe zum Glück. © S. Fischer Verlage, Frankfurt am Main 2006

Peseschkian, N., Boessmann, U.: Positive Ordnungstherapie. © Hippocrates Verlag, Stuttgart 1995

Peseschkian, N., Clever, C.: Goldene Regeln der Lebenskunst. © Herder Verlag, Freiburg 2012

Rosenberg, Marshall B.: Nonviolent Communication. © PuddleDancer Press Encinitas 2003

Seligman, Martin: Flourish. © Simon & Schuster Inc. New York 2011

Seligman, Martin: Learned optimism. © Simon & Schuster Inc. New York 1990

Sincero, Jen: You are a badass. © Running Press 2016

von Witzleben, Gabriele: Enneagramm kompakt. © tao.de Bielefeld 2014

von Witzleben, Gabriele: Das systemische Enneagramm. © tao.de 2014

Wilber, Ken: Integral Spirituality. © Shambhala 2007

Wilber, Ken: Integral Psychology. © Shambhala 2000

Williams, M., Teasdale, J., Segal, Z., Kabat-Zinn, J.: The Mindful Way through Depression. © The Guildford Press New York, 2007

APPENDIX

WIPPF 2.0
Wiesbaden Inventar for Positive Psychotherapy and Family Therapy
International Version 2.04 Arno Remmers 1995

on the following pages you will find expressions and meanings of different people, from different ages, of women as well as of men.

Please value these expressions from your point of view. In this way you can describe your own point of view by filling out the form. You can not do anything „wrong", because every human being can have an own opinion. the results of this questionnaire can be helpful for consultation or treatment. Of course this information will be treated confidentially by therapists or consultants.

We ask you to mark one answer for each question. There are four possibilities:

	Yes			No
Full agreement with the expression mark th 0 on the elf under „yes"	X	0	0	0
Disagreement with the expression mark the 0 on the right under „no"	0	0	0	X
If you agree more than to disagree mark the second 0 closer to the „yes"	0	X	0	0
If you disagree more than to agree, mark the third 0 closer to „no"	0	0	X	0

Thank you

		Yes			No	
1	I have read the instructions and I am ready to answer all questions openly	0	0	0	0	
2	I feel it in my whole body, when I am angry or excited	0	0	0	0	20a
3	I leave my working place/office/household always orderly	0	0	0	0	1a
4	In my childhood I experienced my parents having many social contact	0	0	0	0	26a
5	When I'm in trouble, I can not stop thinking of all that possibly could follow	0	0	0	0	23a
6	Reliability is extraordinarily important in profession and society	0	0	0	0	7c
7	When I made a decision, I keep to it in any case, despite of all that could come up	0	0	0	0	11a
8	When my relatives spend too much money, I feel easily irritated	0	0	0	0	8b
9	Openness and honesty are more important than too much respectfulness for others	0	0	0	0	5c
		4	3	2	1	

WIPPF 2.0
Wiesbaden Inventar for Positive Psychotherapy and Family Therapy
International Version 2.04

		Yes		No		
10	In a hopeless looking situation there is always a way out	0	0	0	0	16c
11	When my parents had a conflict, they always tried to find a common solution	0	0	0	0	25a
12	Performance for me is the most important, especially when I have problems	0	0	0	0	21a
13	I prefer people with good behavior	0	0	0	0	4b
14	I feel only well and clean, when I can wash my body entirely every day	0	0	0	0	2a
15	I can always be patient, even If something irritates me	0	0	0	0	12a
16	I follow orders of a boss or an advise of a person with authority	0	0	0	0	9a
17	I like to be tender very much	0	0	0	0	17a
18	Usually I trust other people when coming into contact with them	0	0	0	0	15b
19	My father was very patient with me when I had been a child	0	0	0	0	24e
20	When I'm in trouble, I try always to contact others	0	0	0	0	22a
21	I will always take my time to meet with others	0	0	0	0	13b
22	To share my questions about life and death with others is very important	0	0	0	0	19b
23	I stay patient with others even if somebody bothers me	0	0	0	0	12b
24	I believe in a good future for me and my family	0	0	0	0	16b
25	Even having enough money I don't like to spend it	0	0	0	0	8a
26	My parents talked with us about questions of life philosophy or faith	0	0	0	0	27a
27	Under all circumstances you should treat others with justice and fairness	0	0	0	0	10c
28	I can always truss myself	0	0	0	0	15a
29	Being lazy causes often bad consequences	0	0	0	0	6c
30	Having good relations is much more important than having money	0	0	0	0	14c
31	I can accept myself like I am	0	0	0	0	18a
32	The partnership of my parents was a partnership of love	0	0	0	0	25b
33	When I am in trouble, I'm very much thinking about it all day and night	0	0	0	0	23b
34	My mother had been very patient with me as a child	0	0	0	0	24b
35	I expect my partner to always be faithful and loyal to me	0	0	0	0	11b
36	The meaning of my life concerns me much	0	0	0	0	19a
37	You will never manage your life without punctuality	0	0	0	0	3c
		4	3	2	1	

WIPPF 2.0
Wiesbaden Inventar for Positive Psychotherapy and Family Therapy
International Version 2.04

		Yes			No	
38	With patience you will reach everything	0	0	0	0	12c
39	My parents had been very tolerant and open with others	0	0	0	0	26b
40	I could go mad when everything is in a mess	0	0	0	0	1b
41	It is always important to regard the opinion of others	0	0	0	0	4c
42	A person on which you can not rely absolutely, never can become my friend	0	0	0	0	7b
43	I have the feeling that my parents treated one another always with justice	0	0	0	0	25c
44	I like people telling very directly and openly what they think	0	0	0	0	5b
45	I see myself as very much work and achievement oriented	0	0	0	0	6a
46	Children should always obey and care about what their parents say	0	0	0	0	9c
47	For me there is a life moto: Everything needs time	0	0	0	0	13c
48	I prefer to be ten minutes earlier than five minutes too late	0	0	0	0	3a
49	My father had been an important model/example for me in my childhood	0	0	0	0	24f
50	Every time I am excited or angry I feel tension or body complaints	0	0	0	0	20b
51	When I have difficulties in my job or at home I need the help of others	0	0	0	0	22b
52	When I have problems I prefer to work harder	0	0	0	0	21b
53	Faithfulness is indispensable for a good human character	0	0	0	0	11c
54	My life philosophy or faith is very important to give ways to my life	0	0	0	0	19c
55	My parents life philosophy or faith was a strong basis for them	0	0	0	0	27b
56	I only feel well, when everybody in my home keeps it tidily clean	0	0	0	0	2b
57	It makes me angry when people are late	0	0	0	0	3b
58	When I'm in trouble I think very much about the meaning of life	0	0	0	0	23c
59	Tenderness and sexuality are necessary conditions for a partnership	0	0	0	0	17c
60	I expect discipline in family or profession	0	0	0	0	9b
61	I can also feel we'll with a person having opinions that differ from mine	0	0	0	0	18b
62	I often have guests	0	0	0	0	14b
63	Trustfulness is a necessary precondition for community life	0	0	0	0	15c
64	My mother had much time for me when I had been little	0	0	0	0	24a
65	I am very sensitive when somebody is not fair	0	0	0	0	10b
66	The best basis for being rich is to save	0	0	0	0	8c
		4	3	2	1	

WIPPF 2.0
Wiesbaden Inventar for Positive Psychotherapy and Family Therapy
International Version 2.04

		Yes		No		
67	Cleanliness of a person shows a clean character	0	0	0	0	2c
68	I always keep to what I promised	0	0	0	0	7a
69	I always have plan for my life	0	0	0	0	16a
70	For me it is easier to say „yes" than to say „no"	0	0	0	0	4a
71	When I'm working I can forget about my problems	0	0	0	0	21c
72	A home should always look orderly	0	0	0	0	1c
73	Despite of my work I have enough time for my interests and hobbies	0	0	0	0	13a
74	My parens had many guests and friends	0	0	0	0	26c
75	My father took time for me when I had been little	0	0	0	0	24d
76	In every person there is something good	0	0	0	0	18c
77	Often I feel my body in a ways that I would like to take medicaments	0	0	0	0	20c
78	I easily can make friends	0	0	0	0	14a
79	My parents had been veery interested in the meaning of life	0	0	0	0	27c
80	I do not feel well when somebody is lazy	0	0	0	0	6b
81	I judge somebody only when I finally know all reasons for her/his behavior	0	0	0	0	10a
82	When I have private or professional problems I need other people around to forget about the problems	0	0	0	0	22c
83	With the partner whom I love I want to be intimate soon	0	0	0	0	17b
84	My mother had been a model/example for me	0	0	0	0	24c
85	I prefer to say very openly my opinion	0	0	0	0	5a
86	As a child I had been often with a person who had more time for me than father and mother	0	0	0	0	24g
87	There was a person in my childhood, which had more patience with me than father and mother	0	0	0	0	24h
88	There was a person in my childhood that had been of more importance for me than my parents	0	0	0	0	24i
		4	3	2	1	

Name: ....Date of birth: .... Date today: ....

Profession: .... Town, City, place of living: ....

Region/County: .... Married O In partnership O Single O   Children:...........

Scale	Answer			Secondary capabilities	o—o	min			medium				max.			x—x	Answer		
						3	4	5	6	7	8	9	10	11	12				
1	a	b	c	orderliness		0	0	0	0	0	0	0	0	0	0		a	b	c
2				Cleanliness		0	0	0	0	0	0	0	0	0	0				
3				Punctuality		0	0	0	0	0	0	0	0	0	0				
4				Politeness		0	0	0	0	0	0	0	0	0	0				
5				Openness, honesty		0	0	0	0	0	0	0	0	0	0				
6				Achievement		0	0	0	0	0	0	0	0	0	0				
7				Reliability		0	0	0	0	0	0	0	0	0	0				
8				Thrift		0	0	0	0	0	0	0	0	0	0				
9				Obedience		0	0	0	0	0	0	0	0	0	0				
10				justice		0	0	0	0	0	0	0	0	0	0				
11				Faithfulness		0	0	0	0	0	0	0	0	0	0				
Summ	a	r	k	**Primary capabilities**		3	4	5	6	7	8	9	10	11	12	Summ	a	r	k
12				Patience		0	0	0	0	0	0	0	0	0	0		a	b	c
13				Time		0	0	0	0	0	0	0	0	0	0				
14				Contact		0	0	0	0	0	0	0	0	0	0				
15				Trust		0	0	0	0	0	0	0	0	0	0				
16				Hope		0	0	0	0	0	0	0	0	0	0				
17				Tenderness/Sexuality		0	0	0	0	0	0	0	0	0	0				
18				Love		0	0	0	0	0	0	0	0	0	0				
19				Faith/meaning		0	0	0	0	0	0	0	0	0	0				
Summ	a	r	k	**Conflict reactions**		3	4	5	6	7	8	9	10	11	12	Summ	a	r	k
20				Body	alexithym	0	0	0	0	0	0	0	0	0	0	Psychosomatic reaction	a	b	c
21				Work	obstaining	0	0	0	0	0	0	0	0	0	0	Flight in work			
22				Contact	Lonesome decision	0	0	0	0	0	0	0	0	0	0	seeking support			
23				Fantasy	avoiding	0	0	0	0	0	0	0	0	0	0	flight in fantasy			
	time	pat.	model	**Model dimensions**		3	4	5	6	7	8	9	10	11	12		time	pat.	model
24	a	b	c	I-mother	distant	0	0	0	0	0	0	0	0	0	0	attached	a	b	c
	d	e	f	I-father	distant	0	0	0	0	0	0	0	0	0	0	attacched	d	e	f
	g	h	i	I-others	distant	0	0	0	0	0	0	0	0	0	0	attached	g	h	i
25	a	b	c	You - Parents partnership	Opposition	0	0	0	0	0	0	0	0	0	0	symbiotic	a	b	c
26				We - Parents- other people	closed	0	0	0	0	0	0	0	0	0	0	open for contact			
27				Primary We - values	insecure	0	0	0	0	0	0	0	0	0	0	absolute ideals			

Social behavior			11	16	21	26	31	36	41	44	
Scale	Answer	Secondary capabilities									Answer
a	**active**	passive-adaptive	oooooooooooooooooooooooooooooooooooo								overly self-control
r	**reactive**	tolerance with others	ooooooooooooooooooooooooooooooooooo								expecting more of others
k	**concept**	free of concepts and ideas	ooooooooooooooooooooooooooooooooo								fixed to concepts/ideas
	Emotional reactions with		minimum			medium			maximum		
e	**ego**	...with oneself	ooooooooooooooooooooooooooooo								e
w	**we/you**	...others	oooooooooooooooooooooooooooo								w
i	**ideals**	...ideals and concepts	oooooooooooooooooooooooooo								i
			8	12	16	20	24	28	32		

Actual Capabilities	I + + / + / + - / - / - -	Partner + + / + / + - / - / - -	Spontaneous ideas
Punctuality			
Cleanliness			
Orderliness			
Obedience			
Courtesy			
Honesty			
Faithfulness			
Justice			
Thrift			
Reliability			
Love			
Sexuality			
Time			
Contact			
Patience			
Doubt			
Faith			

Actual Capabilities	I + + / + / + - / - / - -	Partner + + / + / + - / - / - -	Spontaneous ideas
Punctuality	+ +	+ -	P: „Every time we want to go out you're late!"
Cleanliness	+ -	+ +	I: „I hate it when the dishes are left unattended!"
Orderliness			
Obedience			
Courtesy			
Honesty			
Faithfulness			
Justice			
Thrift			
Reliability			
Love			
Sexuality			
Time			
Contact			
Patience			
Doubt			
Faith